Henry James

AND AMERICAN PAINTING

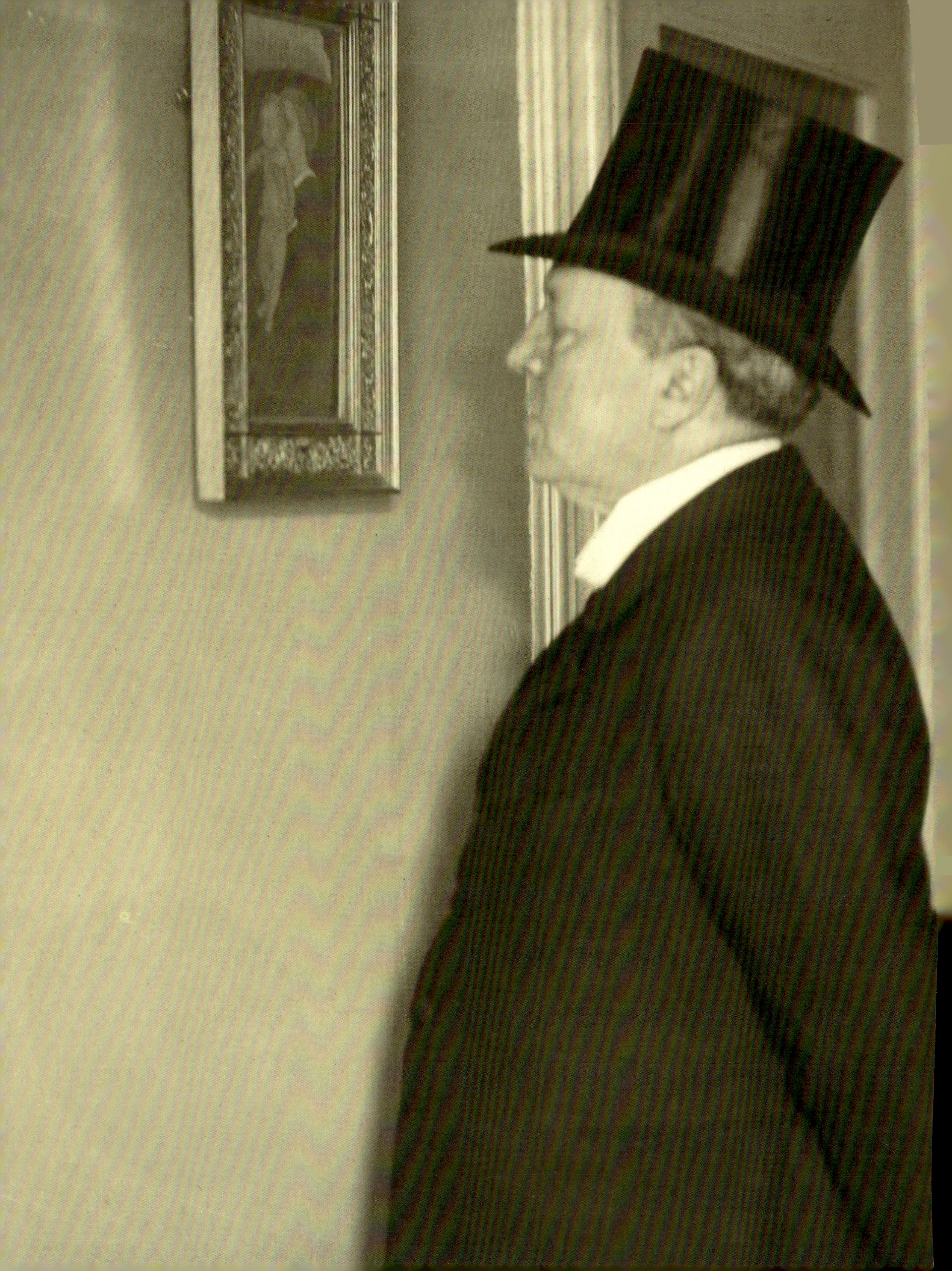

COLM TÓIBÍN

MARC SIMPSON

DECLAN KIELY

Henry James

AND AMERICAN PAINTING

The Pennsylvania State University Press, University Park, Pennsylvania
and The Morgan Library & Museum, New York, New York

Exhibition at the Morgan Library & Museum, New York
9 June–10 September 2017

Henry James and American Painting is made possible with a lead gift from the Jerome L. Greene Foundation.

JLGreene

Major funding is provided by the Henry Luce Foundation.

Generous support is provided by Karen H. Bechtel, the Mr. and Mrs. Raymond J. Horowitz Foundation for the Arts, and the Franklin Jasper Walls Lecture Fund, and assistance from Barbara G. Fleischman and the Wyeth Foundation for American Art.

Library of Congress Cataloging-in-Publication Data
Names: Tóibín, Colm, 1955– , author. | Simpson, Marc, author. | Kiely, Declan, author. | Pierpont Morgan Library.
Title: Henry James and American painting / Colm Tóibín, Marc Simpson, Declan Kiely.
Other titles: Penn State series in the history of the book.
Description: University Park, Pennsylvania : The Pennsylvania State University Press ; New York, New York : The Morgan Library & Museum, [2017] | Series: The Penn State series in the history of the book | "Exhibition at the Morgan Library & Museum, New York, 9 June–10 September 2017."—Title page verso. | Includes bibliographical references and index.
Summary: "Explores how the novels of Henry James reflect the significance of the visual culture of his society, and how essential the language and imagery of the arts, as well as friendships with artists, were to James's writing"—Provided by publisher.
Identifiers: LCCN 2017005749 | ISBN 9780271078526 (cloth : alk. paper)
Subjects: LCSH: James, Henry, 1843–1916—Criticism and interpretation. | James, Henry, 1843–1916—Knowledge—Art. | James, Henry, 1843–1916—Friends and associates. | James, Henry, 1843–1916—Manuscripts. | James, Henry, 1843–1916—Correspondence. | Painting, American—19th century. | Painting, American—20th century. | Painting in literature. | Art and literature.
Classification: LCC PS2127.A75 T65 2017 | DDC 813/.4—dc23
LC record available at https://lccn.loc.gov/2017005749

Printed in Canada
Published by The Pennsylvania State University Press,
University Park, PA 16802-1003

Second printing, October 2017

Front: John Singer Sargent (1856–1925). *Henry James,* 1913 (Fig. 16, p. 38).

Frontispiece and back: Alice Boughton (1865–1943). *Henry James,* 1906 (Fig. 3, p. 106).

Page viii: Photograph of Elizabeth Boott Duveneck, Francis Boott, Frank Duveneck, and Ann Shenston at Bellosguardo, Florence, ca. 1886 (Fig. 8, p. 14).

Page 48: Jervis McEntee (1828–1891), *Saturday Afternoon,* 1875 (Fig. 8, p. 69).

Page 98: Henry James, group of autograph letters, signed, to George Higginson, 1892–1911 (Fig. 25, p. 128).

Page 134: William Morris Hunt (1824–1879), *Girl at the Fountain,* 1852–54 (Fig. 5, p. 59).

Page 152: John Singer Sargent (1856–1925), *An Interior in Venice,* 1899 (Fig. 20, p. 43).

Page 162: Hendrik C. Andersen and Henry James, Rome, ca. 1907; by permission of Ministerio dei Beni e delle Attività Culturali e del Turismo.

Page 170: John La Farge (1835–1910), *Henry James,* 1862 (Fig. 3, p. 8).

The Pennsylvania State University Press is a member of the Association of American University Presses.

It is the policy of The Pennsylvania State University Press to use acid-free paper. Publications on uncoated stock satisfy the minimum requirements of American National Standard for Information Sciences—Permanence of Paper for Printed Library Material, ANSI Z39.48–1992.

Contents

Director's Foreword

The visual arts were part of the bedrock on which Henry James built his house of fiction. He wrote a number of stories about painters and sculptors. His early novel *Roderick Hudson* (1875) deals with the life of a sculptor in Rome. In *The Portrait of a Lady* (1881), Isabel Archer's response to the paintings in the gallery at Gardencourt remains one of the most haunting scenes in the novel. Visual culture plays a significant role in James's late novels. For example, in *The Wings of the Dove* (1902), some of the central scenes take place in art galleries. In *The Ambassadors* (1903), Lambert Strether meets Madame de Vionnet in the garden of the sculptor Gloriani in Paris, whose house is loosely based on Whistler's studio. In *The Golden Bowl* (1904), Adam Verver is an art collector in the tradition of a Morgan or a Frick who plans to ship his collection to the United States.

James used subtlety and nuance in the creation of his characters. He allowed the moment when one of his protagonists sees another—and realizes something fresh and dramatic—to animate and nourish his fiction. Often, these dramatic scenes are like pictures, compositions that a painter might create. He let facial expression carry enormous weight, as he did the sudden glance or something significant noticed in the distance. These moments occur in James's work almost as though they were brushstrokes, a play with perspective, or an added piece of tonal or textured complexity.

From early in his life, James counted a great number of painters among his friends. In his work, he also used the gallery space as a place of pilgrimage, where his characters could spend time alone or encounter one another in a setting that was both public and richly resonant. The visual arts were at the very center of his life, and his relationship to painting and sculpture, and to artists, enriched his sensibility and inspired his own art as a novelist.

James had grown up with a landscape by Thomas Cole on the parlor wall of his family's Washington Square home and died in possession of one of John Singer Sargent's last great portrait paintings. And, just as works by eminent American painters framed his life, his friendships and many close associations with American artists provided important experiences and inspiration for his fiction. He took lessons from the painter John La Farge, who painted his portrait. A number of women artists, such as Elizabeth Boott and Lilla Cabot Perry, were friends. His cousin Ellen Emmet Rand, who did portraits of him, and his nephew William James, Jr., were painters. In Rome during the 1870s, James knew the sculptor William Wetmore Story and later wrote his two-volume biography. Later, he became close to Hendrik Andersen, a young sculptor with whom James enjoyed an extensive and revealing correspondence. He also knew Whistler and used his Paris studio in his novel *The Ambassadors*. In two of his major novels, *The Portrait of a Lady* and *The Golden Bowl*, he transformed his friends Francis Boott and his daughter, Lizzie Boott, into literary characters. Lizzie, who was married to the painter Frank Duveneck, was also a painter.

The exhibition *Henry James and American Painting* was organized by Colm Tóibín, the Irene and Sidney B. Silverman Professor of the Humanities at Columbia University, and Declan Kiely, Robert H. Taylor Curator of Literary and Historical Manuscripts at the Morgan Library & Museum. I am most grateful to Colm Tóibín, whose essay, "Henry James: Shadow and Substance," charts the theme of the exhibition and James's relationships and associations with American artists. I am also pleased to acknowledge art historian Marc Simpson, who collaborated extensively as curatorial advisor, and whose essay, "'I like ambiguities and detest great glares': Henry James and American Paintings," elucidates how, throughout his lifetime, James regarded American art and used his familiarity with it to enrich his life and inform his writings. Declan Kiely's essay, "'Pardon my too many words': Henry James Manuscripts and Letters at the Morgan Library & Museum," discusses both the growth and development of the Morgan's Henry James collection and the author's occasional intersections with members of the Morgan family.

I am also grateful for the support and encouragement of our collaborators in this undertaking: Peggy Fogelman, Norma Jean Calderwood Director of the Isabella Stewart Gardner Museum, Boston, and Christina Nielsen, William and Lia Poorvu Curator of the Collection and Exhibition Program of the Isabella Stewart Gardner Museum.

Henry James and American Painting would not have been possible without the generosity of several important donors. A lead gift from the Jerome L. Greene Foundation provided early and substantial support for the project. Major funding from the Henry Luce Foundation also covered a significant portion of the project's expenses. We are also grateful for the generous support of Karen H. Bechtel and the Mr. and Mrs. Raymond J. Horowitz Foundation for the Arts, assistance from Barbara G. Fleischman, and support for this publication from the Wyeth Foundation for American Art. The Franklin Jasper Walls Lecture Fund has made possible lectures on James and his relationship with American artists.

Colin B. Bailey
The Morgan Library & Museum

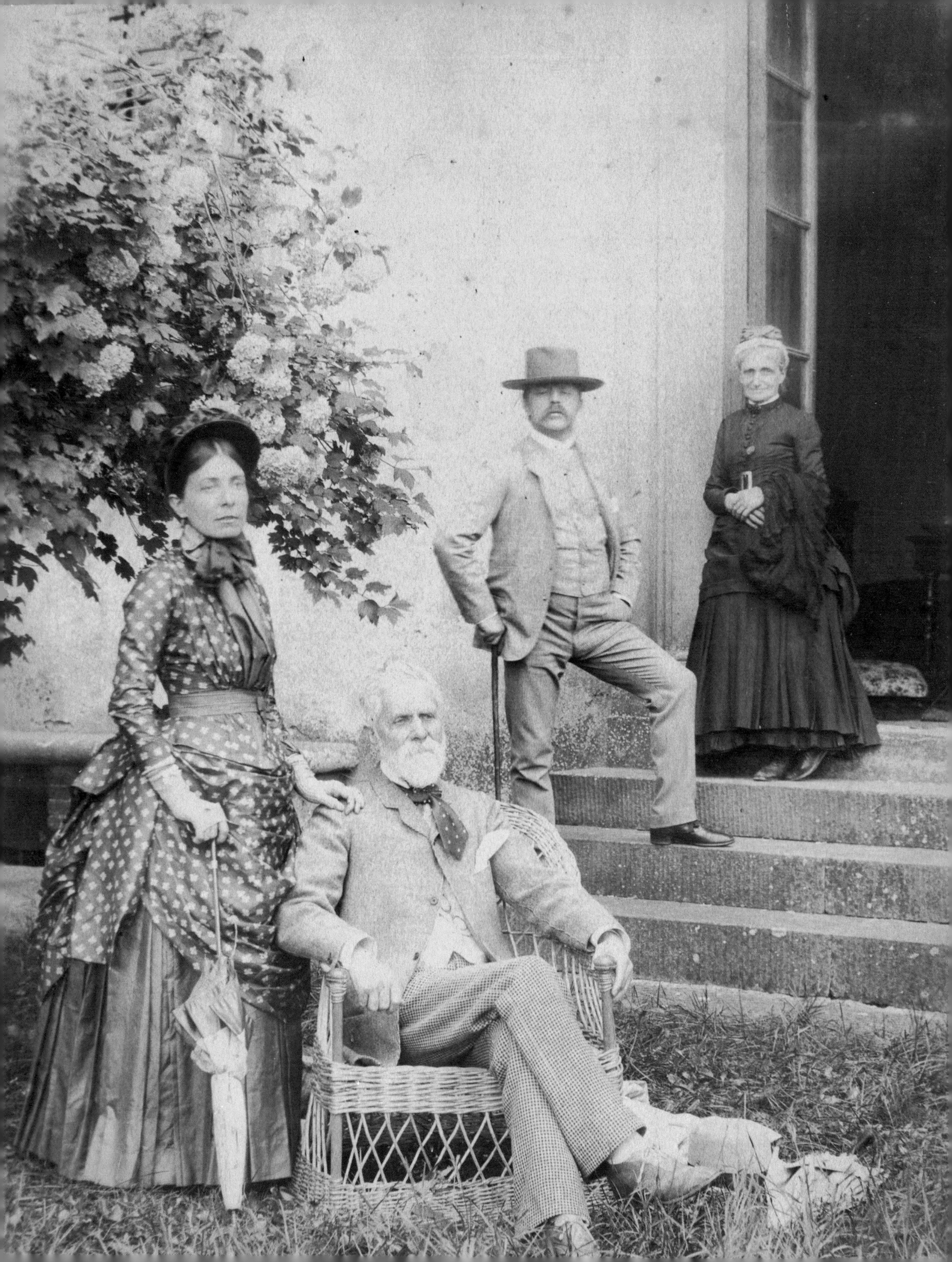

COLM TÓIBÍN

Henry James
Shadow and Substance

Lamb House in Rye, which Henry James began to lease in 1897, is now owned by the National Trust. Although more than a century has passed since James's death, and although other inhabitants have been and gone, and although the large detached garden room, where James often wrote in the summer, was destroyed by a bomb in the Second World War, to this day the house itself has traces of James's presence. In a corner in the small dining room on the ground floor, for example, the small terra-cotta bust of Count Alberto Bevilacqua by the sculptor Hendrik Andersen (1872–1940) is still perched over the mantelpiece where James placed it when it was shipped to Lamb House from Rome in 1899 (Fig. 2).

Hendrik Andersen appears almost as a character out of James's fiction. James met him in the spring of 1899 in Rome in the apartment of the artist John Elliott (1858–1925) and his wife, Maud Howe Elliott, the daughter of Julia Ward Howe. James was fifty-six, Andersen almost thirty years his junior. Andersen had been born in Norway but raised in Newport, Rhode Island, where the James family had also lived between sojourns in Europe. He had studied in Paris and then Naples, and moved to Rome in 1897. According to Olivia Cushing, Andersen's sister-in-law, Maud Howe Elliott welcomed the young sculptor "as a special pet and charge whose golden hair and graceful figure . . . could add a picturesque note to her salon."[1]

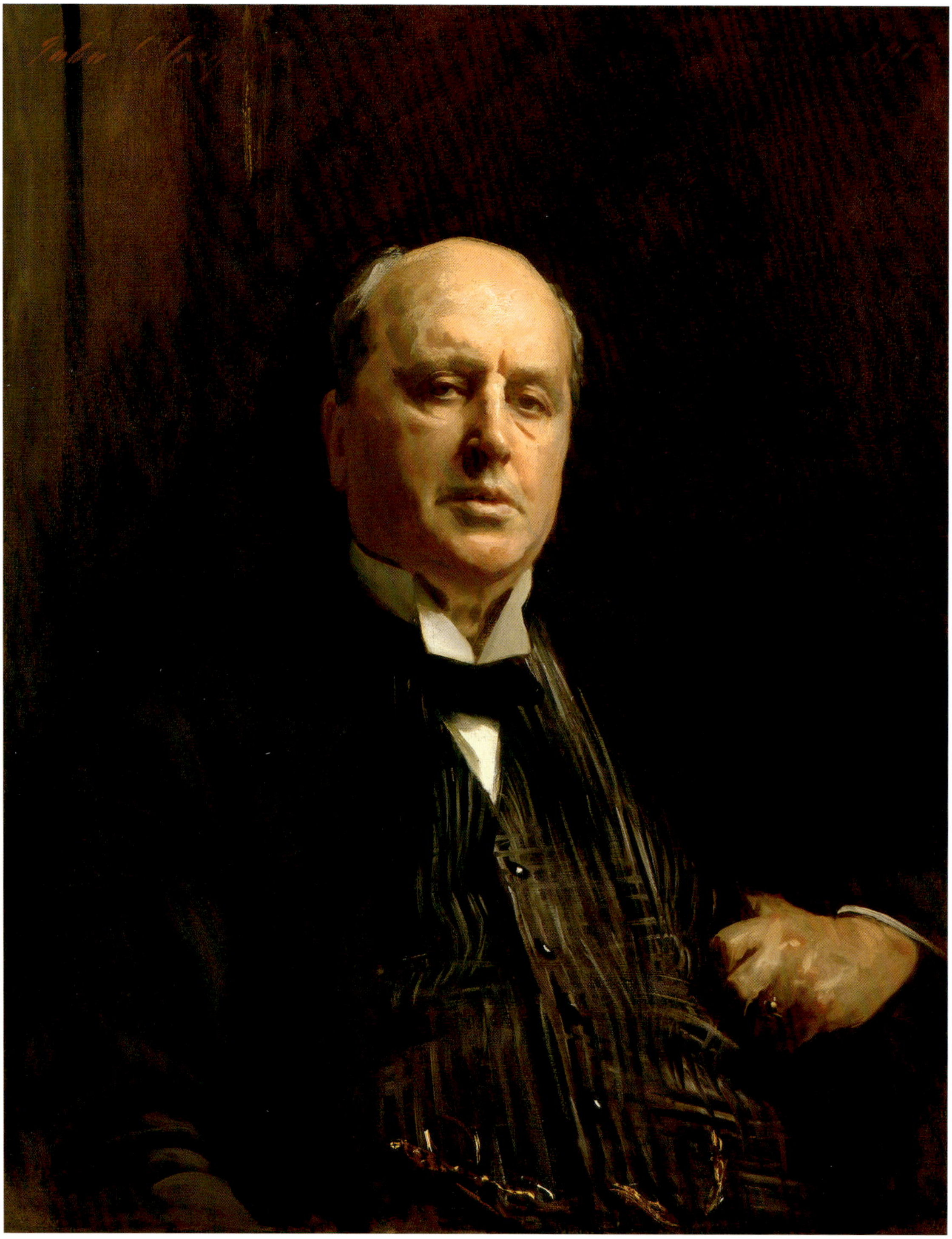

FIG. 1. John Singer Sargent (1856–1925), *Henry James*, 1913, National Portrait Gallery, London.

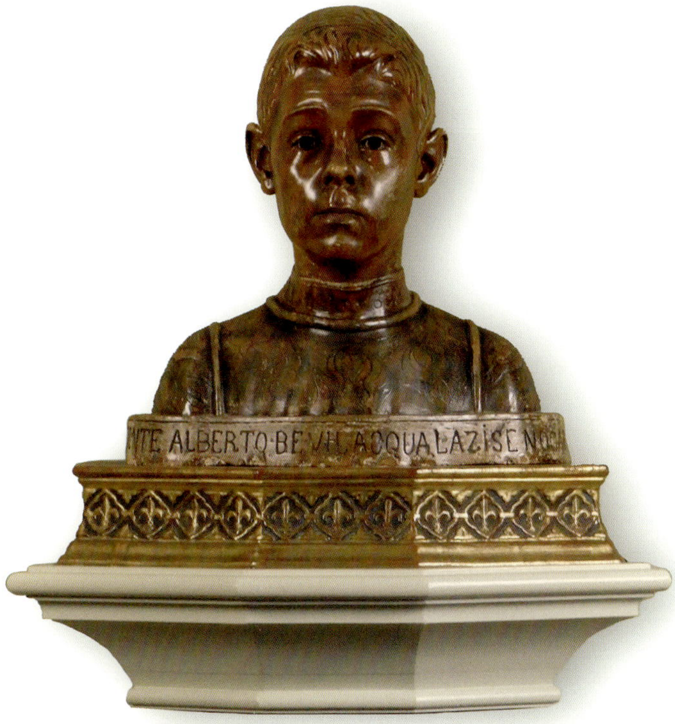

FIG. 2. Hendrik Christian Andersen (1872–1940), *Count Alberto Bevilacqua*, 1899, Lamb House (The National Trust).

James and Andersen remained in contact; Andersen visited James in Rye six times between 1899 and 1908 and James saw him in Newport in 1905 and in Rome in 1907. James's letters to Andersen constitute the most important legacy of their relationship. While James seems to have destroyed Andersen's letters to him, seventy-six letters from James to the sculptor survive. They contain some of James's most heartfelt and passionate writing about art and, because they were provoked by the work of a sculptor, attest to James's close engagement and serious involvement with the visual arts.

After James's death, Andersen wrote: "Deeply as the loss of Henry James was felt by his innumerable friends and the literary world at large, to me it was an unutterable sorrow for no one has ever understood me as he had done, or sympathised so sincerely with my struggle and my aim in life."[2]

James's art and that of Andersen, however, could not have been more different. While James believed in subtlety, nuance, psychological insight, intricate and complex phrasing, deliberate structure and much revision, Andersen made enormous, fleshy figures, paying no attention to detail. He was vastly ambitious without any sense of the painstaking work required to make a human likeness, a human figure. While James was stoical about fame and success, Andersen was optimistic, often megalomaniacal. While James slowly chiseled his sentences one by one, Andersen planned to design a world city, a utopian urban space that would transform humanity.

On 10 August 1904, James wrote to Andersen, having received some photographs of pieces of sculpture from him, expressing his concern about the scale of Andersen's works: "They terrify me so with their evidence as of *madness* (almost) in the scale on which you are working! It is magnificent—it is sublime, it is heroic; & the idea & composition of your group-circled fountain, evidently a very big thing. Only I feel as if it were let loose into space like a blazing comet—with you, personally, dangling after like the tail. . . . And I yearn, too, for the *smaller* masterpiece; the condensed, consummate, caressed, intensely filled-out thing."[3]

The following year, when James alluded to Andersen's work not finding favor with the public, it is interesting that he did not insist on the pure freedom of the artist to work without thought for commerce: "*Make the pot boil at any price, as the only real basis* of freedom & sanity. Stop building in the air for a while & build on the ground. *Earn* the money that will give you the right to conceptions (and still more to executions,) like your fountain—though I am still wondering *what* American community is going to want to pay for 30 & 40 stark naked men & women, of whatever beauty, lifted into the raw light of one of their public places."[4]

In January 1906, James wrote to Andersen, who had sent him a photograph of a piece called *The Kiss,* about the need for him to put more life into his figures: "I don't think I find the *hands,* on the backs, *living* enough & participant enough in the kiss." He advised him to keep at "the flesh & the devil & the rest of it; make the creatures palpitate, & their flesh tingle & flush . . . & their bellies ache & their bladders fill."[5] Later that year, he wrote of his concern about the lack of attention to faces in Andersen's work and of finding not enough difference between the way in which the men and the women were shaped, "the ladies resembling a shade too much the gentlemen."[6]

In November 1906, as James became more impatient with Andersen's work, he wrote with revealing candor about the marketplace in a tone that is not repeated with the same fervor anywhere else in his writing: "You are not even realizing that benefit of *friction with the market* which is so true a one for solitary artists too much steeped in their mere personal dreams, & which wakes them up to a measure of where they are and what they are doing & not doing. . . . You are attempting to do what no young artist *ever* did—to live on air indefinitely." He then referred to the need for artists to produce "the potboiler," and went on: "the potboiler which represents, in the lives of all artists, some of the most beautiful things ever done by them." He advised his young friend to "stop your multiplication of unsaleable nakednesses for a while & hurl yourself, by every cunning art you can command, into the production of the interesting, the charming, the vendible, the *placeable* small thing." He suggested that Andersen concentrate more on the face, instead of "adding Belly to Belly—however beautiful—& Bottom to Bottom, however sublime."[7]

As the correspondence began to peter out, Andersen's ambition to build a world city inspired James to write about what we might call his own micromania as an artist: "The World is a prodigious & portentous & immeasurable affair, & I can't for a moment pretend to sit in my little corner here and 'sympathise with' proposals for dealing with it."[8] He emphasized his own painstaking method as a writer and his own belief in the connection between the art he produced and life, or reality. He deplored Andersen's "mania for the colossal, the swelling & the huge, the monotonously & repeatedly huge."[9] He went on: "I live myself in the very intensity of reality and can only conceive of any art-work as producing itself piece by piece and touch by touch, in close relation to some immediate form of life that may be open to it."[10] In another letter, James impressed upon Andersen his own belief in the connection between art and "sound & sane Reality . . . Reality, Reality, the seeing of things as they *are,* & not in the light of the loosest simplifications."[11]

Also notable about this correspondence is—despite the artistic differences—a tone of fondness and real affection. James is the older man overseeing with care and at times generosity the work and life of a younger artist. It must have struck James at certain moments in the sixteen years when he knew Hendrik Andersen how the relationship between himself and the sculptor seemed almost modeled on that between Rowland Mallet and the young Roderick Hudson in James's novel *Roderick Hudson,* first published in 1875. Thus almost a quarter of a century before James laid eyes on Andersen in Rome, the fictional Rowland Mallet brought Roderick Hudson, who was also a sculptor, to the city. And between Mallet and Hudson there is some of that same connection between an older man and a young artist, a relationship almost sexual as well as watchful and avuncular. What is strange is that James wrote the story when he himself was in his early thirties. Like Rowland Mallet, while in Rome, James "spent long afternoons in the saddle, ranging over the grassy desolation of the Campagna."[12] In the novel *Roderick Hudson,* as he contemplated the life of a young artist and an older man, he was almost imagining his own future.

Some of the same tropes are played out and issues dramatized in the book as in the actual relationship that occurred in life. Hudson, like Andersen, came from a reasonably poor family and a provincial background in the northeastern part of the United States. Both figures were all ego, all boastful ambition. ("I mean to go in for big things; that is my notion of my art," Roderick Hudson says. "I mean to do things that will be simple and vast and infinite."[13])

Just as James in his letters dampened down Andersen's large sense of his destiny, he offered in his novel the figure of Sam Singleton, who worked on his modest watercolors slowly and painstakingly, as a foil for Hudson. (Singleton took weeks to complete a small work and "took a devout satisfaction in his hard-earned knowledge and his happy frugality."[14]) Just as James wrote to Andersen about the bust he made of the novelist himself, the young Roderick Hudson makes a bust of the beguiling Christina Light, who appears in the studio in Rome and with whom Roderick falls in love. (Christina Light reappeared in James's novel *The Princess Casamassima,* 1886.) Another painter in the small circle of invented expatriate artists in Rome, Miss Blanchard, has the same problem as Andersen: "She did backs very well but she was a little weak in faces."[15]

When Henry James first came to Italy in 1869, at the age of twenty-six, it was Italian art that he noted more than, say, Italian landscape or Italian society, or indeed Italian literature or music. In Milan, he described Leonardo's *Last Supper:* "I have looked at no other picture with an emotion equal to that which rose within me as this great creation of Leonardo slowly began to dawn upon my intelligence from the tragical twilight of its ruin."[16] He was also deeply impressed by Raphael's *Marriage of the Virgin* at the Brera. In Venice, in September 1869, he was disappointed by Titian's *Assumption* but more impressed by the work of Tintoretto, of whose *Crucifixion* at the Scuola di San Rocco, he wrote: "Surely no single picture in the world contains more of human life; there is everything in it, including the most exquisite beauty. It is one of the greatest things of art; it is always interesting."[17]

Having spent time in Florence, in late October he arrived in Rome from where he wrote an ecstatic letter to his brother William: "At last—for the first time—I live! It beats everything: it leaves the Rome of your fancy—your education—nowhere. It makes Venice—Florence—Oxford—London—seem like little cities of pasteboard. I went reeling and moaning thro' the streets, in a fever of enjoyment."[18] He wrote to his sister about Raphael's *Transfiguration* in the Vatican: "I sat staring stupidly at the *Transfiguration* and actually *surprised* at its thinness—asking myself whether *this* was the pretended greatest of pictures."[19] On 27 December he wrote to William in raptures about Michelangelo's *Moses*. It had, he believed, "a more melting, exalting power than I have ever perceived in a work of art. It was a great sensation—the greatest a work can give."[20]

During that first stay in Rome, James also visited the American sculptor William Wetmore Story (1819–1895) and his family in their grand apartment in Palazzo Barberini. The Storys were from Boston and had many friends in common with James. Story's *Cleopatra* had been used by Nathaniel Hawthorne in his 1860 novel *The Marble Faun*, which was set among painters in Rome.

In 1869, before the Catholic Church retreated to the Vatican, James witnessed the last days of Rome as a fully papal city. When he went back to the city in December 1873, it had changed, become more secular, almost ordinary, almost provincial. He spent most of his time with American expatriates, having dinner on Christmas Eve with the Bostonian Francis Boott (1813–1904) and his daughter, Lizzie (1846–1888), two figures who would come to matter a great deal to him and who would make their way into three of his best novels, *Washington Square*, *The Portrait of a Lady*, and *The Golden Bowl*. He also began to visit the apartment of the painter Luther Terry, who had lived in Rome for almost forty years, in Palazzo Odescalchi. He also became a regular visitor to the Storys. Much of his social life in Rome revolved around what he called "the rival houses of Terry and Story."[21]

In 1903, James, despite his misgivings about Story's talents, would publish an account, using letters and journals, of the career of William Wetmore Story, commissioned by his family. But what was more significant for James was the general atmosphere he encountered among these American artists and collectors, which he used in both *Roderick Hudson* and *The Portrait of a Lady*, as well as a number of short stories, and encouraged him to make judgments—some severe, others harsh indeed—of the work being made by American expatriates in Rome.

Spending time with American artists in Rome in the early 1870s allowed James to ripen his tone, enjoy his own phrasemaking, and begin to luxuriate in the pleasure to be derived from remaining unimpressed. When he visited Story's studio, for example, which Hawthorne had used for Kenyon's studio in *The Marble Faun*, he told his Boston friend Grace Norton that he found Story "in the midst of an army of marble heroines, which were not altogether unsuggestive of Mrs Jarley's waxworks."[22] To Charles Eliot Norton, he wrote: "So you're acquainted with Story's muse—that brazen hussy—to put it plainly. I have rarely seen such a case of *prosperous* pretention as Story. His cleverness is great, the world's good nature to him is greater."[23]

On visiting Terry's studio on Via Margutta, James would note "the queerest old survivals of the American art of thirty years ago. It is an agreeable curiosity to see their author sit and look at them seriously and expound his intentions and yet to be on the whole a sensible man of the world."[24]

James met or visited the studios of other American artists in Rome, including the sculptor Harriet Hosmer (1830–1908), who had also known Hawthorne; the painter Eugene Benson (1839–1908), whom his father had known, who painted landscapes in the classical mode; and others such as Edward Darley Boit (1840–1915), Frederic Crowninshield (1845–1918), Sarah Freeman Clarke (1808–1896), and J. Rollin Tilton (1828–1888). On most of these painters, James made comments in his letters home; he used aspects of many of them in the creation of the Rome to which Roderick Hudson, with all his vaulting ambition, arrives. What is interesting is that the artistic milieu in which James moved in Rome included very few writers and no composers—although Francis Boott was an amateur composer—but many painters and sculptors. This connection to the visual arts would nourish James's fiction in different ways, providing him with a social and intellectual hinterland he otherwise lacked, allowing the gallery and the studio space, the expatriate dilettante and the collector, a privileged place in his work but also offering the scene—a single, significant moment in the narrative, captured as though by a painter—a central pillar in his house of fiction.

Although his relationship with the visual arts became more intense once James went to Italy, paintings and painters were not new to him. When he was still in his teens in Newport, James got to know the painter John La Farge (1835–1910), who had come to study there with William Morris Hunt (1824–1879). In October 1858, William James, Henry's older brother, despite his father's disapproval, began to study painting with Hunt. Henry spent time with both William and La Farge in Hunt's studio, dabbling with paintbrush and pencil. William, he later wrote, drew "because he could, while I did so in the main only because he did."[25] It was in Hunt's studio that James observed his cousin Gus Barker, who was to be killed in the Civil War, "the beautiful young manly form of our cousin Gus Barker . . . perched on a pedestal and divested of every garment . . . the gayest as well as the neatest of models" being drawn by William.[26]

Hunt's studio on Church Street in Newport was, Leon Edel writes, "filled with plaster casts, canvases and the presence of the Quixote-like figure of the American master. William Morris Hunt had been a pupil of Couture whose 'Romains de la Decadence' Henry had seen in Paris; he had studied later with Millet in Barbizon. In Newport he was the embodiment of the artist, the flowing beard, the velvet jacket, the scarlet sash."[27]

John La Farge, eight years older than Henry James, had lived in France and knew the work of French writers such as Sainte-Beuve, Baudelaire, and Flaubert; he shared with the young Henry James the latest copies of the *Revue des Deux Mondes* and introduced James to the work of Balzac. "He opened up to us," James later wrote, "though perhaps to me in particular . . . prospects and possibilities that made the future flush and swarm. . . . He revealed to us Balzac. . . . To reread, even after long years, the introductory pages of *Eugenie Grandet*, breathlessly seized and earnestly absorbed under his instruction, is to see my initiator's youthful face, so irregular but so refined, look out at me between the lines as through prison bars."[28] James wrote to a friend: "If La Farge is within hail, please tell him that I feel the loss of him, always, as one of the greatest pangs of my long exile."[29]

La Farge, who later became a close friend of historian Henry Adams, did a portrait of Henry James when

James was in his late teens (Fig. 3). After La Farge died in 1910, James attended a commemorative exhibition of his work. He remembered a day in Newport almost half a century earlier when La Farge had proposed to him "that we should drive out to the Glen, some six miles off, to breakfast and should afterwards paint—*we* paint!—in the bosky open air. It looks at this distance a mythic time."[30]

On La Farge's death in 1910, James wrote to the painter's daughter, remembering "the old years when I saw him so much oftener and when the interest and fascination of his wondrous intelligence and rare and distinguished personality were really a feature of my life . . . I think of him as one of the very small number of *truly* extraordinary men whom I've known. . . . He was the intellectual or temperamental artist as no one else has ever been here."[31]

Many of the accounts of La Farge tell what a great talker he was. "I have heard some brilliant talkers, Whistler amongst them," one associate remembered, "but I have never heard one remotely comparable to La Farge." Henry Adams believed La Farge to be the best conversationalist of his time. But others noted how refined, distilled, and baroque La Farge's tone could be. "La Farge," one wrote, "was a past master of the parenthesis and he hated to let go of his collateral lines of thought." William James remembered that "his sentences when they do come forth are often worth the throes of concentration which attend their birth." Henry Adams observed: "In conversation, La Farge's mind was opaline with infinite shades and refractions of light and with color toned down to its finest gradations" (Fig. 4).[32]

Since this is precisely how those who knew Henry James spoke of James's conversational style, and since it also manages to describe James's epistolary style and his style as a writer of fiction, it is interesting that, as an

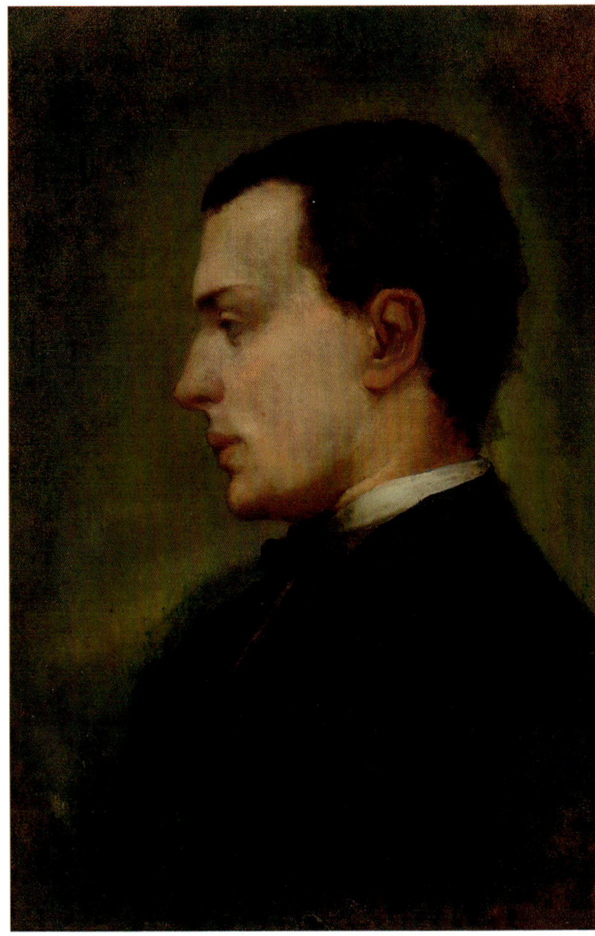

FIG. 3. John La Farge (1835–1910), *Henry James*, 1862, The Century Association, New York.

impressionable teenager, he spent so much time with La Farge. Had La Farge been a novelist, James would have set about competing with him, or at least observing him with some suspicion or with worry about his worth. But since La Farge was a painter who knew about literature, he could have a much greater and clearer effect on his young friend and the direction he would take, including his very tone. Henry James did not have to measure himself against a painter and thus La Farge, in the years when James was uncertain about his talent and his future, became perhaps the most significant mentor James ever had (Fig. 5).

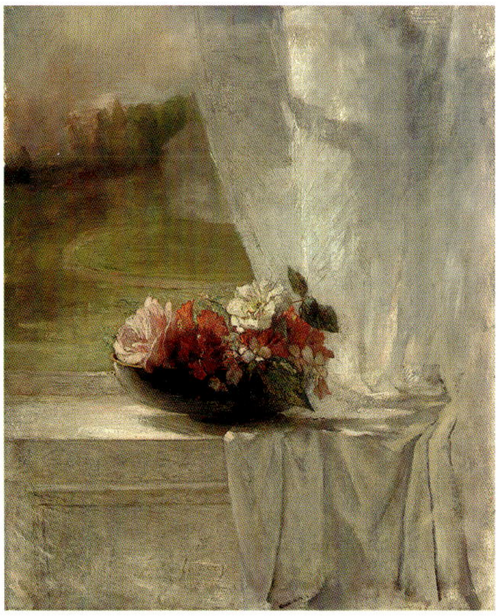

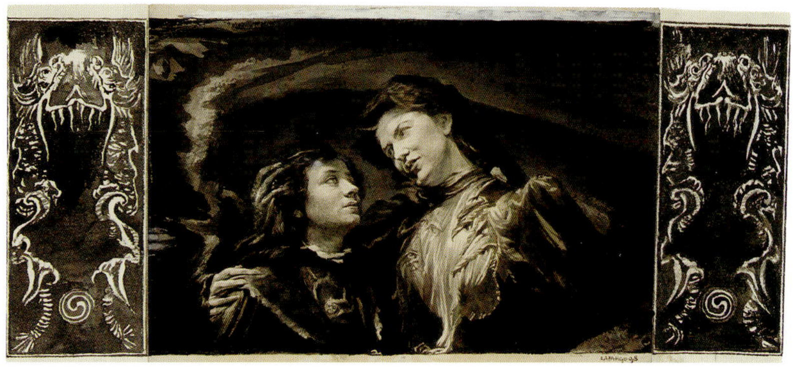

FIG. 4. John La Farge (1835–1910), *Flowers on a Window Ledge,* ca. 1861, National Gallery of Art, Washington, DC.

FIG. 5. John La Farge (1835–1910), *The Child Magnetized by the Nurse, for "The Turn of the Screw,"* 1898, Fogg Art Museum, Harvard University Art Museums, Cambridge, Massachusetts.

While James wrote with great acuity about the novel, indeed became one of the greatest theorists of fictional form, his writing about visual art, mainly done in his early years in Europe, failed to recognize the significance of Impressionism. Thus while he moved among artists and wrote about artists' lives in his work, he did not know the main French artists of the age, even though he knew most of the French novelists. The work that interested him most was Anglo-American, or pre-Impressionist. What mattered to him was perhaps the atmosphere that visual artists created and the world they inhabited more than any new systems or innovations.

In his account of books and writers, James generally wrote with admiration, appreciation, even mildness. Even when he took a dim view, he expressed himself with great care and made many distinctions. When he wrote about visual art, on the other hand, his tone could be astringent, often acid; he was often ready to judge the work he saw harshly. When he wrote about painting and sculpture, he tended to use a tone almost absent elsewhere in his writing. He seemed willing to deplore. In his writing about visual art, he was setting a standard that was easy for him to outline. Looking at a bad painting did not take much time, compared to reading a bad book. Writing about visual art allowed James to get things off his chest, so to speak, without having to go to too much trouble.

James took a benign, if rather offensively patronizing, view of the American need for European paintings. In 1874, when he was thirty-one, he wrote in an unsigned piece for the *Atlantic Monthly:* "It has been proved that there is no reason in the essence of things why a room full of old masters should not be walked into from an American street and appear to proper advantage in spite of what in harmonious phrase we should call its location. There is something we like, moreover, in our sending out at a venture for half a million dollars' worth of pictorial entertainment."[33]

Especially when he was young, James reserved some of his greatest disapproving moments for paintings he did not like. These included a painting by the French painter Jean-Léon Gérôme (1824–1904) of a cockfight, which James saw in Boston when he was twenty-nine. "A young man," James wrote in another unsigned piece for the *Atlantic Monthly*, "entirely naked, is stooping upon one knee, and stirring two bristling game cocks to battle. A young woman, also naked—more than naked, as one somehow feels Gerome's figures to be—reclines beside him and looks lazily on. . . . There is a total lack of what one might call moral atmosphere. . . . The horrid little game in the centre, the brassy nudity of the youth, the peculiarly sensible carnality of the young woman, the happy combination of moral and physical shamelessness, spiced with the most triumphant cleverness, conduce to an impression from which no element of interest is absent, save the good old-fashioned sense of being pleased."[34]

So too in a long essay, also written in 1872, on the collection that became the germ of the Metropolitan Museum of Art, a collection James believed "contains no first-rate example of a first-rate genius,"[35] James stood in front of a painting by Jacob Jordaens and commented: "The Virgin is a sweet-faced young woman whom the painter evidently meant to make pretty within the limits of Flemish probability, and the child has an odd look of having just waked up the least bit cross from a nap."[36] Two years later, from Florence, he had this to say about Rubens: "Was Rubens lawfully married to Nature, or did he merely keep up the most unregulated of flirtations? Three or four of his great carnal cataracts ornament the walls of the Pitti. If the union was really solemnized it must be said that the ménage was at best a stormy one. He is a strangely impossible jumble of the true and the false. He paints a full flesh surface that radiates and palpitates with illusion, and into the midst of it he thrusts a mouth, a nose, an eye, which you would call your latest-born a blockhead for perpetrating."[37]

But as time went on the enemy ceased to be the limits of Flemish probability and became the limits of painting itself. In 1876 James saw an early showing of the work of Renoir, Monet, Sisley, Pissarro, and Morisot. "This little band," he wrote in a dispatch to the *New-York Tribune*, "is on all grounds less interesting than the group out of which Millais and Holman Hunt rose into fame. None of its members show signs of possessing first-rate talent, and indeed the 'Impressionist' doctrines strike me as incompatible, in an artist's mind, with the existence of first-rate talent. . . . The Impressionists . . . abjure virtue altogether, and declare that a subject which has been crudely chosen shall be loosely treated. They send detail to the dogs and concentrate themselves on general expression."[38]

In his writing about painting, James made many definite statements. "There is no greater work of art than a great portrait";[39] or "A picture should have some relation to life as well as to painting";[40] or "A picture is not an impression but an expression—just as a poem or a piece of music is."[41] But in his stories about painters, he tended to be more exploratory and tentative, more fascinated by the action of art itself and by what the making of art did to a personality than interested in making judgments. He left his astringent tone aside when he came to work as a writer of fiction.

—

Above the city of Florence sits Bellosguardo, which would become an important place for James. Elizabeth Barrett Browning invoked it in her poem *Aurora Leigh:*

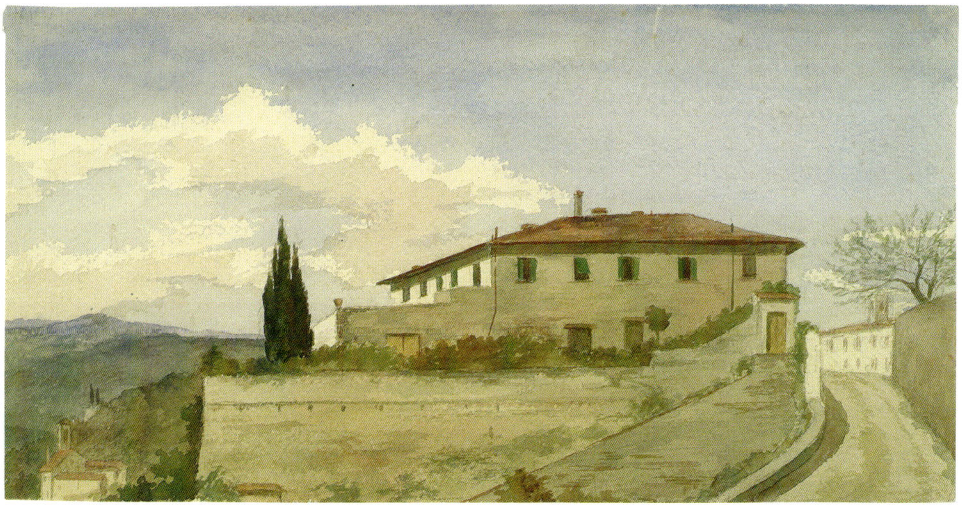

FIG. 6. Elizabeth Boott Duveneck (1846–1888), *Villa Castellani at Bellosguardo,* 1886, National Museum of Women in the Arts, Washington, DC.

I found a house, at Florence, on the hill
Of Bellosguardo. 'Tis a tower that keeps
A post of double-observation o'er
The valley of Arno (holding as a hand
The outspread city) straight towards Fiesole
And Mount Morello and the setting sun,—
The Vallombrosan mountains to the right,

No sun could die, nor yet be born, unseen
By dwellers at my villa: morn and eve
Were magnified before us in the pure
Illimitable space and pause of sky.[42]

Villas studded into the hill at Bellosguardo have, as Browning says, a majestic view over the city and the Arno valley below. In 1888 James wrote *The Aspern Papers* in the Villa Brichieri-Colombi on Bellosguardo, which James's friend Constance Fenimore Woolson (1840–1894) had rented. Farther up the hill, there is a small square with a large villa, previously called Villa Castellani, which, from the front, looks like a barracks. The apartment—which James's friends Francis Boott and his daughter, Lizzie, rented—in this house has not changed to this day; the house itself and indeed the gardens also are still much as James described them in *The Portrait of a Lady.* The "imposing front," James wrote, "had a somewhat incommunicative character. It was the mask, not the face of the house. It had heavy lids, but no eyes; the house in reality looked another way—looked off behind, into splendid openness and the range of the afternoon light. In that quarter the villa overhung the slope of its hill and the long valley of the Arno, hazy with Italian colour. It had a narrow garden, in the manner of a terrace, productive chiefly of tangles of wild roses and other old stone benches, mossy and sun-warmed. The parapet of the terrace was just the height to lean upon, and beneath it the ground declined into the vagueness of olive-crops and vineyards" (Figs. 6 and 7).[43]

James had also used this house in *Roderick Hudson,* calling it the Villa Pandolfini, which "stood directly upon a small grass-grown piazza on the top of a hill which sloped straight from one of the gates of Florence. It offered to the outer world a long rather low façade, coloured a dull, dark yellow and pierced with windows of various sizes. . . .

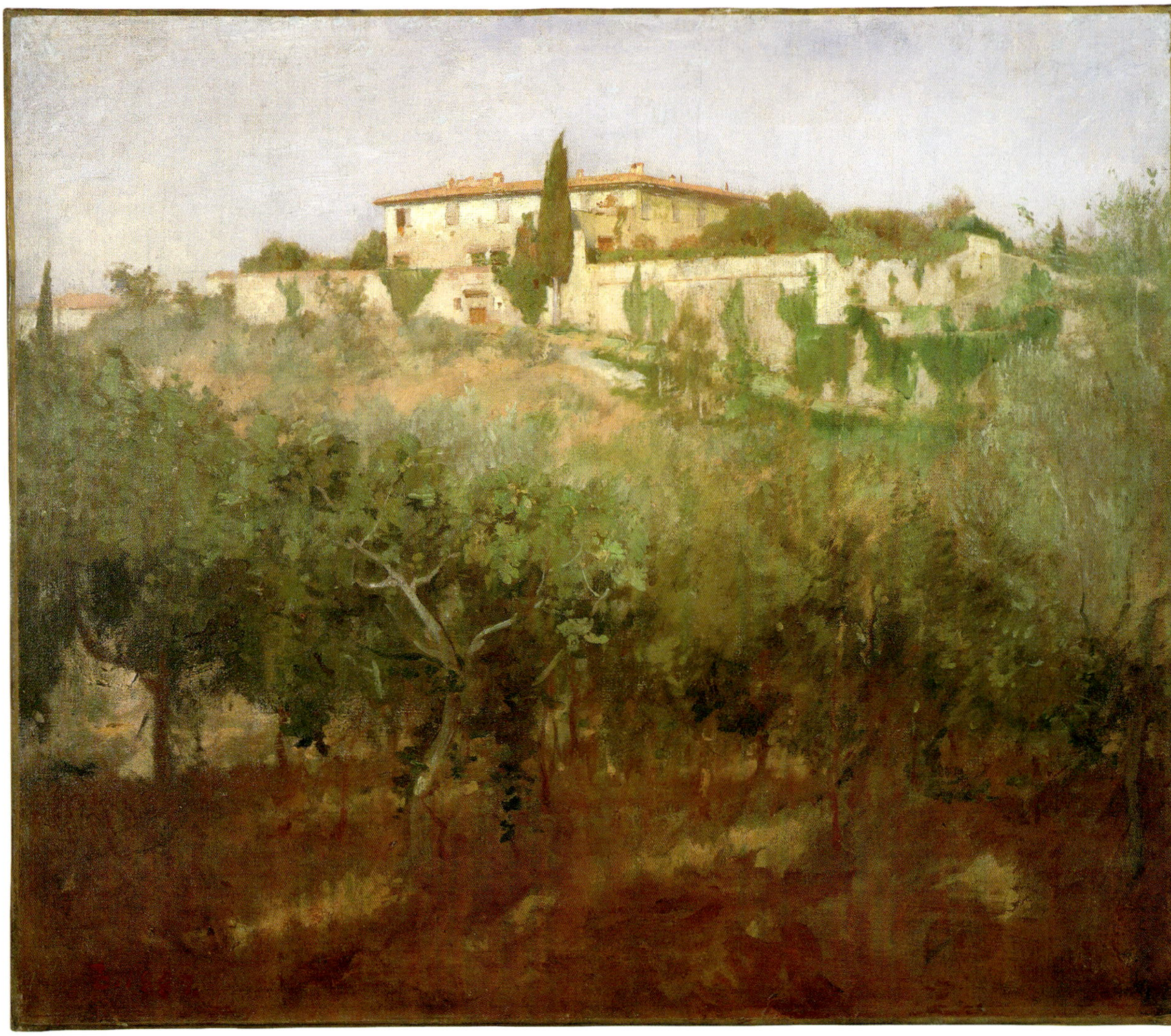

FIG. 7. Frank Duveneck (1848–1919), *Villa Castellani at Bellosguardo,* 1887, Brooklyn Museum.

Mrs Hudson's rooms opened into a small garden. . . . Silence, peace and security seemed to abide in the ancient house and make it an ideal refuge for unsuccessful lives."[44]

The reader often has, with James, as with most novelists, an urge to find an autobiographical base, or a source in real life, for his best fiction and a fascination about why certain themes and topics continued to interest him. Finding characters from James's life, however, and suggesting that he based fictional characters on them is often to miss the point of his art. As he imagined his books, James saw life as shadow and the work he produced as substance. He believed that language and form, the tapestry of the novel, could produce something richer and more substantial than mere life. He believed that art could offer what was chaotic and incomplete a complex and golden completion.

When his friend Grace Norton wrote to him about *The Portrait of a Lady* as its serialization began, suggesting that the character of Isabel Archer was based on his dead cousin Minny Temple, James replied: "You are both right and wrong about Minny Temple. I had her in mind and there is in the heroine a considerable infusion of my impression of her remarkable nature. But the thing is not a portrait. Poor Minny was essentially *incomplete* and I have attempted to make my young woman more rounded, more finished. In truth everyone, in life, is incomplete, and it is [in] the work of art that in reproducing them one feels the desire to fill them out, to justify them, as it were."[45]

In three of his novels, James dramatized the close relationship between a father and his only child, a daughter. In a letter to Lizzie Boott in 1874, after a visit to her father's apartment in the Villa Castellani, James wrote how pleasant it might be "to live in that grave, picturesque old house." He added: "I have a vague foreboding that I shall, some day."[46] It is notable, then, how intensely this space and the people who lived in it began to inhabit and nourish his imagination.

Gilbert Osmond and his daughter, Pansy, who reside in that house in *The Portrait of a Lady* would not, Leon Edel wrote, actually "resemble Frank and Lizzie Boott; but the image of the villa, and the couple in it was to serve [James's] need in the novel that was slowly taking shape in his consciousness." Edel went on: "Perhaps we may discern also . . . the germ of a much later subject . . . for in the observed relationship of a father and daughter leading a self-sufficient life, he had the theme of an ultimate novel as well."[47] This novel would be *The Golden Bowl.*

It would be too crude then to suggest that James based any of his characters on his friends Francis and Lizzie Boott; rather he allowed their relationship to enter into the spirit of some of his fiction, become the "germ" for it. James allowed himself to reimagine the relationship between these figures whom he knew and offer it to characters whom he began to imagine in the light of what he knew, or in its shadow, or the space between.

Although James created fictional characters with their own autonomy, he moved very close to the shape of how the Bootts lived. In *The Portrait of a Lady,* he used not only their apartment and gardens, describing these spaces down to the letter, but also aspects of the hothouse relationship between the father and the daughter. In *Washington Square* and *The Golden Bowl,* he found a different setting, but in both novels he also dramatized an intense relationship between a rich, widowed father and his only child, a daughter. And in all three novels, James introduced a man less grand or rich than the father—an outsider who wanted to marry the daughter. Thus in all three of these novels James used the actual shape of the relationship between Francis Boott, his daughter, Lizzie, and the American painter Frank Duveneck (1848–1919), who eventually married Lizzie, to create drama (Fig. 8).

If Hendrik Andersen was the American artist with whom James had the most intense correspondence, and if John La Farge was the artist who had the greatest influence on James, then Frank Duveneck was the American artist whom James filled out most in his fiction, the artist whom he most reimagined, whom he made most use of, whom he, to use his own term, most completed.

As much as he was interested in character, James was interested in configuration. He was concerned with what would happen to a character placed in association with others. In general, he found an intensity and produced greater fictional energy when working with a small number of characters and placing them in association with each other, much as a painter might do in a group portrait, using light and shade, color, arrangement, and perspective.

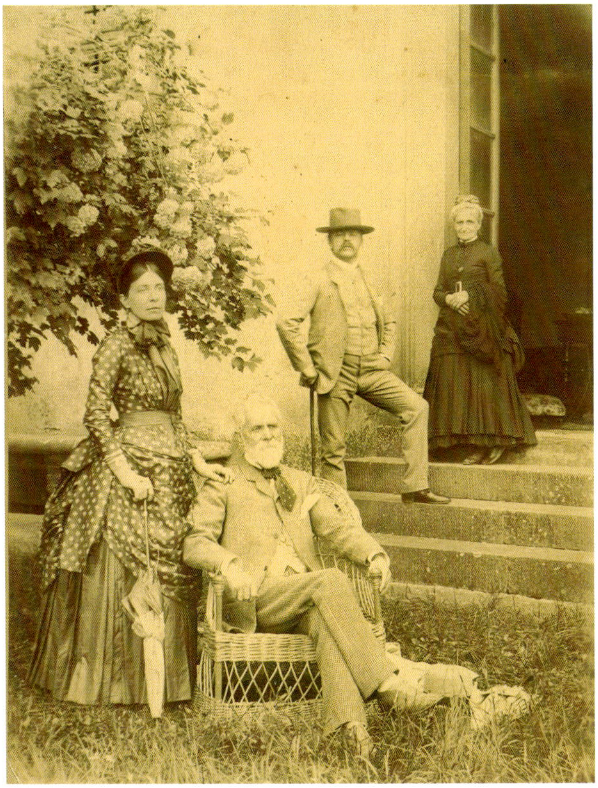

FIG. 8. *Photograph of Elizabeth Boott Duveneck, Francis Boott, Frank Duveneck, and Ann Shenston at Bellosguardo, Florence,* ca. 1886, Archives of American Art, Smithsonian Institution, Washington, DC.

It is often possible to find in James's own personal relations a shadow that became substance as he created these configurations. For example, the relationship between John La Farge and the young Henry James made its way into the relationship between Rowland Mallet and Roderick Hudson—the older mentor and the young genius. And to find this again as the relationship between James himself and the young Hendrik Andersen became substance in the connection between Chad Newsome and Lambert Strether in *The Ambassadors.*

James, of course, used his imagination more than he used anything else; he also had other sources or shadows to work from in both *Roderick Hudson* and *The Ambassadors.* But La Farge and Andersen mattered to James over certain periods of his life. It is thus clear that they, or their spirits, entered as one element into the body or bloodstream of his fiction.

In a way, these beginnings, this set of shadowy, unformed shapes, were essential for James. They were pressing, ghostly presences that he could imbue with substance, changing details, adding weight, but using always something intense that had captured the imagination in the first place or mattered somehow to the hidden self or appeared as intensely interesting.

Thus the figure of the American painter Frank Duveneck and his relations with Francis Boott and his daughter, Lizzie, require some consideration when we think of *Washington Square, The Portrait of a Lady,* and *The Golden Bowl.*

This in turn leads us to the idea that the very figure of the painter, or the visual artist, found a way to haunt and nourish James's imagination more than, say, the image of the writer, even though James wrote several stories about writers, or even the actual life of the author himself.

James knew a number of visual artists and studied them closely. Because their temperament and system of work were not his, he was not confined by his knowledge as he started to imagine what such a temperament could do in a piece of fiction. In considering Duveneck, James could see the energy such a figure could release—a figure who worked with his hands for the benefit of wealthy patrons, allowing him to move from untidy studio to polished salon, thus allowing him to appear both humble and grand, or be caught, by virtue of his work, between two classes.

In some of his fiction James dramatized such an artist directly, allowing the sculptor Roderick Hudson, for example, to have, even though he is poor, a glamor that his rival the wealthy Prince Casamassima lacks, thus attracting the beautiful Christina Light, who becomes involved with both men in the novel, all the more. Thus the artist in the novel has a sexual allure and a sense of entitlement that attracts the young woman and, at the same time, a lack of a fixed position in society that repels her family. In other books, James transformed such energy, or allowed it to become the seed for another form of ambiguous and troublesome energy.

For example, he changed Frank Duveneck, whom he saw as a penniless expatriate provincial, into a handsome, penniless fortune hunter (*Washington Square*), a timid expatriate collector of artifacts (*The Portrait of a Lady*), and a penniless and untrustworthy Roman prince (*The Golden Bowl*). In each of the novels, the man seeks to marry above his station, or to a young woman richer than he is, as Duveneck did, and thus causes chaos, as Duveneck did, too; and in each novel the young woman is an only child who has been brought up by her formidable, protective, patrician, and widowed father. And in each case, too, the young woman has deep, stubborn feelings that are carefully masked. Despite a paleness and an innocence, when it comes to love she is someone who will not easily give in.

Francis Boott was born in Boston in 1813 (Fig. 9). His family owned the Boott Mills, which produced textiles, in Lowell, Massachusetts. In 1844 he married Elizabeth Lynam, who also came from a wealthy Boston family. His daughter, Lizzie, was born in 1846; a year later Boott's wife, Elizabeth, died. When Lizzie was a year and five months old, Francis Boott traveled to Europe with her and her nurse, who was to remain with them for the next forty years. (William Wetmore Story was on the same boat.) They lived in Italy, where Francis Boott began to compose music. His first string quartet had its initial performance at William Wetmore Story's apartment in Rome. In 1858, the Bootts rented the apartment on Bellosguardo above Florence that James used as Osmond's apartment in *The Portrait of a Lady*. Lizzie wrote poems and a novel and began to study art with Giorgio Mignaty (1824–1895), a Greek painter who had lived for many years in Florence. (In 1861, Mignaty was commissioned by Robert Browning to make a painting of the drawing room of the Casa Guidi in Florence, the room where *Aurora Leigh* had been written.)

The Bootts returned to Boston in 1865, when Henry James first met them. (Lizzie became close to Minny Temple, whose spirit—she died in 1870—was one of the inspirations for Isabel Archer in *The Portrait of a Lady*.) In 1869, Lizzie studied with William Morris Hunt—with whom William James and John La Farge had also studied—when he opened the first painting classes for women in the United States. That year, William James wrote to a friend: "Miss Boott though not overpoweringly beautiful, is one of the best members of her sex I ever met. . . . She has a great talent for drawing and was very busy painting here, which, as she is in just about the same helpless state in which I was when I abandoned the art, made her particularly interesting to me. You had better come home soon and make her acquaintance for you know these first class young spinsters do not always keep forever, although on the whole they tend to in Boston."[48]

In *Notes of a Son and Brother*, Henry James remembered the Bootts when he first met them: "It mattered enormously for such a pair as the Bootts, intimately associated father and daughter, that what had lain nearest *their* hand,

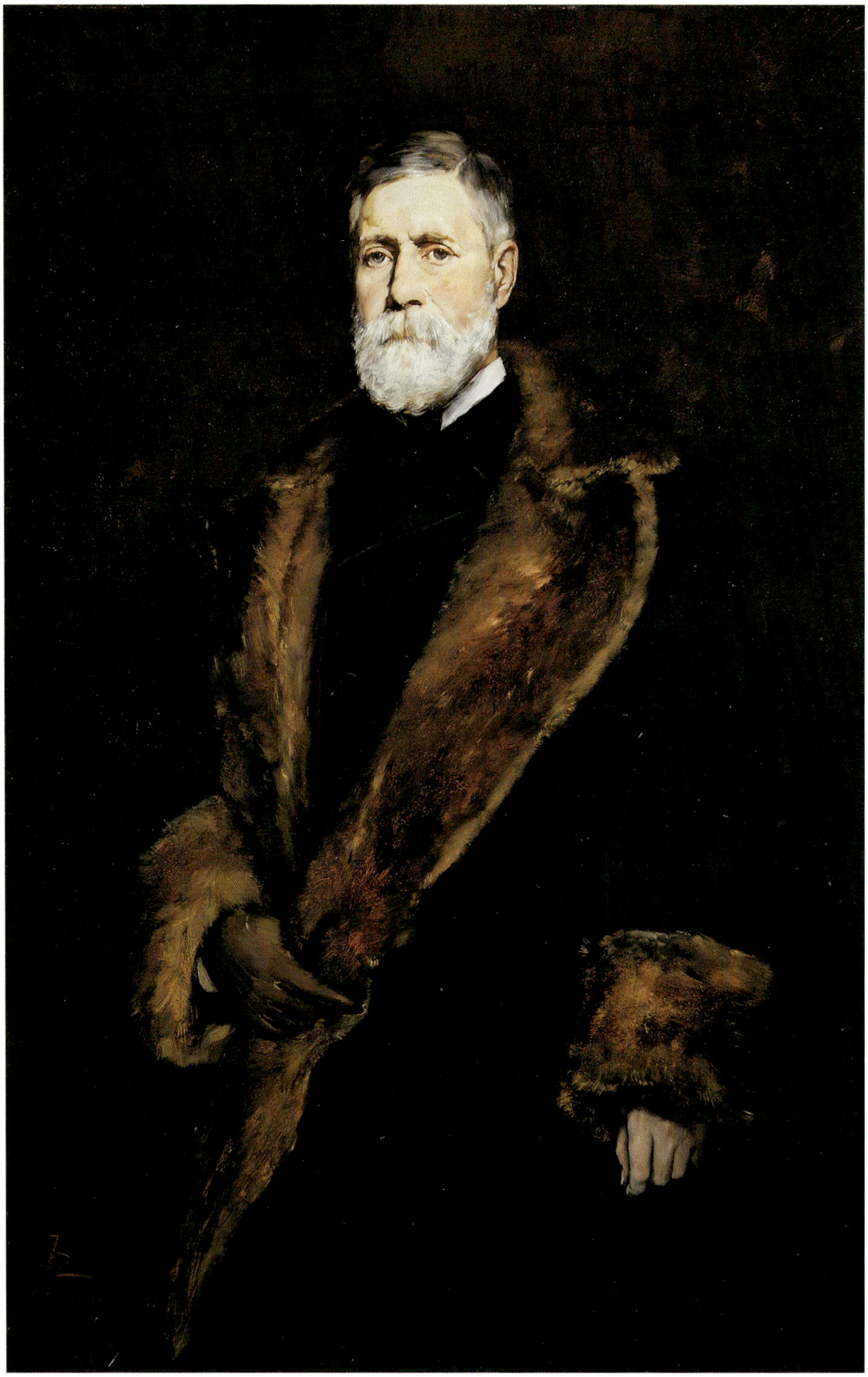

FIG. 9. Frank Duveneck (1848–1919), *Francis Boott,* 1881, Cincinnati Art Museum.

or at least that of conspiring nature and fortune in preparing them for our consumption, had been the things of old Italy, of the inconceivable Tuscany . . . and that when originally alighting among us *en plein* Newport they had seemed fairly to reek with a saturation, esthetic, historic, romantic that everything roundabout made precious."[49]

Of Lizzie he wrote: "This delightful girl, educated, cultivated, accomplished, toned above all, as from steeping in a rich old medium, to a degree of the rarer among her coevals 'on our side,' had the further, the supreme grace that she melted into American opportunities of friendship . . . with the glee of a sudden scarce believing discoverer."[50]

Even Henry James's mother noticed Lizzie's charms. In the summer of 1869, she wrote to Henry about her: "What a striking instance she is of what a careful and thorough education can accomplish. . . . Of course she could never be formed as she is in America" (Fig. 10).[51]

The Bootts crossed and recrossed the Atlantic a number of times. Henry James, while traveling with his aunt and his sister, Alice, met them in Paris, Switzerland, and Rome, where he spent Christmas Eve with them in 1872. The following year, when he was again in Rome, James continued to see them. He wrote home: "Lizzie is as sweet as ever. She has a little studio. . . . I had an errand this morning . . . and found Lizzie in her studio, *en tete a tete* with one of the very swell models—a wondrous youth in a sheepskin jacket and bandaged legs and flowing curls and the most pictorial complexion." James was present when Lizzie showed her sepia and watercolor sketches to Edward Boit and Frederic Crowninshield. "They, like myself, were much surprised at her fertility and general skill."[52] Lizzie Boott became one of James's regular correspondents.

In 1876, the Bootts, father and daughter, settled finally in Europe, living first in France, where James also was and where Lizzie became a student of Couture, with whom Hunt in turn had studied three decades earlier. James thought Couture "a vulgar little fat and dirty old man," but Lizzie liked him as a teacher.[53]

The artist Frank Duveneck, whom Lizzie would eventually marry, was born in 1848 and brought up in a poor family in Cincinnati, Ohio. At the age of twenty-one, he went to the Munich Academy to study art. In Munich he became close to William Merritt Chase (1849–1916), with whom he shared a studio. As the art historian Francesca Bardazzi has written: "Both assimilated the lesson of the academy through the teaching of Wilhelm von Diez: the dark palette, the dense brushwork, the admiration for the psychological penetration of the old Northern European portraitists. While from Wilhelm Leibl they learned about the more modern French models of Courbet and Manet."[54]

In 1878 Duveneck began an art school in Bavaria. His American students, who painted in Bavaria and later in Venice and Florence, included Otto Henry Bacher (1856–1909), John Twachtman (1853–1902), John White Alexander (1856–1915), Charles Abel Corwin (1857–1938), and Julius Rolshoven (1858–1930). They became known as the Duveneck Boys. Ralph Curtis (1854–1922), whose family would later own the Palazzo Barbaro in Venice, also studied with Duveneck in Munich.

When Duveneck exhibited five paintings at the Boston Art Club in 1875, James wrote in *The Galaxy:* "The good people of Boston have recently been flattering themselves that they have discovered an American Velasquez. In the rooms of the Boston Art Club hang some five remarkable portraits by Mr. Frank Duveneck of Cincinnati. This young man, who is not yet, we believe, in his twenty-fifth year, took his first steps in painting in the Bavarian capital, and it is hardly hyperbolical to say that

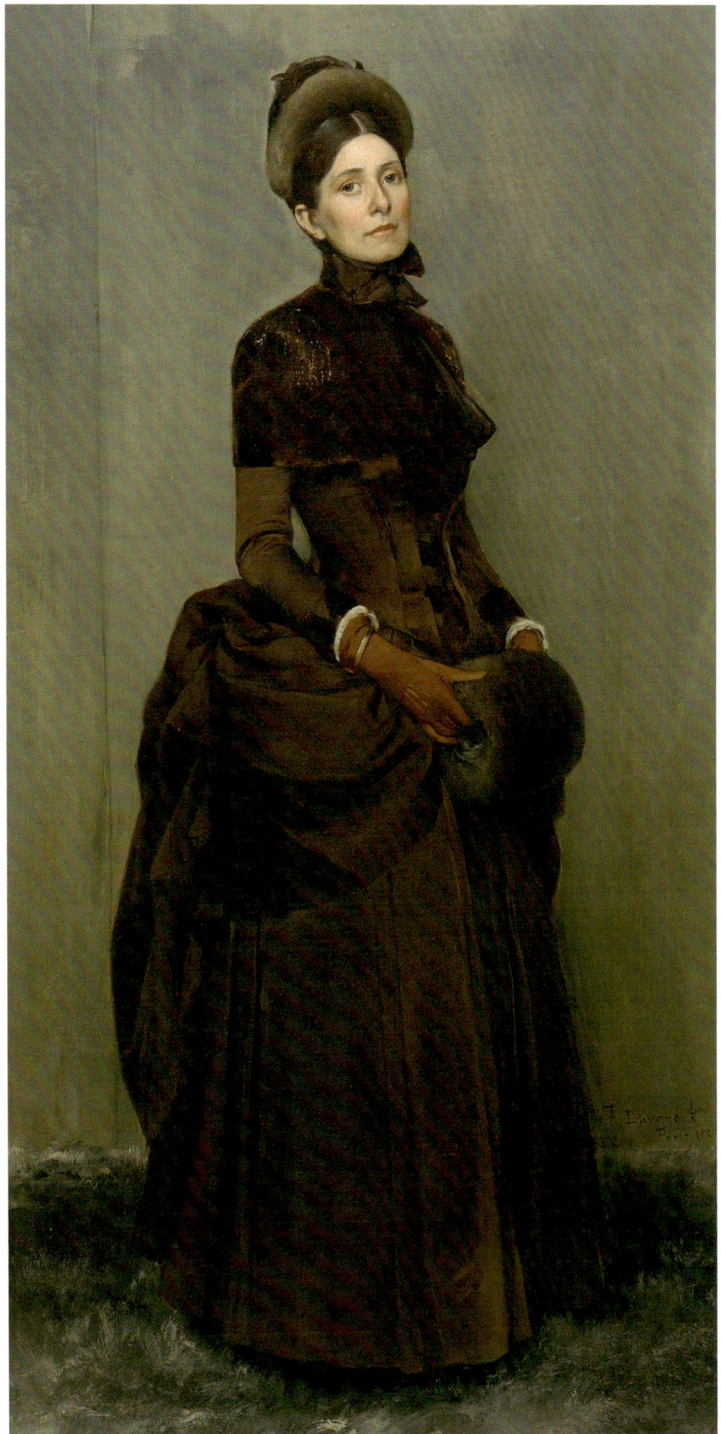

FIG. 10. Frank Duveneck (1848–1919), *Elizabeth Boott Duveneck*, 1888, Cincinnati Art Museum.

these steps were, for a mere lad, giant strides. He came back a while since, if we are not mistaken, to his native city, where his genius was not highly appreciated, and where depressing obscurity was his portion, until aesthetic Boston held out a friendly hand. It is of course of supreme importance that Mr. Duveneck should not be talked about intemperately, though we shall be surprised if his head is not too firmly set upon his shoulders to be easily turned. We speak in reason when we say that the half dozen portraits in question have an extraordinary interest. They are all portraits of men—and of very ugly men; they have little grace, little finish, little elegance, none of the relatively superfluous qualities. But they have a most remarkable reality and directness, and Velasquez is in fact the name that rises to your lips as you look at them. It is very evident that in so far as there is any question of Velasquez in the matter, the analogy of Mr. Duveneck's talent with that of the great Spaniard is a natural, instinctive one."

James went on to comment on the "extreme naturalness" of the works, "their unmixed, unredeemed reality." They contained, he wrote, "the material of an excellent foundation" and he looked forward to Duveneck doing something "first rate."[55]

In Boston that season, Lizzie Boott purchased a portrait of William Adams from Duveneck. Three years later, when she visited Duveneck's studio in Venice, she wrote to a Boston acquaintance: "He is a remarkable looking young man. He has a fine head and a keen eye and the perceptions strongly developed."[56]

At some stage toward the end of the 1870s, Lizzie Boott fell in love with Frank Duveneck. Later, she wrote of him: "He is a child of Nature, but a natural gentleman. He seems to have led the queerest, most vagrant sort of life among monks and nuns and convents in America, and rough art students here. . . . He is the frankest, kindest-hearted of mortals and the least likely to make his way in the world. He is rather lazy, I fancy, and besides never looks at all to the main chance, so I suppose he will always be out at elbow as he seems to be now."[57]

It is easy to imagine how shocked Francis Boott must have been. Not only was Duveneck penniless and unrefined, he was Catholic, and not only that but had developed a reputation for carousing in beer halls with his friends. He was hardly the sort of person whom the Bootts had left Boston to consort with.

In the summer of 1879, in Munich, Frank Duveneck became Lizzie's art teacher. It was agreed that she would take a studio in the city and he would visit her at the weekend from the town of Polling, where he was teaching his male students, and thus comment on her progress. Lizzie's father accompanied her to Munich. She wrote to a friend in Boston: "We have now been here four days and in that time have taken and moved into an apartment, hired a studio and engaged Duveneck as a teacher." She had been told, she wrote, that Duveneck "had a real genius for imparting to others and had many scholars among young Americans." Her informant did not know, she wrote, if Duveneck "would take any more but I had better try. So try we did and he accepted at once and is to come tomorrow to my studio. Joy! Do you not all envy me?"[58]

On 28 June, James wrote to Lizzie from London: "I am delighted that you have fallen on your feet so speedily in Munich. I congratulate you on everything, and I congratulate Duveneck on *you!* I am rather sorry that you are not going to a more famous instructor—an acknowledged Master—or to a man who goes in rather more for 'high finish' . . . but I have no doubt that Duveneck will be able to show you a good many things and that under his genial influence your powers will increase and multiply."[59]

Lizzie borrowed the word *genial* when she wrote to a friend about her new teacher: "He is very nice, genial, simple, and friendly and ready to talk by the hour and tell me all he knows. He seems to me a born painter, perfect in technique, too realistic to be interested ever in sentiment, perhaps in fact making things invariably uglier than they are. Ugly always, but the bare startling fact he gives you with such force and truth that it is admirable."[60]

She wrote again, this time emphasizing some of her own primness: "I watched Duveneck paint and some of his boys. . . . The reverence and love which they bear to their master is delightful to behold. He is a man who endears himself to all who know him and apart from his artistic power the moral restraint which he exercises on these young men who are in Europe without friends or relatives is very great." She compared this to some of the French schools and went on: "And this must convince us all the more that the standard of morals is higher among Americans than any other nation." She described meetings of students for drawing with music and tea. "We banished all parents quite in the American fashion and the meetings turned out to be very pleasant."[61]

During the summer Francis Boott returned to Italy alone. At the end of September, Lizzie, it seems, convinced Duveneck to move to Florence, and he, in turn, invited all his students to follow him there. At the end of September, she wrote to a friend: "Duveneck is to migrate to Florence with ten of his pupils next month. He is tired of Munich. Florence for a time will be a better place for him, though he ought finally to go to Paris."[62]

Since neither Duveneck nor any of his students spoke Italian, Lizzie arranged living and studio spaces for them in Florence. They were a raw group of art students, ambitious and serious, but also opinionated and somewhat uncouth. The effect they had on Florence was described by William Dean Howells in his novel *Indian Summer,* where they were called the Inglehart boys, as one of the characters explains to Colville, the main protagonist of the novel, an American visiting Florence: "'They were here all last winter and they've just got back. It's rather exciting for Florence.' She gave him a rapid sketch of that interesting exodus of a score of young painters from the art school in Munich, under the head of the singular and fascinating genius by whose name they became known. 'They had their own school for a while in Munich, and then they all came down into Italy in a body. They had their studio things with them, and they travelled third class, and they made the greatest excitement everywhere, and had the greatest fun. They were a great sensation in Florence. I hope they are going to stay.'"[63]

Later, Colville sees this version of the Duveneck Boys in a Florentine restaurant. "They all talked at once, each man of his own interests, except when they joined in a shout of mockery and welcome for some newcomer. Colville . . . could hear what they thought of Botticelli and Michelangelo . . . of whether Inglehart had probably got to Venice yet . . . all the voices joined in jolly uproar."[64]

In *Indian Summer,* Inglehart is presented as very popular among the young ladies of Florence, who made him so much tea that they almost killed him, causing him to move to Venice. But there may have been another reason why Duveneck and his boys went to Florence. It is suggested first in a letter Henry James wrote to his brother William in November 1879: "The natural and logical thing now seems . . . for Lizzie to marry Duveneck."[65] In January 1880, in a single sentence at the end of a postscript in a letter to his mother, also written from London, James wrote: "I wish Lizzie *would* wed Duveneck!"[66] This is significant because it makes clear that there was open talk between Boston and London late in 1879 about

Lizzie's relationship with Duveneck, a relationship of which, later evidence makes clear, her wealthy father disapproved. This was the period in which James was writing *Washington Square.* While there were other sources for the book, including a story told to him by Fanny Kemble about her brother jilting an heiress when he discovered that her father would disinherit her, it is fascinating that the short book was written during a period when Lizzie Boott was fraternizing in Florence with Frank Duveneck, whom she had lured from Munich while her father remained apart in Bellosguardo. At the time he was writing the short novel, James in two letters made clear that there was a possibility of marriage between the heiress and the penniless provincial.

—

In the autumn of 1879, as Duveneck and his boys were making their way in Florence, James McNeill Whistler (1834–1903) was arriving in Venice. Henry James had met Whistler a number of times in London the previous year during that famous season when James had dined out 140 times. In April 1878, James wrote to his father about a breakfast at Whistler's "queer little house in Chelsea, on the river," noting that his "Sunday morning breakfasts are somewhat classical. He is a queer little Londonized Southerner, and paints abominably. But his breakfasts are easy and pleasant, and he has tomatoes and buckwheat cakes."[67] In that same year, James had attacked Whistler's *Nocturnes* and *Arrangements* in an anonymous article published in *The Nation:* "Mr. Whistler's productions are pleasant things to have about, so long as one regards them as simple objects—as incidents of furniture or decoration. The spectator's quarrel with them begins when he feels it to be expected of him to regard them as pictures."[68]

James's line on Whistler was not unusual. In November 1878 Whistler was awarded a farthing damages in a libel action he took against John Ruskin, who had insulted his work. Ruskin had written: "For Mr. Whistler's own sake, no less than for the protection of the purchaser, Sir Coutts Lindsay [founder of the Grosvenor Gallery] ought not to have admitted works into the gallery in which the ill-educated conceit of the artist so nearly approached the aspect of willful imposture. I have seen, and heard, much of Cockney impudence before now; but never expected to hear a coxcomb ask two hundred guineas for flinging a pot of paint in the public's face."[69]

Whistler did not take to Venice immediately, as James had. On 1 January 1880, he wrote to his sister, wishing he were in London: "Of course, if things were as they ought to be all would be fit and well and I should be resting happily in the only city in the world fit to live in instead of struggling on in a sort of Opera Comique country where the audience is absent and the season is over."[70] It was one of the coldest winters ever recorded in Venice, and Whistler blamed the cold for his failure to deliver twelve etchings but promised that they would be "superb. . . . I have learned to know a Venice in Venice that the others seem never to have perceived. . . . The etchings themselves are far more delicate in execution, more beautiful in subject, and more important in interest than any of the old set."[71]

Whistler hired a gondolier and began to make his way into the lesser-known parts of the city with his materials for etching. He saw a number of artists who lived in the city, including Ralph Curtis, whose parents had begun to rent the palace that they eventually bought. In the spring, when Frank Duveneck and his friends arrived in Venice from Florence, Whistler, despite having manners rather more smooth than theirs and social ambitions more lofty, began to consort with them. Otto Henry Bacher, one of the

Duveneck Boys, described Whistler as "a curious sailor-like stranger . . . short, thick and wiry, with a head that seemed large and out of proportion to the lithe figure. His large wide-brimmed hat was tilted far back, and suggested a brown halo. It was a background for his curly black hair and singular white lock, high over his right eye, like a fluffy feather carelessly left where it had lodged. A dark sack coat almost covered an extremely low turned-down collar, while the narrow black ribbon did service as a tie, the long pennant-like ends of which, flapping about, now and then hit his single eye-glass."[72]

Compared to this, Frank Duveneck was less refined. Henry James commented on his "roughness, want of education."[73] But Whistler was broke, down on his luck. He was indeed the most famous pauper in the world, having had to sell his house in London to pay his debts. He moved into lodgings close to Duveneck and his friends in the Casa Jankovitz at the end of the Riva degli Schiavoni, which was not the fashionable part of the city. The Duveneck Boys looked up to Whistler and helped him with his etchings. Whistler, his biographer has written, "sometimes played shamelessly" on the idolatry of the Duveneck Boys. "He borrowed money and paints from the boys, and made use of the high quality printer's ink and portable press [Otto] Bacher had brought from Germany."[74]

The etchings Whistler made were more loose and free than the works he had made in London; he allowed what was not at the very center to dissolve and become indistinct. He wrote: "I began first of all by seizing upon the chief point of interest. Perhaps it might have been the extreme distance—the little palaces and the shipping beneath the bridge. If so I would begin drawing that distance in elaborately and then would expand from it until I came to the bridge, which I would draw in one broad sweep. If by chance I did not see the whole of the bridge, I would not put it in. In this way, the picture must necessarily be a perfect thing from start to finish."[75]

In his eighteen months in Venice, Whistler made some of the best etchings of his career. In his book *With Whistler in Venice*, Otto Bacher described the meticulous work that Whistler put into the process of preparing and printing the etchings: "He made his etched lines feel like air against solids; that is the impression some of his rich doorways of Venice gave me. He was the first to show me how to etch a deep, variegated door with a deeper figure somewhere in that darkness, all contrasted against something in the near opening that was much darker and which made the doorway effective. If he etched a doorway, he played with the lines and allowed them to jumble themselves into beautiful forms and contrasts, but was always very careful of the general direction they should run as a whole. In the partial darkness he could put in a hazy figure, the values being adjusted by the biting. He worked for hours on figures, and at times became quite excited over some success attained after much painstaking labor."[76]

Whistler also produced over a hundred pastels and some oil paintings. Otto Bacher watched him making the pastels: "He had quantities of vari-colored papers, browns, reds, greys, uniform in size. In beginning a pastel he drew his subject crisply and carefully in outline with black crayon upon one of those sheets of tinted paper which fitted the general color of the motive. A few touches with sky-tinted pastels, corresponding to nature, produced a remarkable effect, with touches of reds, greys and yellows for the buildings here and there. Some motives were finished at one sitting, but more often he made only the crayon outline . . . leaving the unfinished sketch for days . . . to be filled in later with pastels."[77]

In January 1881, Whistler's showing of fifty-three of these pastels in London offered him a triumphant return to

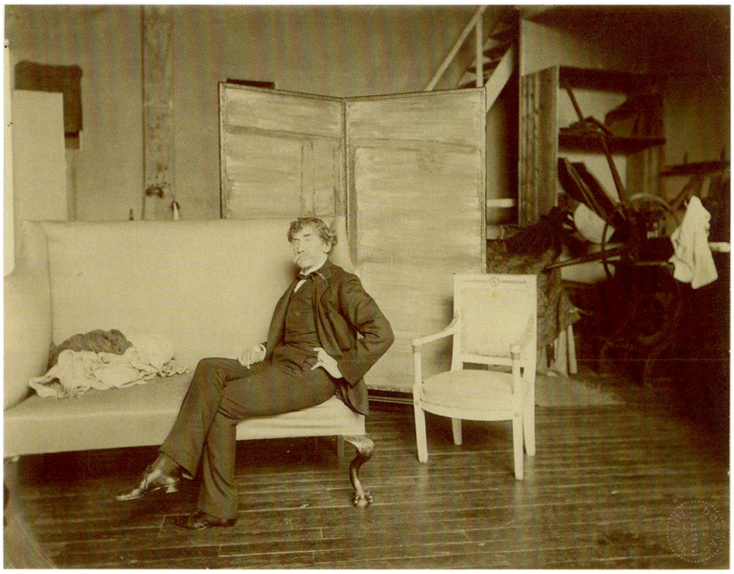

FIG. 11. M. Dornac (1858–1941), *Photograph of James McNeill Whistler in His Paris Studio at 86 rue Notre Dame des Champs*, 1890s, Charles Lang Freer Papers, Freer Gallery of Art and Arthur M. Sackler Archives, Smithsonian Institution, Washington, DC.

the city after the disastrous libel action. His etchings were also a great success. Since some of Duveneck's etchings of Venice had arrived in London at the same time, they were mistaken for Whistler's etchings, and it was presumed that Duveneck had copied Whistler. But in his book, Otto Bacher wrote: "It is only fair to say that Duveneck made the etchings of the Riva before Whistler made his. Whistler saw them as I was helping Duveneck bite the plates, and frankly said: 'Whistler must do the Riva also.'"[78]

Within a few years, Henry James had come around to taking a favorable view of Whistler's work. In June 1884 James wrote to Lizzie Boott from London about the exhibitions he had seen: "The Academy full of poor stuff, and the Grosvenor no better. The best thing at the latter—putting Sargent's Mrs Leigh apart—is an adorable big Whistler, a portrait of Lady Archibald Campbell. It is almost as good as the portrait of his Mother."[79]

In July the following year, on the suggestion of John Singer Sargent (1856–1925), James spent an evening in London in the company of Whistler and Count Robert de Montesquiou, on whom Huysmans had based the character of Des Esseintes in *A Rebours* and on whom Proust later modeled for Baron de Charlus and whose portrait Whistler would later paint. More than a decade later, when Whistler sent James a gift of an etching, James responded by sending him a copy of *The Spoils of Poynton*. When James moved to Lamb House in Rye in 1897, he hung the etching there. In his letter to Whistler of 18 February 1897 he told the artist that his etching (*Mairie, Loches*, 1888) was "already swinging in glory on a poorly-populated wall, where a liberal space has been made for it, and where it is quite the fair high aristocrat of the collection."[80]

A few years later, James used Whistler's apartment and garden in rue du Bac in Paris for a crucial scene in his novel *The Ambassadors* that takes place in the studio and garden of the sculptor Gloriani, a figure who also appears in the novel *Roderick Hudson* and the story "A Velvet Glove" (Fig. 11). Lambert Strether in *The Ambassadors*, on seeing the garden, "had the sense of names in the air, of ghosts at the windows, of signs and tokens, a whole range of expression, all about him, too thick for prompt discrimination." One of the "ghosts at the windows" was, in fact, James himself, as his familiarity with this particular garden stemmed from his 1876 visits to his friend

Madame Mohl, the famous Parisian *salonnière.* From the vantage point of Madame Mohl's home, James could look into this garden. Later, on 1 May 1893, James wrote to Isabella Stewart Gardner: "I went to tea yesterday with the Whistlers in their queer little garden-house off the rue du Bac, where the only furniture is the paint on the walls and the smile on the lady's broad face."[81]

As Duveneck and his followers were working in Venice, Henry James was leaving London. He appeared in Florence on 28 March 1880. As Leon Edel writes: "He lost no time in calling on the 'gentle and pure minded' Bootts."[82] He wrote to his father on March 30: "The Bootts are the same old Bootts as ever—gentle and affectionate and appreciative, but exhaling a kind of impression of sadness. Frank is less irrepressible (which is an improvement) and Lizzie is if possible even more mouselike. . . . [She] has thrown herself completely into the ministrations of Duveneck. She seems to spend her life in learning, or rather in studying without learning, and in commencing afresh, to paint in someone else's manner. I have not seen any of her new things yet, but, I believe, am to go to the studio today, and make the acquaintance of Duveneck."[83]

The following day James wrote to Charles Eliot Norton in Boston, making clear that he had seen Duveneck, and rehearsing some of the elaborate praise he had showered on his work in 1875: "I was interested very much in going to see a compatriotic artist, Frank Duveneck, who was very many years at Munich and has lately established himself here with a number of pupils. He is 'a child of nature and a child of freedom,' as Martin Chuzzlewit says; but he also struck me as much the most highly-developed phenomenon in the way of a painter that the U.S.A. has given birth to. His work is remarkably strong and brilliant, with a completeness about it that I should not have suspected from some unfinished things that were exhibited a long time since in Boston. I don't understand why he has not made more reputation—unless it be that he has apparently an almost *slovenly* modesty and want of pretention. I am told however that he was the pride and joy of the Munich School, which has been much depressed by his departure. I shall urge upon him the importance of his making himself known in Paris and London."[84]

James then left Florence to go south, returning to the city at the end of April. On 3 May, he wrote to his Aunt Kate about how Lizzie Boott seemed to stand to Duveneck "in a sort of double relation of pupil & adoptive mother—or at least adoptive sister. I hope she won't ever become his adoptive any-thing-else, as, though an excellent fellow, he is terribly earthy and unlicked."[85]

In his 30 March letter to his father, James had referred to his plan to return to Florence and work on what he called his "big novel," which would be *The Portrait of a Lady.* He had begun the book in Florence in late March. By early May, as he worked on the novel in earnest, living in the Hotel de l'Arno, Frank Duveneck was in Venice and Lizzie Boott was traveling in Spain with three women friends from the Hunt art classes in Boston. It is clear from a letter that James wrote to his mother from Genoa in March the following year that there was still discussion about the romance between Lizzie and Duveneck: "Perhaps you . . . know that (as I am told) Lizzie is much 'talked of,' in Florence in the matter of Duveneck. I have no 'inside view' of the case. Her marrying him would be, given the man, strange (I mean given his roughness, want of education, of a language, etc.) But the closeness of her intimacy is hardly less so. I take it, however, that the said intimacy is simply the result of the total unconventionality of the three persons concerned,—the third being Francis Boott. The latter thinks everything that Lizzie does all right, and is himself as simple as a milkmaid. Lizzie likes Duveneck, who is a very good fellow, and Duveneck likes her (no wonder, after all she has done for him); and none of them have any consciousness of appearances."[86]

James may have been exercising discretion is telling his mother that Francis Boott thought that everything his daughter did was "all right." It was clear that Francis Boott did not want Lizzie to marry Duveneck. In order to end what may have been an informal engagement between Lizzie and Duveneck, Francis Boott took his daughter back to Boston, where she concentrated on her painting. Although she and Duveneck may have met a number of times between 1881 and 1885, it was presumed that the romance between them was over. In this period, as for all of their lives since the death of his wife, Francis Boott had, as far as he was concerned, the full attention and loyalty of his only child.

As is the case to this day, and was also true when the Bootts lived there, the Villa Castellani was "divided into several distinct apartments."[87] The rooms on the ground floor were inhabited by the Bootts as, in the novel, they were occupied by Gilbert Osmond and his daughter Pansy. Gilbert Osmond, like Francis Boott, was a dilettante. He worked on his watercolors in the same way as Boott did on his musical compositions. Both men looked after their daughter, an only child, with the same immense zeal. In the novel, as in the life of the Bootts, the close connection between father and daughter was noted by all.

In *The Portrait of a Lady*, Ralph Touchett speaks about Osmond to his cousin Isabel Archer: "Who is he—what is he? He is a mysterious American, who has been living these twenty years, or more, in Italy. . . . For all I know he may be a prince in disguise; he rather looks like one."[88]

There were also, of course, differences between Francis Boott and Gilbert Osmond. One was money. Francis Boott was rich; Gilbert Osmond was more or less penniless. Another was manners. Francis Boott was known for his natural sweetness; Gilbert Osmond for his rudeness and his manufactured charm.

In the novel, Osmond, once he has married Isabel Archer and settled in Rome, is determined that his daughter will not marry Ned Rosier, who is in love with her and whom she loves too. Rosier comes again and again to the Osmonds' palace as Duveneck came to the Villa Castellani. Finally, Osmond decides that his daughter should return to the convent where she has been educated, as Francis Boott decided to take his daughter back to America.

Although James used the Bootts' living quarters in Florence with absolute transparency, neither the Bootts themselves, nor indeed Duveneck, interested him as precise figures on whom he could model characters. It is often more useful, in any case, to look at a drama already in the making rather than an individual character as the seed for James's work. James was interested, as his initial inspiration, in scenes rather than souls; he made his characters out of the dramatic moments he created for them, treating moral conflicts and matters of secrecy, infidelity, and power with infinite subtlety. In his work, a single look, a single moment of recognition, a single ambiguous resolution took on enormous force, became the fuel that powered the great engine of his novels. In his novels, he dramatized the intensity in the relations between people, playing freedom against pattern, restriction against openness, and dark chaos against harmony.

As he worked on *The Portrait of a Lady,* the drama that was closest to James was the drama of Francis Boott believing that his daughter, Lizzie, was making a mistake with Frank Duveneck, partly because of Duveneck's manners, but also because Duveneck had no money.

Thus in *The Portrait of a Lady* there are two configurations, one is Ralph Touchett, who believes that his cousin Isabel should not marry Gilbert Osmond partly because he dislikes Osmond's manners and also because he (and indeed his mother) sense that Osmond is marrying Isabel for money. The second configuration is Osmond himself and his daughter, whom he has raised like a hothouse flower, and Ned Rosier, whom Osmond does not think is grand enough or rich enough for his daughter.

James found the shapes and shadows, the configurations he needed for his novel in Bellosguardo. Thus the painter Frank Duveneck, who had already nourished *Washington Square,* subtly made his way into *The Portrait of a Lady* as someone who was seen as a fortune hunter wooing an heiress and also as an unsuitable match for a woman who was strangely, almost unhealthily, allied with her rich, idle father. As though Duveneck were a ghost, James created from him a living figure. From the chaos that existed in the relationship between Francis Boott and his daughter, Lizzie, in the shifting relationship between Lizzie and Frank Duveneck, and then in the uneasy relationship between all three, James, with all his guile as a novelist, created order. From the raw materials they gave him, he built his house of fiction.

Just as in the early 1880s James was making art from his interaction with the Bootts and from his observation of Duveneck, so, too, Duveneck made a grave and dignified formal portrait of Francis Boott in 1881, which is one of his best paintings (see Fig. 9), as he later made a formal portrait of Lizzie (see Fig. 10) as well as paintings of the Villa Castellani itself (see Fig. 7). Lizzie Boott, too, made paintings and sketches and watercolors of the Villa Castellani (see Fig. 6).

Early in 1886, Lizzie Boott finally agreed to marry Frank Duveneck. She wrote to a friend: "It has been a long affair for years. The thing was given up entirely at one time but on meeting again we find that the old feeling is not dead and we are going to take up life together as we did not like it very well apart. . . . This is a very solemn and momentous step for me and it involved, I felt, so much that was dear to me in my past life. I could not have been separated from my father after all these long years together. As it fortunately happens, this will not be. We shall all live together, most happily, I hope."[89]

They married in March 1886, with Lizzie a month away from her fortieth birthday. Her father made Duveneck sign a contract specifying that Lizzie's fortune was to remain hers "for her sole and separate use forever."[90] Francis Boott also created a trust in Lizzie's name that would remain in his keeping. Among the few who attended the civil ceremony in Paris was the artist Edward Darley Boit, a friend to both from Boston. (John Singer Sargent made a famous portrait of Edward Darley Boit's daughters; see Simpson, Fig. 16.) Ralph Curtis also attended as well as the artist George Henry Clements (1854–1935).

James was in London when he heard the news of the engagement. He wrote to Lizzie to congratulate her, saying that his "interest in you, dear Lizzie, will be so much greater as may be possible in a sentiment in which there was so little margin for increase." He then went on: "If your Father doesn't like it, he must come over and live with me—I have a room for him."[91] On the same day, he wrote to her father: "I hasten to express my sympathy in all you must feel on the subject of her engagement. . . . Take care lest between two easels you fall to the ground, you can so easily trip over their legs. . . . You will be a delightful *beau pere*—that is what strikes me most, and if you shouldn't be appreciated come and be that of your ever affectionately, Henry James."[92]

A few weeks later, James wrote to a friend about the marriage: "Duveneck won't beat her, nor *la rudoyer* [treat her badly], nor perhaps even neglect her, and will be completely under her influence and control; but he is illiterate, ignorant, and not a gentleman (though an excellent fellow, kindly, simple etc.) and she gives away to him her independence and freedom. His talent is great, though without delicacy, but I fear his indolence is greater still. . . . For him it is all gain—for her it is very brave. You see I am far from enthusiastic, but I await results with a certain confidence, thinking they may be considerably better than some of the elements would promise."[93]

James's next letter to Francis Boott, written on 25 May 1886, is, for readers of his fiction, one of his most intriguing; it is also a letter that makes the figure of Frank Duveneck even more important as shadow and inspiration in James's fiction. The letter reads: "I wonder, my good Francis, whether you will do me rather a favour. My excellent and amiable friend Constance Fenimore Woolson is in Florence, and I want to pay her your compliment and administer her some social comfort." James proposed that his friend go and visit Woolson and then went on "by which I don't mean that I want you to 'propose' to her, either for me or for yourself."

He went on to refer to Lizzie and Frank Duveneck, adding that he had three paintings by Lizzie on the wall of his apartment in London and hoped to have more. "They furnish my *apartment,* simply—or rather richly."[94]

As Lyndall Gordon has written about this letter of introduction, James "had no wish to promote a marriage between Boott and Miss Woolson; his interest lay in their capacities to generate an alternative world which could house his imagination."[95] In other words, in London James could contemplate a new configuration in Florence—his friend Francis Boott severed from his only daughter, to whom he was devoted, by her marriage to Duveneck, and the arrival of the outsider—also a close friend of James—and the father getting to know this woman, offering her "social comfort."

Duveneck and Lizzie were living with Francis Boott on Bellosguardo. They both had studios in the Villa Castellani. Under the influence of Italian light and Italian painting, Duveneck's dark palette was lightening. In the catalogue for a joint show of Frank Duveneck and Lizzie Boott's paintings in 1996, Carol M. Osborne wrote: "Golden light saturates the atmosphere of Duveneck's genre paintings dating from the two halcyon seasons he spent at Bellosguardo with his wife. . . . [Lizzie] Boott had always disliked the dark realism of his Munich portraits and now, undoubtedly encouraged by her taste for Salon painting, Duveneck too spun out sunny peasant women in the picturesque costume of the region. Occasionally, husband and wife painted from the same model."[96]

Between June and December 1886, James stayed in London knowing that his four friends—or rather his three friends and Duveneck—were seeing one another regularly and living in close proximity to each other in Florence. He had met the novelist Constance Fenimore Woolson, who was three years his senior, in Florence in the spring of 1880. He spent time with her visiting churches and museums. Something of her fresh and original response to what she saw made its way into the spirit of Isabel Archer whom James was then in the process of creating. On 3 May 1880, he wrote to his aunt: "This morning I took an American authoress [on] a drive—Constance Fenimore Woolson, whose productions you may know. . . . Constance is old-maidish, deaf, & intense; but a good little woman and a perfect lady."[97] She, in turn, wrote to a friend that Henry James "has been perfectly charming to me for the last three weeks."[98] There is no evidence that Woolson saw the Bootts during this sojourn in Florence.

James and Woolson soon became friends, and saw one another a great deal in England and on the Continent. In her biography of Woolson, Anne Boyd Rioux wrote about what happened in Florence once James wrote his letter to Boott in May 1886: "The fatherly Francis Boott appears to have called at the Casa Molini [where Woolson was staying] as soon as he received James's letter, and shortly afterwards she made the trip up to the Villa Castellani where she also met Lizzie and her new husband Frank Duveneck, both of whom were artists. The three were so taken with Woolson that they encouraged her to take an apartment in the villa. . . . Woolson thrilled at the thought of living across the courtyard from her new friends. She envisioned them painting in their garden and herself writing in her own, with the heavenly view laid out before her."[99]

A few months later, Woolson took a lease on the nearby Villa Brichieri-Colombi. When James came to Florence in December 1886, she suggested that he move into that house for a month while she remained in the Villa Castellani. James asked the Bootts and Woolson not to tell anyone in Florence of his advent as he did not want, he insisted, to enter the social whirl of the expatriate community in Florence. He would thus be able to concentrate on his work. He would also be able to take a very close look at his friends. He had, up to now, only ever seen Woolson alone; he had not seen the Bootts or Duveneck since the marriage.

From stray sentences in letters it is clear that the idea of Francis Boott and Constance Fenimore Woolson together had begun to intrigue James. In a letter to Boott when Woolson had gone to Geneva, he imagined her, he wrote, "in a balcony of the Hotel National, hanging over the lake and thinking of—you!"[100] In November, when Woolson was living in the Villa Castellani, James wrote to Boott about his imminent arrival: "She is a gallant friend, but I am afraid she has bored you with me. Never mind, you will have your revenge; she will bore *me* with *you*!"[101]

"It is easy to see," Anne Boyd Rioux wrote of the correspondence between Francis Boott and Woolson in subsequent years, "that during the three years Woolson lived at Bellosguardo she grew very attached to him . . . now that his daughter had married, Boott needed a companion, and Woolson liked feeling needed. . . . He wrote her a poem about her name, playing on the confusion many people had between her and her great-uncle James Fenimore Cooper, but stressing the 'world-wide fame' she had already achieved."[102]

When Henry James arrived in Bellosguardo on 8 December 1886, the Bootts had already decamped to the city below to await the birth of Lizzie's baby. Once the child—also called Frank—was born on 18 December, Francis Boott revoked the prenuptial agreement he had Frank Duveneck sign at the time of the wedding. Peace, it seemed, had broken out. The Duvenecks asked Woolson to be godmother to the new baby. In January, James moved into the city center himself and then moved to Venice, leaving Woolson to take up residence in the Villa Brichieri-Colombi. But in April, after an illness, James returned and moved into an apartment in Woolson's house where, over a six-week stay, he completed his long story *The Aspern Papers*.

During this period, Francis Boott and the rest of the family moved back into the Villa Castellani, completing the game of musical chairs. They were, it seemed, the

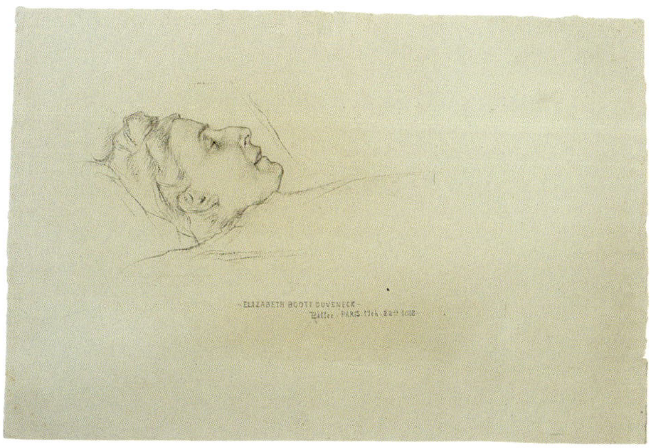

FIG. 12. Louis Ritter (1854–1892), *Post-Mortem Portrait of Elizabeth Boott Duveneck,* 1888, Cincinnati Art Museum.

only ones who actually knew where James was living in these six weeks, as in his letters to others he attempted to suggest that he was elsewhere. Thus he had briefly joined as a secret member the strange quasi family he himself had helped to create.

In March 1888 the jury of the Salon in Paris accepted both Frank Duveneck's ambitious portrait of Lizzie Boott (see Fig. 10) and Lizzie's watercolor study of the Villa Castellani (see Fig. 6). They were to be exhibited the following May, when Duveneck's portrait won honorable mention. On the day the jury met, Lizzie fell ill in Paris. She died of pneumonia there on 23 March 1888 (Fig. 12).

Her father and her husband brought her body back to Florence, where she was buried at the Allori Cemetery outside the Roman Gate. They also brought the fifteen-month-old baby back to Bellosguardo, where Woolson was waiting for them.

On 3 April, from London, James wrote to Francis Boott, using a tone that one might say was less than helpful, the sort of tone he would also use at times after the death of his cousin Minny Temple in 1870 and also in moments after Woolson's 1894 suicide in Venice. The tone, as Lyndall Gordon has described in her book *A Private Life,* was cold, analytical, oddly merciless, as though he were an observer, from a place apart.

"It is essentially true," he wrote of Lizzie, "that she had undertaken an effort beyond her strength, and she staggered under it and was broken down by it. I was conscious of this as long ago as during those months in Florence when superficially she seemed so happy and hopeful. The infirmity was visible beneath the optimism—and the whole thing seemed to me without an issue. This particular issue is the most violent—but perhaps after all it is not the most cruel—the most painful to witness—for perpetual struggle and disappointment would have been her portion. I mean on account of the terrible *specific gravity* of the mass she had proposed to herself to float and carry.—It is no fault of *his*—but simply the stuff he is made of. There is something unspeakably pathetic to me in all the little heroisms of her plans, her faiths, her view of the future—quenched for ever—but quenched in a void—that is in a soundless rest—far sweeter than anything the hard ache of life had to give." James ended his letter with: "Please say to Duveneck that he is very frequently in my thoughts."[103]

Two days earlier, he had written to his friend Henrietta Reubell in Paris: "Lizzie's sudden death was an unspeakable shock to me—and I scarcely *see* it, scarcely believe in it yet. . . . And the unnatural and most unhappy situation she has left behind her—those two poor uncongenial men tied together by that helpless baby—is something of which I don't see the solution."

Since Reubell was in Paris, where Lizzie had died, James then asked her for information about Francis Boott:

"I have only wanted to ask you to send me three words when you *do* see Boott (whenever that is) and tell me what impression he makes on you—what he intends to do—what relation appears to exist between Duveneck and himself? Had you seen poor Lizzie long—or shortly?—before her death? . . . Have you seen any of D's [Duveneck's] work this winter—and especially the portrait of Lizzie? Is it good or interesting?"[104]

In the middle of May, James wrote to Boott again: "I am very glad too that you and Duveneck are able—or you at any rate—to remain for the present at Bellosguardo—in the midst of all that beauty and peace, out of the roughness of things elsewhere and with Lizzie's presence in every room and her voice in every air. . . . I needn't express the hope that Fenimore shows herself a good and friendly neighbour to you—she was too full of affection for Lizzie and is always so of every benevolent impulse not to hold out her hand to you in all sorts of soothing ways. It is a great satisfaction to me to think that you are within her bountiful sphere."[105]

In September, Woolson wrote a letter to Boott, with whom she would correspond for the rest of her life, setting out her version of the last years of Lizzie Duveneck, in flat contradiction to the letter that James had sent: "In all your grief and loneliness it must still be a pleasure to you to remember how happy her life was during those last 2yrs; a woman understands a woman & I think she was one of the happiest wives I have ever known. Her whole life was unusually happy,—first with you,—& then with you & her husband.[106]

The following month, Boott and Duveneck had taken the baby back to America, where he would be raised by relatives of Boott's. Boott returned to live in Boston (where he would see a great deal of William James). Duveneck, whom John Singer Sargent called "the greatest talent of the brush of this generation,"[107] went back to Covington, Kentucky. At that time, James wrote again to Boott from Geneva: "If I were addicted to saying that, I should say to you now that your 'ears must have burned' a good deal lately, for you have been a daily theme of conversation with me for the past ten days, with Fenimore. That excellent and obliging woman is plying her pen hard on the other side of this lake and I am doing the same on this one. Our hotels are a mile apart but we meet in the evening, and when we meet she tells me, even at the risk of repetition to which I am far from objecting, the story of your last months, weeks, days, hours etc. at Bellosguardo. We often talk of Lizzie, and it is a great pleasure to me to do so with one who had entered so much into her life in so short a time. She had known you only a year or two—but the rate at which she went with you made it practically much longer."[108]

In January 1889, James wrote again to Boott: "Fenimore's mind and talk are indeed full of her last year or two at Bellosguardo, and especially of the period of your return and your tragic departure. I questioned her so much on all this that that is partly why she dwelt upon it."[109] More than a year after the death of Lizzie Boott, Alice James, Henry's sister, noted in her diary: "Henry says he misses Lizzie Duveneck more and more."[110]

When Woolson returned to Bellosguardo for another year, she moved some of Francis Boott's furniture into her house. "I read your books," she wrote to him, "& write at your table; & sit in your chairs; I admire your marbles & bronzes and your hanging lamp." In the ground floor apartment, where Henry James had written *The Aspern Papers*, she installed Boott's bedroom furniture to "be ready for *you*, when you come over to pay me a visit."[111] She had a key to his garden and took walks there, in the very garden where Pansy Osmond had once poured tea

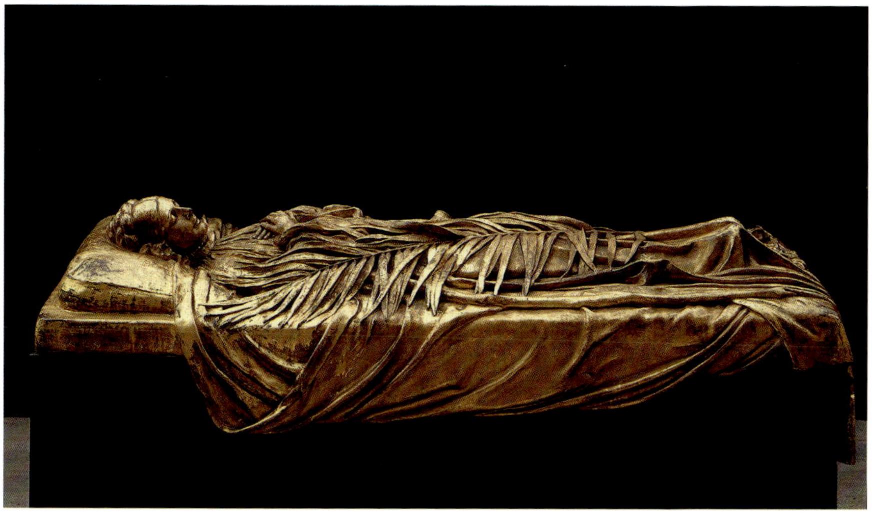

FIG. 13. Frank Duveneck (1848–1919), *Tomb Effigy of Elizabeth Boott Duveneck*, 1891, The Metropolitan Museum of Art, New York.

in *The Portrait of a Lady* for Gilbert Osmond and the Countess Gemini, Isabel Archer, and Madame Merle.

Two monuments were made for Lizzie Boott. The first is on her grave outside Florence. It depicts her, life size, as a figure almost out of some medieval heroic story. It was made by Duveneck in Covington with the aid of a young sculptor, Clement Barnhorn (1857–1935). (They would later collaborate on a statue of Emerson for Harvard in 1905.) Duveneck chose as a model for his monument the tomb of Ilaria del Carretto done in the early fifteenth century by Jacopo della Quercia (1374–1438), the original of which is in the cathedral in Lucca. Casts of it could be seen in Florence.

In a catalogue essay for *Americans in Florence: Sargent and the American Impressionists,* Grazia Gobi Sicca described the monument: "The painter is sculpted in bronze on the marble bier; her figure seems bodiless, as the drapery that covers her reveals little of the human body within. Only the hands, crossed on her breast and clasping a palm frond, and the face, closed in the mystery of death, lend physical substance to the figure. In this statue, of which her father Francis Boott had several copies made—one in marble, donated to the Museum of Fine Arts in Boston; one in bronze, at the Cincinnati Art Museum; and another still, in gilded bronze, at the Metropolitan Museum in New York [Fig. 13]—as if to ensure a more lasting memory for his daughter, is contained the story of his daughter."[112] The marble version of the tomb, which is now in Boston, was first shipped to Paris, where it was shown in the Salon of 1895 and awarded Honorable Mention. It was seen there by Francis Boott and his young grandson.

Both William and Henry James wrote about the monument. William admired it when he went to see it in Florence. He wrote to Duveneck: "All I can say is that it is *beautiful, beautiful, beautiful!* The face with its solemn half-smile, the position of the head, the hands upon the somewhat flattened form as if sunk into the couch, the simple delicate drapery, the serenity and peace of the whole thing! It is a great work and a great monument."[113] In July 1893, when Henry James was sent a photograph of the monument by Duveneck, he wrote to Boott: "One sees, in its place, and its *ambiente,* what a meaning and eloquence the whole thing has—and one is touched to tears by this particular example which comes home to one so—of the jolly great truth that it is *art* alone that triumphs over fate. Poor long-silent Lizzie speaks and lives there again and will be present to generations and generations and have a continuity and a beauty superior to ours."[114]

A year later, James saw Frank Duveneck near Venice. He wrote to Francis Boott in December: "I went to Chioggia to see Duveneck and spent several hot and rather smelly hours with him—unrewarded, I grieve to say, with the sight of a single stroke of his brush. He would 'show' us nothing—save the beauties of Chioggia and his robust and pleasant self." James then saw the monument in situ at the Allori Cemetery. In that same letter, he wrote: "In Florence, where I spent a few days on my way to Rome, I made an intensely pious pilgrimage to the spot where Lizzie lies in majestic and perennial bronze. Strange, strange it seemed, still to see her only so—but so she will be seen for ages to come. I climbed to Bellosguardo . . . but the whole place is now such a perfect cemetery of ghosts that there is little joy in it left for me—or rather there would be little if I had not deep-seated disposition to find myself secretly, even whenever so sadly, fond of the company of the relics of the dead."[115] By this time, Constance Fenimore Woolson was dead as well. On that trip to Italy, James had also visited the place in Venice where she had fallen to her death in January 1894.

James's last great novel, *The Golden Bowl*, published in 1904, represents the other monument to Lizzie Boott made after her death. Like all of his books, its inspiration came from several sources, including, of course, his imagination. In 1887, in a notebook entry, James set down the first vague shadow of a new scenario. It arose from something that James's sister, Alice, had mentioned to him—the story that a widower's daughter was opposing her father's remarriage. This became the story "The Marriages," which was published in 1891. The protagonist of "The Marriages" was Adela Chart, whose father was about to remarry a woman named Mrs. Churchley, much to Adela's consternation, which was partly based on the pious memory of her dead mother but also arose from something powerful that pervades the story: Adela's closeness to her father and her sexual jealousy of the woman who had won her father's affections.

The first real entry, however, in James's notebooks that offers us a shadow of Adam Verver in *The Golden Bowl* appeared on 22 May 1892. James had been reading an article in *Revue des Deux Mondes* on *"La Vie Americaine."* He began to think of somebody "civilized, large, rich, complete, but strongly characterised, but essentially a *product*. Get the action—the action in which to launch him—it should be a big one. I have no difficulty in *seeing* the figure—it *comes*, as I look at it."[116]

James, like many writers before him, managed to embody in his characters themes and ideas that Sigmund Freud would subsequently formulate. Thus the idea of a widowed father and his only child, a young unmarried daughter, dramatized in a shifting set of scenes, each with an aura of something unsettlingly sexual, would have intrigued James once it occurred to him. It occurred to him for his story "The Marriages," and once again on 28 November 1892, when he wrote in his notebook of "a simultaneous marriage, in Paris, (or only 'engagement' as yet I believe) of a father and daughter—an only daughter. The daughter—American of course—is engaged to a young Englishman, and the father, a widower and still youngish, has sought in marriage at exactly the same time an American girl very much the same age as his daughter."[117]

In this scenario that James set out, the father did not lose his daughter because of the two new arrivals into their family, rather they were thrown together a great deal more. This was because the daughter's husband and the father's wife had already known each other; the young husband "would have married [the father's new wife] if she had had any money. She was poor—the father was very rich and *that* was her inducement for marrying the father." Thus as the father and daughter spent time together, so too did the new husband and the young wife. "The whole situation," James wrote, "works in a kind of inevitable rotary way—in what would be called a vicious cycle."

James went on to note that "a necessary basis for all of this must have been an intense and exceptional degree of attachment between father and daughter—he peculiarly paternal, she passionately filial." He saw the story as being "a short tale" and the son-in-law as being French and poor "but has some high position or name [and is] clever, various, inconstant, amiable, cynical, unscrupulous." His other three characters, James thought, would be "all intensely American."[118]

Three years later, as James took stock of the ideas for new books that were in his head, he listed six possibilities, two of which he did not write, but four of which became novels. One, he named as "The Marriages," adding in parentheses: "What a pity I've used that name." He summarized the plot: "The Father and Daughter, with the husband of one and the wife of the other entangled in a mutual passion, an intrigue."[119]

It is important to remember that James used his notebooks to write down stories and details that he might otherwise have forgotten. The notes were often scrappy and seldom elaborate. It is clear from these notes that he paid attention to two stories about a father and a daughter who were deeply attached to each other, the drama then arising from the marriage of one or both. He seemed to have no sense in these notes that they would lead to a book as long, intricate, and intense as *The Golden Bowl.*

In the introduction to *The Golden Bowl* written for the New York Edition in 1909, James apologized for the "fewness" of the characters in the book, "the fact that my large demand is made for a group of agents who may be counted on the fingers of one hand . . . but the scheme of the book, to make up for that, is that we shall really see about as much of them as a coherent literary form permits."[120]

In the two years between Lizzie Boott's marriage and her death, four characters, including herself, circled each other almost to the exclusion of the rest of the world, as the characters did later in James's novel. They were Francis and Lizzie Boott, Frank Duveneck, and Constance Fenimore Woolson. Lizzie and Duveneck spent their days in the studio working until Lizzie had her baby. Woolson spent her days working on her fiction. Francis Boott, we presume, wrote songs and music. There is evidence that these four people did not see anyone else much, other than servants, during most of this time. They did not accept or send out invitations, for example. They saw only each other.

As in *The Golden Bowl,* the daughter was rich, but her new husband's name meant something. In the novel, he was a Roman prince; in life he was a well-known artist. As in the novel, the father was rich indeed and American and cared about art. He was at a loss once his only daughter's marriage was announced, as they had been very close. He thus sought solace from a younger woman, recently arrived on the scene. As in the novel, the daughter had a child. As in the novel, all four characters dined together a great deal; they worked out a set of new patterns and configurations since their circumstances had changed. No one in the novel had to travel to work, as none of the four people whose flickering, shadowy lives became bright lights in the novel had to leave the enclosing environs of Bellosguardo. They were thus all the more useful to James because two of them were artists, one a writer.

They gave nourishment to *The Golden Bowl.* Francis Boott slowly gave shape to Adam Verver, as his daughter, Lizzie, did to Maggie Verver; Frank Duveneck slowly gave shape to the prince, as Constance Fenimore Woolson did to Charlotte Stant. James, of course, also had the other sources he jotted down in his notebooks.

Rather than use the simple term *gave shape,* it is perhaps more true to say that the strange and unusually intense relations between all four of James's friends in the hothouse world they had invented for themselves on Bellosguardo in those years shifted from shadow toward substance in James's imagination over more than a decade. They moved from being incomplete to completion as he thought about them, imagined them, and learned to see them and indeed resee them as he gave them physical characteristics quite different than the four people he had actually known.

But he also, of course, came to visit them. The Bootts, father and daughter, were by this time James's oldest friends in Europe, and Woolson was the person to whom he was closest. Duveneck was the outsider, the interloper. Being an artist gave him mobility, allowed him to move from his provincial background to Florence. This mobility meant that James never quite came to trust him, or fully appreciate him, or become friends with him. James used this sense of foreignness and distance in the making of Prince Amerigo in *The Golden Bowl.*

As is clear from his letters, James himself took on the role of Fanny Assingham, the outsider in *The Golden Bowl* who watches the four. When he came to Florence and asked that no one in the city be apprised of his presence there, James was furthering the closed atmosphere that his arrival could easily have diluted. There were no big parties or outings. All five remained intensely close; their relations were complex and open to change as they circled each other.

As is clear from James's letters to Francis Boott in October 1888 and January 1889, he and Woolson discussed what happened on Bellosguardo in those two years a great deal after Lizzie's death. Constance had all the information or most of it, as Maggie Verver did in *The Golden Bowl;* James had all the curiosity, all the insatiable need for news, as Fanny Assingham did in the novel.

In *The Golden Bowl,* Maggie Verver appears in two guises. In the first half of the book, she is the innocent heiress, vulnerable, easily broken. In the second part, she becomes vastly more subtle and interesting and morally powerful as she attempts to mold the lives of those around her into a shape that suits her purposes. She begins to notice everything. Since, after Lizzie's death, James and Woolson wrote to her father with precisely opposing versions of who Lizzie was, how she lived in those two years after her marriage, and since they discussed her, as we know, at some length after her death with each other as well, then these two versions of Lizzie Boott became part of the shadowy, ghostly world that James began to explore and bring to life for Maggie Verver, as she appeared in two versions in *The Golden Bowl.*

Once more, as with *Washington Square,* and more emphatically with *The Portrait of a Lady,* James did not "base" his characters in *The Golden Bowl* on the Bootts and Duveneck. Instead, he allowed the richly edged shape they made as a group to emerge; he used their configuration; he used something close and then distant that he could mull over, guess at, dream about, imagine, watch. Because this group intrigued him, captured his imagination, then he could work.

But it is important to emphasize that while these figures were essential for James, they were only the beginning, a sort of dim light by which he worked to create complex colors. His imagination was, by the time he began to write *The Golden Bowl* in Lamb House in Rye in 1903, at its most delicate and refined. His interest in the mechanics of the novel was also at its most ironic and pure. He saw the immense dramatic possibilities in withholding what was expected in a novel about treachery and discovery, innocence and experience. He saw a new shape for the novel in which he would explore questions that went beyond the social toward a dramatization of human motives and interactions that was allegorical, that was to do with salvation, and that was almost religious in its moral seriousness (Fig. 14).

Yet even these terms are too large and vague because it is essential to remember that James sought to offer them, in a tone of full and sweet understanding, to a single and frail human consciousness. Maggie Verver might have been nourished by the ghost of Lizzie Boott, but she stands only for herself. The flickering of her conscious will and the subtlety of her responses cannot be summarized nor easily rendered or explained. She is made with many tones, using many patterns. Each thing thus comes to her in all its complexity; she deals with it accordingly. For this dramatizing of her consciousness, and of the action that takes place around her, we need a language of infinite suggestion and layered nuance.

This language enacts levels of feeling and knowing in ways that are both precise and indirect, both poetic and forensic. This late style of James suggests that feeling and knowing are open ended and can lead, even in the bleakest circumstances, to something like forgiveness, the glossing over of unpure motives, the creation of harmony based on language as an ambiguous way of healing pain. James came to this style gradually and by necessity not because he needed a language that was more playful and vague, but because he needed, despite all his qualms and in a way that mattered to him, a tone that would measure up to and mediate between the yearning of his characters for completion and the limits that life, despite all its intense variety, offered to them.

In James's fiction, the glance, the glimpse, the gaze are essential tools in creating drama. Many of the metaphors he used take their bearings from the visual arts, but more than that, James's way of creating pattern and scenes of recognition are heavily influenced by visual culture. James composed the most dramatic moments in his work as though they were framed, as though his characters were placed in light and shade as a painter might pose figures in a painting. He worked with nuance and tone and indeed with the face itself as though an outward appearance perfectly captured could tell us more than any number of analytical paragraphs about the inner being or state of mind of a character.

James had scant interest in classical music. (He could easily have met Wagner, for example, in Naples in the spring of 1880 but did not seem interested.) There are very few references in his correspondence or his work to concerts or compositions or composers. He seemed more at ease in the company of painters and sculptors and happier, too, using the gallery or the studio space in his fiction and indeed dramatizing the lives of artists and art collectors. His Italy, as we have seen, was a place of visual artists more than writers.

James's imagination seemed most at ease with the image, the idea of light and shade, the sense that he was, as he created his fictional characters, making portraits much in the way that a visual artist might. He was greatly nourished by his friendship with visual artists, and his work took much of its energy from the idea of the visible, of what is suggested by a scene, by how much a single framed moment lets the reader know about motive and psychology and the interior texture of his creations.

Indeed, the visual arts are crucial to his work in many

different ways. In his novel *The Portrait of a Lady,* for example, Isabel Archer's response to the paintings in the gallery at Gardencourt remains one of the most haunting scenes in the book. In James's late novels, visual culture plays a central role. In *The Wings of the Dove,* some of the central scenes are set in places where paintings are hung. In *The Golden Bowl,* Adam Verver is an art collector who plans to ship his valuable collection to the United States.

James's European world is one of painters, sculptors, art collectors, characters who spend time in galleries and allow their lives to be nourished by the visual arts. There are constant references in his fiction to paintings and works of art, much more than, say, novels or pieces of classical music. Art is in his work because it was an essential part of James's own life, as his essays on Italy and his letters make clear. He knew this world and then used it in his fiction with a clarity and a conviction that is often missing, say, when he tried to write about the source of his characters' wealth or about politics and current affairs.

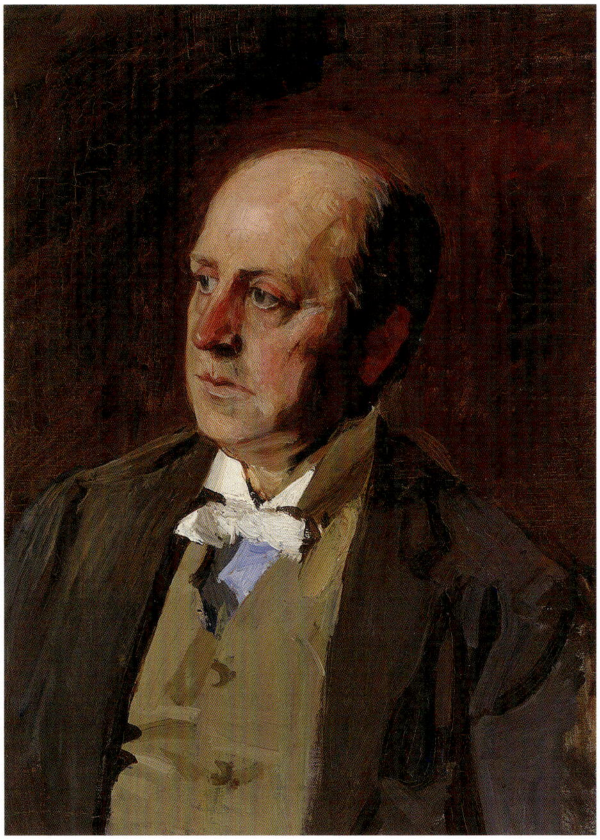

FIG. 14. Ellen Gertrude Emmet Rand (1875–1941), *Henry James,* 1900, National Portrait Gallery, Smithsonian Institution, Washington, DC.

In James's best novels, there was also another matter that he dramatized with great zeal: this was the matter of secrecy, especially sexual secrecy. In novels such as *The Portrait of a Lady, The Ambassadors, The Wings of the Dove,* and *The Golden Bowl,* which are among his greatest works, there is a sexual secret that, when known, will become explosive and animate the novel as nothing else does. Against the high civilization he explored using the visual arts, he placed a world more primitive, more base, treacherous, and strange.

It would be too crude to surmise from this that James himself was in possession of such a secret or that he lived a secret sexual life himself. In the four above-named novels, he also wrote about characters with no money, or very little money, and he dramatized what poverty does to the spirit and what it impels the characters to do. This, too, became an essential element in his best work. Yet James himself was never penniless; he inherited and indeed made a good deal of money, even if he worried about his finances and grumbled about them a good deal (Fig. 15).

More than dealing with his own experience directly, it is more likely that James used the shadowy shape of his own uneasy and ambiguous homosexuality to nourish his work. It is interesting then that he found and befriended a painter whose personal and social life were almost a mirror image of his own and whose ways of navigating the world with an ambiguous sexual presence were similar to James's.

James and this painter came together in one very public moment, when one of them—John Singer Sar-

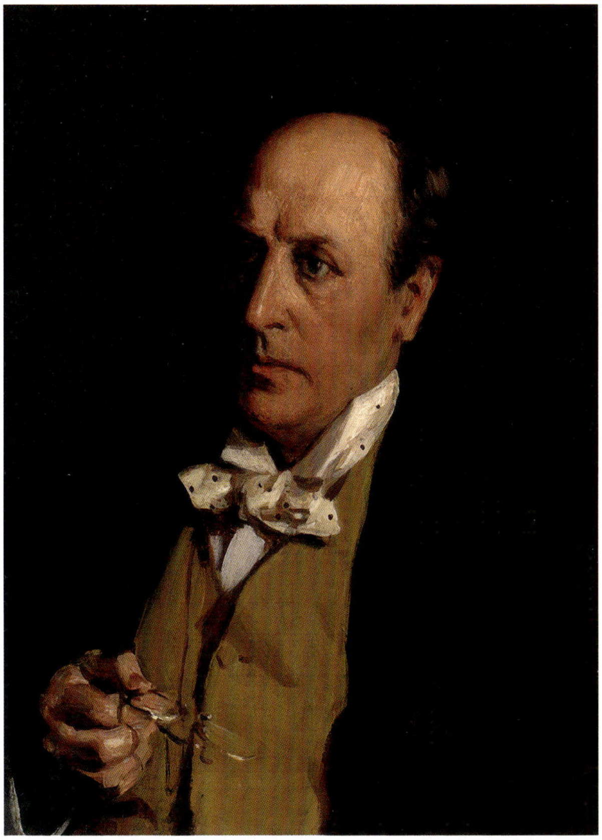

FIG. 15. Ellen Gertrude Emmet Rand (1875–1941), *Henry James*, 1900, National Portrait Gallery, Smithsonian Institution, Washington, DC.

gent—painted a public portrait of the other—Henry James—for his seventieth birthday, offering him a mixture of dignity, reserve, and sensuous intelligence (Fig. 16). The connections between James and Sargent make the latter essential in any consideration of James and painting, as they are also fascinating in any consideration of James's own life in all its rich complexity, ambiguity, and hiddenness. In 1886, one critic noted the connections between them: "He [Sargent] is the Henry James of portraiture; and I can't help wishing he were not—as I can't help wishing that Henry James were not the Sargent of the novel."[121] W. Graham Robertson (1866–1948), who knew both of them, described them as "real friends, they understand each other perfectly and their points of view were in many ways identical. Renegade Americans both . . . they were *plus Anglais que les Anglais* with an added fastidiousness, a mental remoteness that was not English."[122]

John Singer Sargent, who was born in Florence in 1856, the son of expatriate Americans, was a most refined and genteel little boy. He did not see America until he was twenty but spent his childhood wandering with his family in Italy and France, Switzerland, Austria, and Germany. His father had abandoned a medical career; his parents lived on a modest independent income. By the age of eleven, Sargent was fluent in French and Italian and could get by in German. He and his two sisters were provided with piano teachers and sent to dancing classes. While his father had hopes that he would join the American navy, it was clear to Sargent's mother that her only son would become an artist.

As a teenager, Sargent was enrolled in the Accademia delle Belle Arti in Florence and later, when he was eighteen, the family moved to Paris, where Sargent could study at the atelier of the painter Émile Carolus-Duran (1837–1917), of whom he would make one of his best early portraits. Carolus-Duran, an admirer of Velázquez, taught his students not to prepare a painting by making sketches or drawings but instead insisted that the paint be laid directly on unprepared canvas with a broad brush. The emphasis was on capturing the flow of light on surface, seeking inflections and what was shimmering and in flux rather than solid mass or carefully delineated tonal structure.

Sargent's talent was recognized by his fellow students, one of whom wrote in October 1874: "I met this last week a young Mr. Sargent about eighteen years old and one of the most talented fellows I have ever come across; his drawings are like old masters, and his colors are equally fine. . . . Such men wake one up, and as his principles are

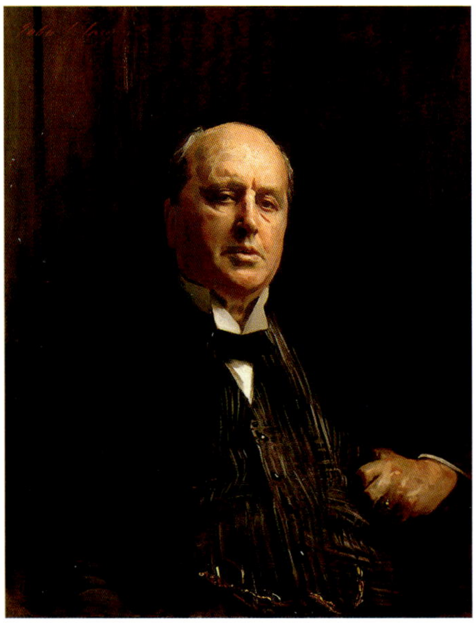

FIG. 16. John Singer Sargent (1856–1925), *Henry James*, 1913, National Portrait Gallery, London.

equal to his talents, I hope to have his friendship."[123] During his time as a student in Paris, Sargent became immensely industrious, as did James, and indeed Sargent remained so until his death in 1925. Unlike his fellow students, Sargent dressed respectably; he tended also to be prim and well-mannered.

In 1878, Sargent began to exhibit at the Salon in Paris. He developed a way of making his subjects seem both close and distant. His way of painting a face appeared to capture a vivid sense of life while also managing to depict a fine detachment. His use of costume and pose was highly theatrical. Thus his portraits had both clarity and mystery; his subjects seemed on display while maintaining a masked inner life and an alluring sense of remoteness. This distance between the face and pose and then the inner life, and the distance, too, between control and looseness in the methods of painting and composing gave Sargent's best portraits a dramatic force that meant that Sargent, by the time he was in his midtwenties, was in high demand as a fashionable portrait painter.

Part of his appeal was that sitting for him was risky. He did not flatter his subjects (Fig. 17). Thus, despite his interest in the famous and the fashionable, there remained a whiff of danger about Sargent. James sought to reassure one sitter, Mrs. Mahlon Sands, before she sat for Sargent at his Tite Street studio in 1894 (see Fig. 18): "I want to give you a bushel of good advice, in short—advice about the supreme wisdom, in a situation like yours, of the policy of self-surrender to the artist—that of giving him his head and letting him utterly alone. Trust him completely and ask no questions. . . . From the moment one trusts him enough to ask for a portrait at all—trust him enough to leave him his ways, his variations, his mysteries and circumgyrations and idiosyncrasies. You can't keep step with him and you can't assist at the process. You can't collaborate or co-operate, except by sitting still and looking beautiful, in your own portrait. You are outside of it altogether and you will—you always *must*—consult the highest interest of the result by preserving this perfectly helpless and detached attitude!! Cultivate indifference, cultivate not looking at it nor thinking about it. Don't challenge him by the way and give him a tremendous margin. It's *his* affair—yours is only to be as difficult for him as possible; and the more difficult you are the more the artist (worthy of the name), will be condemned to worry over you, repainting, revolutionizing, till he, in a rage of ambition and admiration, arrives at the thing that satisfies him and that enshrines and perpetuates you."[124]

In 1884, when he showed his portrait of Madame Pierre Gautreau, or Madame X, at the Paris Salon, it

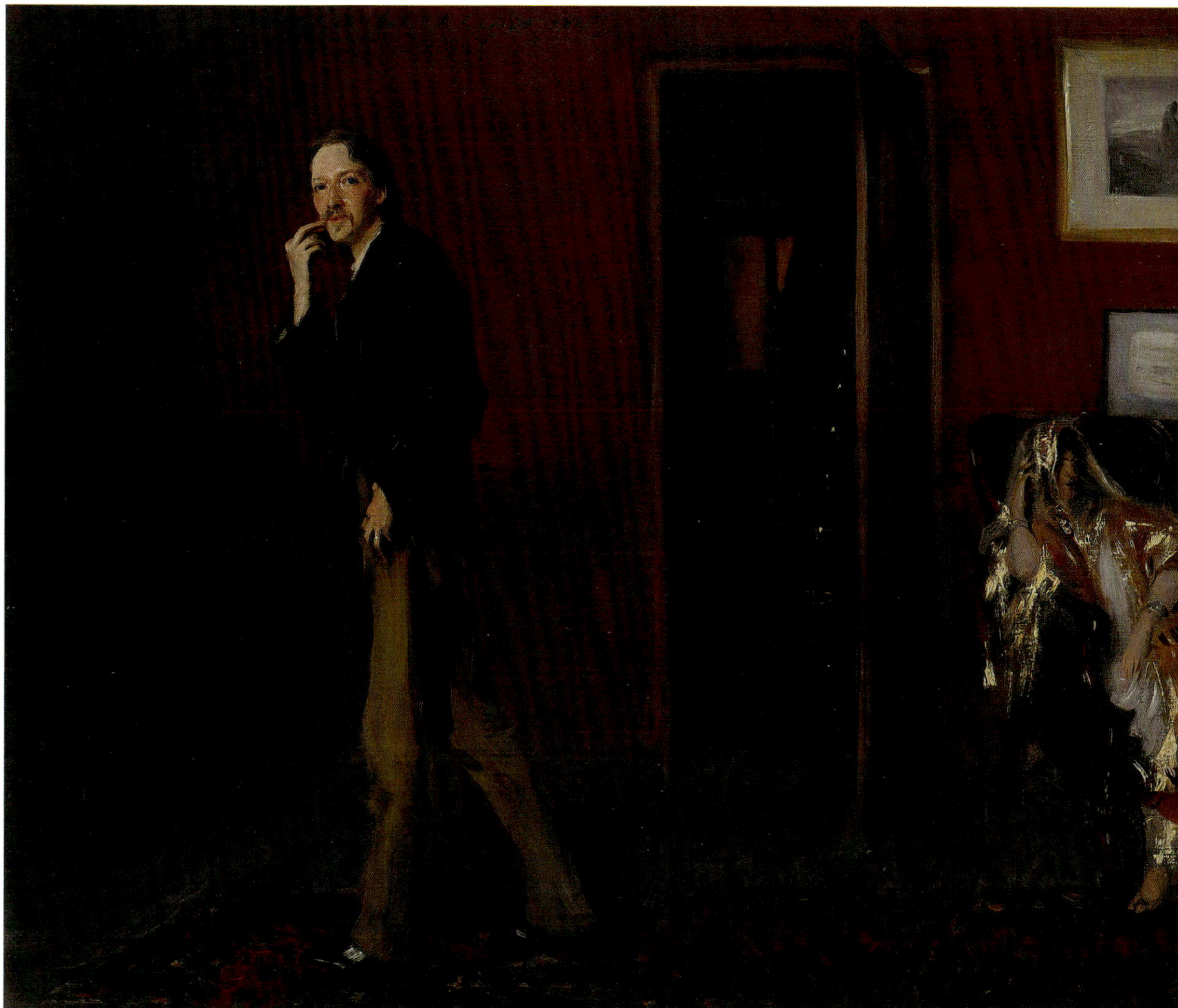

FIG. 17. John Singer Sargent (1856–1925), *Robert Louis Stevenson and His Wife*, 1885, Crystal Bridges Museum of American Art, Bentonville, Arkansas.

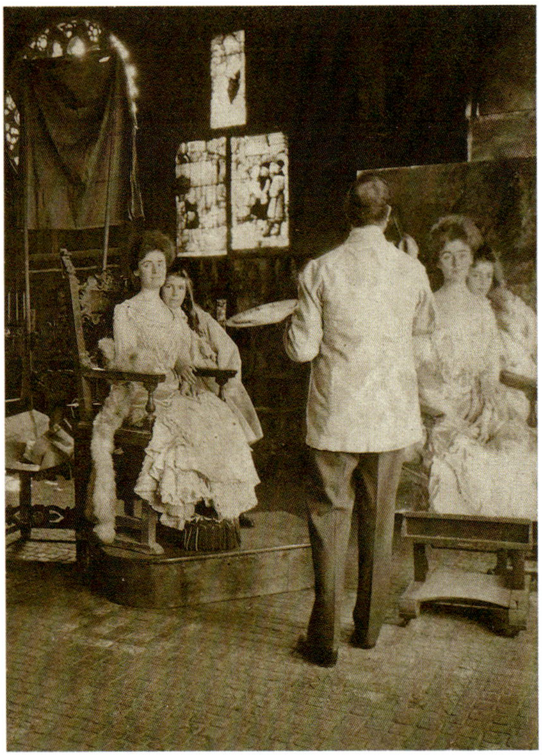

FIG. 18. John Templeton Coolidge (1856–1945), *Photograph of John Singer Sargent Painting Mrs. Fiske-Warren and Her Daughter Rachel in the Gothic Room at Isabella Stewart Gardner's House,* 1903, Isabella Stewart Gardner Museum, Boston.

caused outrage and mockery (see Simpson, Fig. 13). It showed the woman's haughty face in profile, her dress was low-cut, a great deal of flesh was on display. In the original painting, one strap of the dress hung loose, but after all the fuss (Madame Gautreau and her mother went berserk when they saw the painting), the strap was repainted and put back in place.

In that same year in Paris, Sargent met James, who became one of his greatest supporters. James suggested that Sargent move to England, and he began to pave the way for him there. James wrote to a friend: "I want him to come here to live and work—there being such a field in London for a *real* painter of women, and such magnificent subjects, of both sexes."[125]

Sargent and James were both Americans in Europe who had spent much of their childhood abroad. They were both bachelor expatriates, reserved, industrious, careful about their private lives. They both liked society (although James was a great talker, and Sargent often remained silent and seemed awkward); they both took an interest in fashionable women. In the way they dealt with their own rootlessness and their own sexuality—moving between England, France, Italy, and America—in the way they seemed, as artists, both modern and also old-fashioned—concerned with both surface and psychology—they could, some of the time, have been mirror images of each other.

James's short story "The Pupil," first published in 1891, has elements of his own childhood and that of Sargent. The Moreens, in the story, "had a sort of professional acquaintance with Continental cities."[126] The mother, like Sargent's mother, was an amateur painter. The son, the pupil, wonders about his family: "Are they rich, are they poor? . . . Why are they always . . . living one year like ambassadors and the next like paupers? Who are they, anyway, and what are they?"[127] James also used elements of Sargent's personality in his novels *The Tragic Muse,* in which he got aspects of Nick Dormer from Sargent, and *The Reverberator,* in which the expatriate, Impressionist portrait-painter Charles Waterlow also has elements of Sargent.

Besides letting the shape of Sargent's life into his fiction, James wrote about the adult Sargent's art. In 1887, in a long essay in *Harper's Magazine,* he raised the question (that has still not gone away) about how to categorize

Sargent's genius. "From the time of his first success in the Salon," James wrote, "he was hailed, I believe, as a recruit of high value to the camp of the Impressionists, and today he is for many people most conveniently pigeon-holed under that head."[128]

Sargent was fascinated by what was happening in French painting. He bought two paintings by Manet and four by Monet, with whom he developed a friendship in the mid-1880s. Lilla Cabot Perry (1848–1933), from James's circle in Boston, married to his friend Thomas Sergeant Perry, also became close to Monet and helped introduce the work of French Impressionists to America (Fig. 19). But Sargent was considered an outsider by most of the Impressionists. While he refined the systems he had learned from Carolus-Duran, the way he worked with light and shade remained, for the most part, pre-Impressionist, nonetheless—even if he took what he could use from the Impressionists he admired.

Although Degas, while praising his skill, made clear that Sargent was not much different from the better and more fashionable Salon painters, we have to be careful about viewing Sargent as an essentially conservative painter, as we have to be careful about viewing James in this way. Sargent may have been the last in the line that included Velázquez and Ingres, and he may also have been one of the last society portrait painters, but he brought a textural richness, a serious and often startling sense of composition and, at his best, a muscular theatricality, to what he did as a painter.

Sargent painted his friend Monet at work in the open air. He also sought advice from Monet, as Elaine Kilmurray has written, as he began to experiment "with landscape and figures painted under real conditions of light and, technically, beginning to use a brighter palette and more broken brushwork."[129] This seemed to irritate Monet, who wrote to

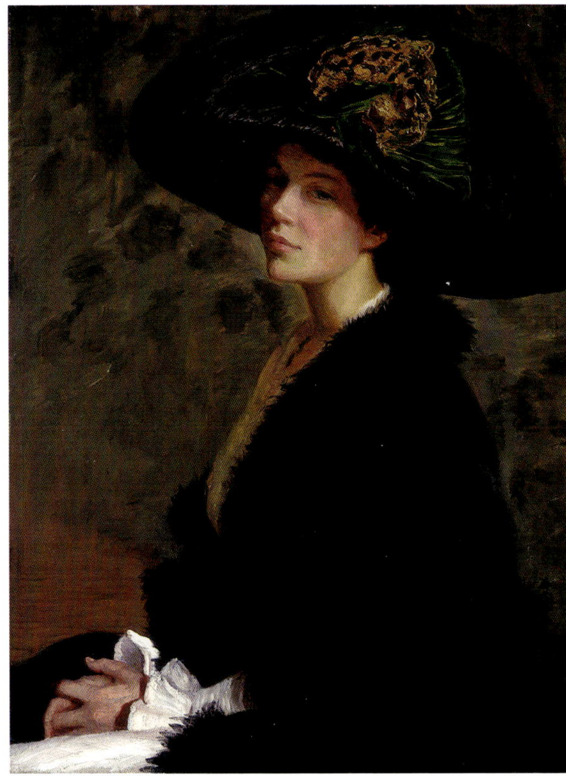

FIG. 19. Lilla Cabot Perry (1848–1933), *The Green Hat,* 1913, Terra Foundation for American Art, Chicago.

his wife complaining that Sargent "is making an extraordinary enquiry about the use of yellow and green and asking me if I am coming to London; he needs me to advise him on the pictures he is working on."[130]

The problem Sargent had was how not to make his portraits formulaic, to prevent them from becoming merely a display of his immense skill. Sometimes, by a mixture of cunning and care, insight and bravery, he managed to make paintings that had extraordinary freshness. At other times, his work had a strange dullness, as though the real world for Sargent were elsewhere, as though the portraits were ways of making money, fulfilling a commission. The same can be said for some of Henry James's short stories.

Both James and Sargent were fascinated by Venice, as Whistler and Duveneck were. What connects all four of them in the city is the painter Ralph Curtis, whose wealthy family lived in Venice for many years. Curtis studied with Duveneck in Munich, attended his wedding, and had his portrait painted by Duveneck.

Whistler knew Ralph Curtis in Venice; Curtis painted a portrait of him at a party and also did a number of sketches of Whistler during his stay in Venice.

John Singer Sargent was a distant cousin of Ralph Curtis, with whom he had studied at Carolus-Duran's studio. He traveled to the Netherlands with him and painted a portrait of Curtis lounging on a beach. In 1898, he did a portrait of Curtis's wife.

James also knew Curtis well. Curtis, like the other three painters, made paintings of Venice, just as James set *The Aspern Papers* and parts of *The Wings of the Dove* in the city. There is an indirect reference to the Curtis family in the latter book when James alludes to the family who rent a Venetian palace to Milly Theale: "Charming people, conscious Venice-lovers, evidently, had given up their house to her. . . . Palazzo Leporelli held its history still in its great lap, even like a painted idol, a solemn puppet hung about with decorations."[131]

Once the Curtis family bought Palazzo Barbaro, James stayed there, using the library at the top of the house as his bedroom, a room still there, in the same condition as when James slept there. James wrote to Ariana Curtis about "the divine old library" asking: "Have you ever lived here? If you haven't, if you haven't gazed upward from your couch, in the rosy dawn, or during the postprandial (that is after luncheon) siesta, at the medallions and arabesques of the ceiling, permit me to tell you that you don't *know* the Barbaro."[132]

Sargent also stayed in the Palazzo Barbaro. In March 1899, James saw Sargent's painting of the Curtis family, *An Interior in Venice,* a group portrait in the grand drawing room of the palace with Ralph Curtis and his wife to the left, Ralph's father, Daniel, who was a wealthy Bostonian, to the right, and Ariana, the daughter of an English admiral, close to the center (Fig. 20).

James wrote to Ariana to tell her that he "absolutely and without reserve adored [it]. I can't help thinking that you have a slightly fallacious impression of the effect of your (*your,* dear Mrs Curtis) indicated head & face. It is an indication so *summaire* that I can't think it speaks for itself—as a simple sketchy hint—& it didn't displease me. . . . I've seen few things that I craved more to possess! I hope you haven't altogether let it go."[133] Ariana, however, disliked it, thought she looked too old in it, and believed her son Ralph's pose was too casual and refused to accept it as a gift from the artist.

Just as Sargent painted the grand salon of Palazzo Barbaro with figures of Anglo-American grandeur in it, so, too, James, a few years later, offered a vivid description of the palace that Sargent had used in his group portrait. He managed the same sort of sumptuous tone as Sargent, as if he were competing or joining forces with him. He wrote about "the high, florid rooms, palatial chambers where hard cool pavements took reflections in their lifelong polish, and where the sun on the stirred sea-water, flickering up through open windows, played over the painted 'subjects' in the splendid ceilings—medallions of purple and brown, of brave old melancholy color, medals as of old reddened gold, embossed and beribboned, all toned with time, and all flourished

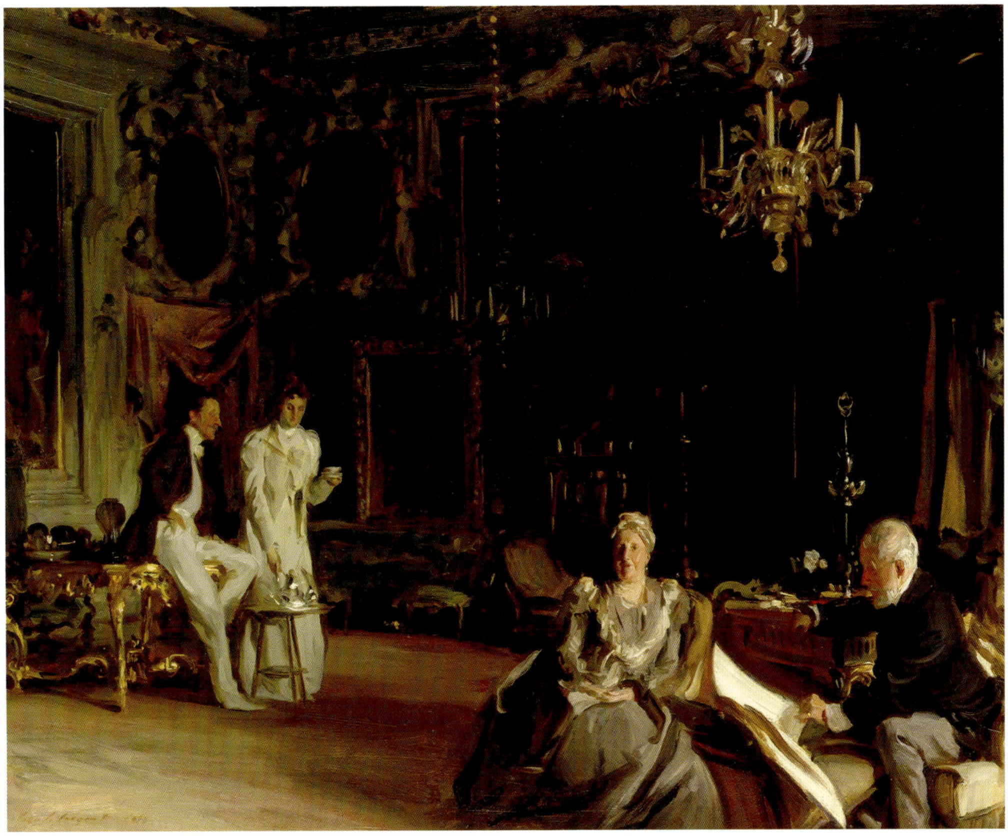

FIG. 20. John Singer Sargent (1856–1925), *An Interior in Venice,* 1899, Royal Academy of Arts, London.

and scalloped and gilded about, set in their great molded and figured concavity. . . . "[134]

In March 1912 James wrote to Edith Wharton about the charcoal portrait that Sargent had just made of him: "I have sat again to Sargent with complete success, and he has made an admirable drawing. He kept on with the work of the two previous séances—and brought it round, beautifully developed, and redeemed and completed. It's a regular first class living, resembling, enduring thing."[135] Sargent's fee for the portrait painting commissioned to mark James's seventieth birthday the following year was paid by a number of James's friends who arranged for James to have the portrait until his death and then for it to be handed over to the National Portrait Gallery. James described the portrait as "Sargent at his very best and poor old H. J. not at his worst; in short a living breathing likeness and a masterpiece of painting."[136]

When the portrait was finished, the subscribers were invited to view it at Sargent's studio in Tite Street in London. James also put himself on view, so that those who had paid for the portrait could compare painting and sitter. He wrote to Sargent's sister: "Such a carnival of glory as I have been seeing enacted in the studio. . . . Such a multitudinous jig-dance round & round the Portrait! Sitting for it was a bliss, but this standing *by* it has been an even richer experience."[137] In May 1914, when the painting was displayed at the Royal Academy, it was badly damaged by Mary Wood, a militant suffragette wielding a hatchet, but it was subsequently restored. Shortly after the attack, responding to a letter from Charles Hagberg Wright, Librarian of the London Library, James wrote: "I am deeply moved by your generous letter & have only not assured you of this sooner because the accursed fury with the cleaver has been the cause of a huge amplification of my daily, or hourly, postal matter. . . . The ravage was great, but it appears that, very wonderfully, it can be made good—to all probability—by some master-restorer into whose hands it is already being put." Looking at the incident in a more positive light, James reflected: "I . . . really owe the vicious hag & her ravage a good mark for having led to my hearing from you."[138]

James, in Sargent's portrait, is enormously present and alive, in possession of a rare and exquisite intelligence. The gaze is clear and direct; parts of the face, especially the lips, are sensuous and full. There is a feeling that James is not merely being captured by a painter; there is a sense that he is not a passive sitter, as many of Sargent's subjects were, but that he, too, is capturing the painter. He is looking fearlessly and openly outward at him, all the more to sympathize, understand, and see. In Canto VII, Ezra Pound described the painting, with "the great domed head" of James and the sense of the novelist in the picture "drinking the tone of things."[139]

While many of the women Sargent painted are beautifully dressed and still have a great sense of life in them, it is, for the most part, a posed life, a life created for them by the painter. While they can seem sexual, their sexuality is often oddly artificial, whereas many of his men don't seem sexual at all, instead appearing as though they were born with suits on and distant or arrogant expressions on their faces, exuding power in a world in which their power was fading.

Some of the exceptions to this are worthy of close attention. They are all portraits of young men. One, a portrait of the painter Albert de Belleroche (1864–1944) done in 1883, remained in Sargent's possession all his life and was hung in the dining room of his house in Tite Street in Chelsea. Almost androgynous in appearance, Belleroche displays a sultry sexual presence. Another interesting painting, of the singer George Henschel, which is softer, more tender, was done six years later.

The key to these works, and indeed to aspects both apparent and hidden in Sargent's personality as an artist, was offered in *John Singer Sargent: The Sensualist,* published in 2000 by Trevor Fairbrother. The publication includes reproductions of drawings of naked men that Sargent never exhibited in his lifetime but kept together in an album. Sargent's family donated the drawings to the Fogg Museum at Harvard, but they were not much noticed until Trevor Fairbrother wrote an article about them in 1981 (Fig. 21).

They really are eye-openers, sexually explicit and filled with open homoerotic desire. "Strapping men," as Fairbrother wrote, "assume showy or exultant poses." He later wrote: "These charcoal drawings are just as vivid and individual as [Sargent's] better-known society portraits. . . . The album's male images are variously immediate, lush, intimate, heroic and tender."[140] These drawings are as openly erotic as Sargent's *Nude Study of Thomas E. McKeller,* painted between 1917 and 1920. (Sargent first noticed McKeller as an elevator operator in a hotel.) This painting was, like the drawings of naked men, not exhibited during Sargent's lifetime. It was first reproduced in a book in 1955 but did not become widely known until it was bought by the Museum of Fine Arts in Boston in 1986 (Fig. 22).

As with James's homosexuality, we have to be careful how we read the clues we have about Sargent's sexuality. It may be a fascinating undercurrent in his work. Keeping

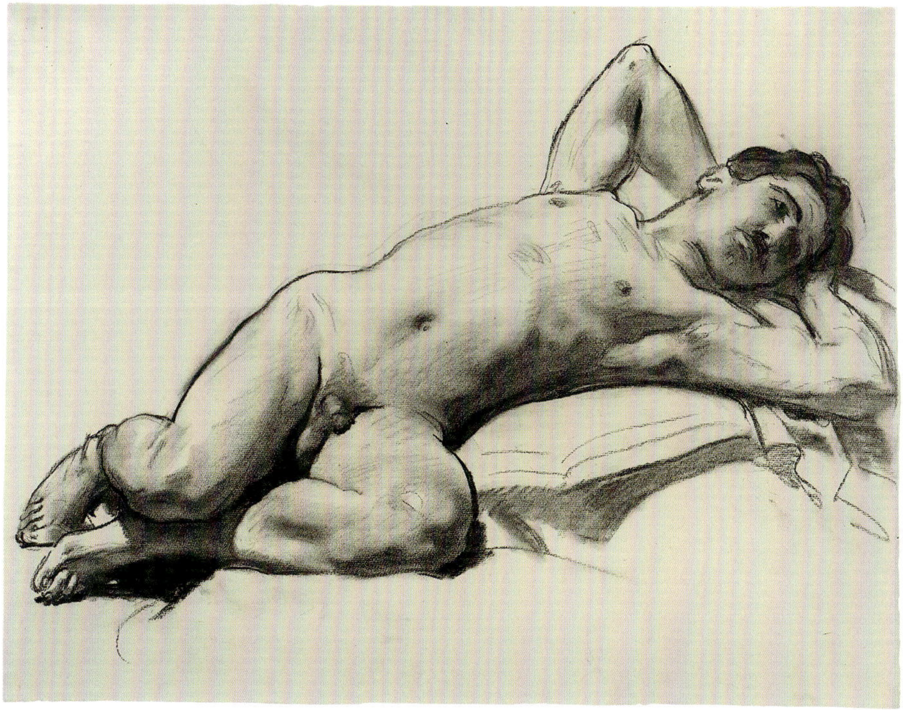

FIG. 21. John Singer Sargent (1856–1925), *Reclining Male Nude with Hands Behind Head,* ca. 1890–1915, Fogg Art Museum, Harvard University Art Museums, Cambridge, Massachusetts.

it secret, as he tried to do in his lifetime, may explain some of the ways he painted and some of the subjects he chose. It may also explain the masked sensuality in some of the work or the sense of the face and the pose as filled with an aura of performance, with as much attention to the dress as to the face. But it may also encourage us to look at Sargent's paintings more subtly and carefully, and indeed may allow the work itself to yield much more.

As Trevor Fairbrother wrote of Sargent in *The Sensualist:* "His images present a vibrant, forceful realism while subtly projecting emotions, desires, and intuitions as their visual subtext. He jabbed, dabbed, smeared, slapped, and scratched his paint surfaces; he deployed brilliant, murky, flashy, peculiar, and ravishing colors. All are the expressions of a man whose instincts and appetites were deeply sensual."[141]

In the afterlife of Henry James, his sexuality, as with that of Sargent, became more apparent. In 2000, the same year as Trevor Fairbrother's book appeared, James's letters to Hendrik Andersen were first published. After his death in 1916, James's family had made an effort to control his reputation. Within two days of his cremation, for example, his sister-in-law was meeting with his literary agent in London to discuss how his estate should be managed. It was decided to publish a volume of his letters, to be edited by Percy Lubbock.

Lubbock was aware, as he told a friend, that even talking to the James family involved moving "in such a cloud of fine discretions and hesitations and precautions that it is difficult altogether to know where one is."[142] James's associates in London also became alert to how little his family actually knew about him and how uneasy they might become at discovering in his letters what Michael Anesko in his book *Monopolizing the Master* calls "his most distinctive qualities: his devastating sharpness of wit, his extravagant inventions of intimacy, his Rabelasian powers of innuendo."[143]

As Lubbock worked on what would become the

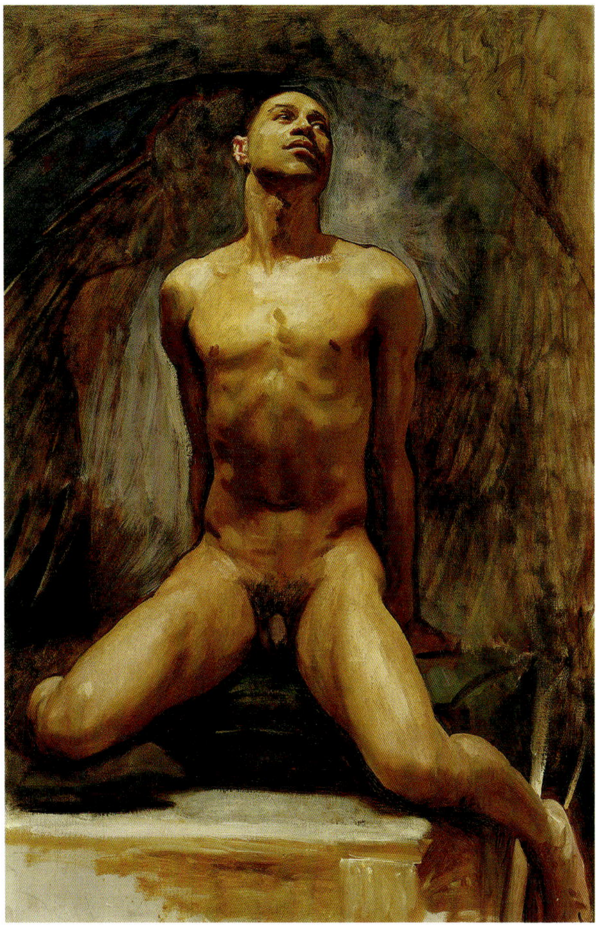

FIG. 22. John Singer Sargent (1856–1925), *Nude Study of Thomas E. McKeller*, ca. 1917–20, Museum of Fine Arts, Boston.

standard edition of James's letters for fifty years, it was agreed that he would excise unpleasant remarks about the living and take out evidence of James's obsession about his health and money. It was also agreed with James's nephew Harry that Lubbock would, as much as possible, omit James's effusive ways of beginning and ending letters, especially missives to younger men, in case the tone might be misconstrued. As the edition in two volumes was going to press, four members of the James family—Harry, his siblings, Billy and Peggy, and their mother—pored over the letters, demanding further cuts. "In almost every instance," Anesko wrote, "Lubbock finally yielded to the family's wishes."[144]

Even though they worked hard at sanitizing the letters, the family still worried that too much had been revealed. A year after the edition appeared, Alice James wrote to Harry: "People are putting a vile interpretation on his silly letters to young men. Poor dear Uncle Henry."[145] Later, Harry James regretted giving permission to E. F. Benson to publish a volume of James's letters to him. They included passages like "Why aren't you here to take a good Devonshire walk with me? I hang over a green garden and a blue sea from a big balcony. . . . There would be room on the balcony even for your inches or cigarettes, even for Apollo's lips" or "I am divided between 2 sensations—panting for to-morrow pm and blushing for all the hours of the past days."[146]

Soon afterward, when Harry was approached by Hendrik Andersen, seeking permission to publish the seventy-eight letters from James he had received, Harry refused.

At that time most readers would not have been comfortable with news of James's complex sexuality, as they might not have responded warmly either to rumors about Sargent. The large collection of James papers housed eventually in the Houghton Library at Harvard was guarded with fierce anxiety by Harry James. Eventually, Leon Edel became a trusted servant of the James estate as well as becoming James's biographer. For example, on one occasion, he informed the family when a scholar he met at a conference expressed an interest in James's homoerotic correspondence. He was assured by the Houghton Library that "she is certainly not going to see anything she's not supposed to see."[147]

Since Edel knew he would have to deal with James's sexuality in his later volumes, he hoped that some other writer would spill the beans first so that it would, as he wrote, "relieve me of the onus of 'breaking' the story."[148]

As their work was reexamined in the light of their sexuality, both James and Sargent became more intriguing. Just as we can look at Sargent's portraits, his sumptuous brushwork, and wonder what hidden desires went into the making of that work, so too with James's heroines and the dramas he created for them. James's artistry, his skill at creating scenes, his sly sexuality, his elaborate prose style, his genius with form and tone and structure make him a subject of fascination not only for ordinary readers but also for students and teachers of literature, and indeed for many, if not all, of the novelists who have come after him. James's dying words—"Tell them to follow, to be faithful, to take me seriously"[149]—continue to resonate a hundred years after his death (Fig. 23).

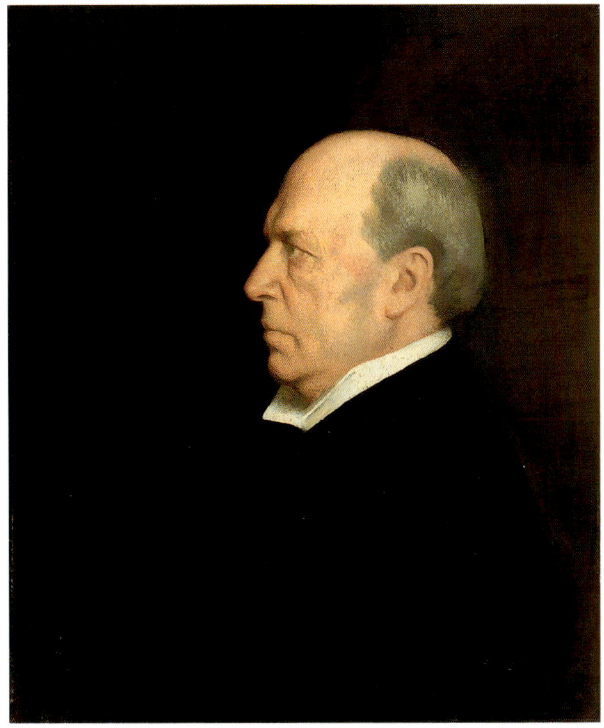

FIG. 23. William James (1882–1961), *Henry James*, 1910, Isabella Stewart Gardner Museum, Boston.

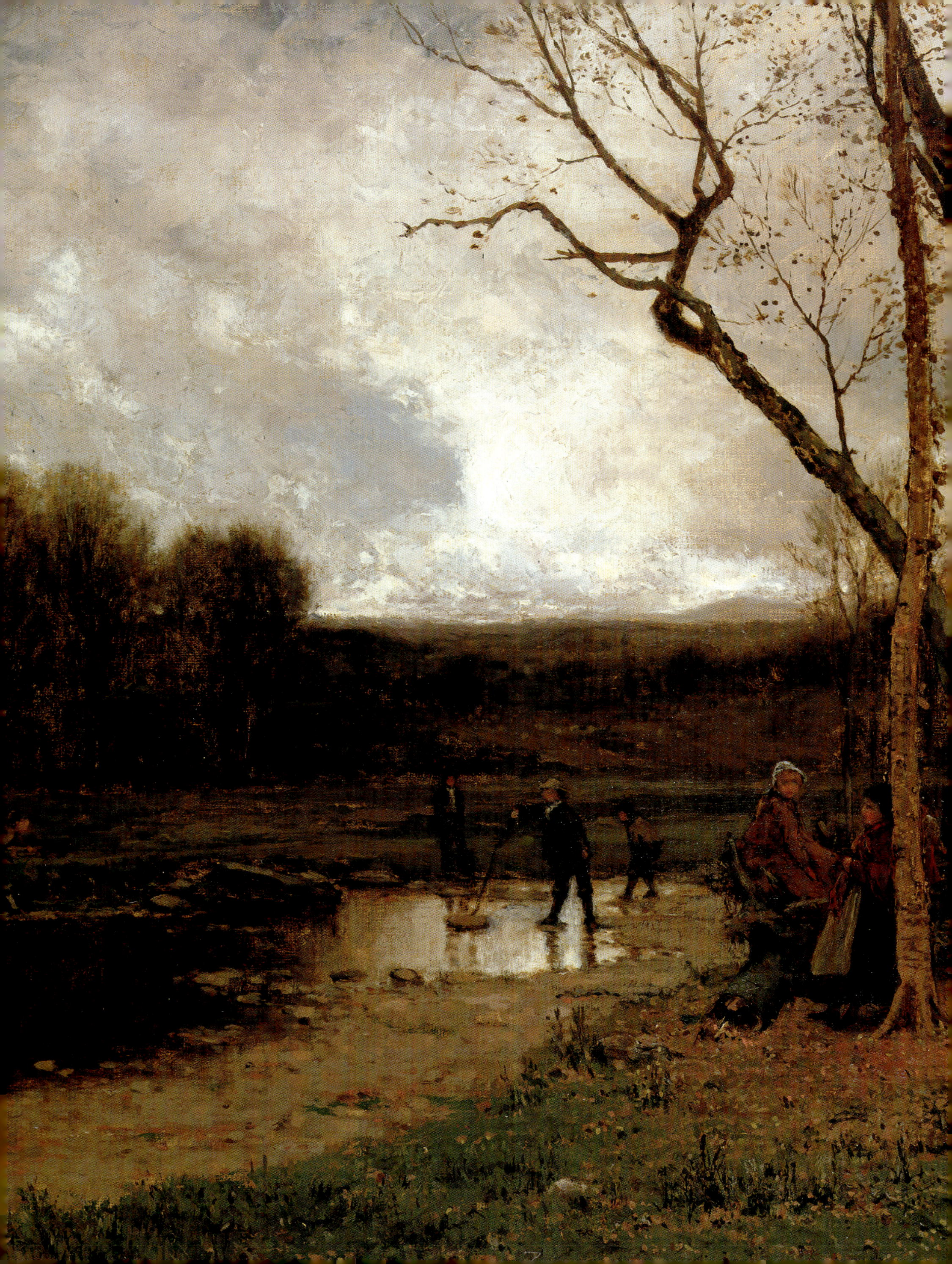

MARC SIMPSON

"I like ambiguities and detest great glares"
Henry James and American Paintings

Through all his days, Henry James knew American artists, saw American art, and used his familiarity with both to enrich his life and inform his writings. From 1866 (with the short story "The Landscape Painter") for the next forty-five years (to *The Outcry* of 1911), James drew on his knowledge of the studio world to give authenticity to the painters and sculptors who populated his fiction. "There is hardly a tale among James's one hundred and twelve stories and twenty novels that does not catch within its net some artifact of status," wrote one distinguished scholar of James's work.[1] Even when the visual arts are not central elements, there is often a pictorial sensibility present on the page; after all, wrote another, "painter of life" was one of James's "favorite metaphors for the novelist."[2] The allusive entwining of the verbal and visual modes of expression in James's writings—painting's figure hidden in the carpet of his fiction—has been the study of many renowned writers and scholars, Colm Tóibín in this volume among their number.[3] Most of them have rightly focused their attention on James's experiences as a boy and young man, when "the house of life and the palace of art became so mixed and interchangeable," with masterworks and masters old and new in various European capitals.[4] On occasion, however—in his art criticism, memoirs, and letters—James wrote directly about his experiences with specific American pictures and their makers.[5] These writings reside at the core of this essay.

James's late-life memoirs set the scene.[6] Looking back more than fifty years, in *A Small Boy and Others* (1913), James noted that such painters and illustrators as Thomas Hicks (1823–1890), Paul Duggan (1810–1861), Christopher Pearse Cranch (1813–1892), and Felix Octavius Darley (1821–1888) virtually haunted the "friendly fireside" of his boyhood home on Washington Square. Through them, he gained an awareness of landscape painters Jasper Francis Cropsey (1823–1900) and John Frederick Kensett (1816–1872) as well as the sculptors Chauncey Bradley Ives (1810–1894), Hiram Powers (1805–1873), and Joseph Mozier (1812–1870).[7] He noted Thomas Cole (1801–1848) as another member of this "outer circle." While James never met Cole, he knew one of his paintings exceedingly well, since *View of Florence from San Miniato* (Fig. 1) "covered half a side of our front parlour." He called the monk sitting in the picture's foreground "a constant friend of my childhood."[8]

Other memories of American art seen in childhood, wrung from his memory like water from a sponge ("the more I squeeze the sponge of memory the more its stored secretions flow"), included, in the James family home, a Neoclassical marble bacchante from an unnamed hand; and, seen elsewhere, portraits by Hicks and Samuel Stillman Osgood (1808–1885).[9] Barring the Cole, however, no American art object from these early years "was half so momentous as . . . the epoch-making masterpiece of Mr. Leutze, which showed us Washington crossing the Delaware in a wondrous flare of projected gaslight and with the effect of a revelation to my young sight of the capacity of accessories to 'stand out.'"[10] James was referring, of course, to *Washington Crossing the Delaware* by Emanuel Leutze (1816–1868; Fig. 2). The visit to this public spectacle "near the Stuyvesant Institute" was all the more thrilling since the expedition took place after James's usual bedtime and was "quite as if going to the theatre."[11] James detailed his childish wonder at the congeries of details that Leutze wrought: "the marvel of the wintery night, of the sharpness of the ice-blocks, of the sickness of the sick soldier, of the protrusion of the minor objects, that of the strands of the rope and the nails of the boots, that, I say, on the part of everything, of its determined purpose of standing out." The inflated language, climaxing in James's ironic admiration of the "profiled national hero's . . . standing *up*, as much as possible, even indeed of doing it almost on one leg, in such difficulties, and successfully balancing," conveys his casting aside of childish things and a gentle mockery of his immature tastes. For he follows immediately on this with the passage:

> *So memorable was that evening to remain for me that nothing could be more strange, in connection with it, than the illustration by the admired work, on its in after years again coming before me, of the cold cruelty with which time may turn and devour its children. The picture, more or less entombed in its relegation, was lividly dead.*[12]

The characteristic that dominated James's childish impression of the Leutze is the picture's power of itemization, the strength and independence of its details over and above demonstrable truths and enhanced unity of effect. In this it became "lividly dead." Of Cole's *View of Florence from San Miniato,* however, he wrote specifically: "not an object represented in it began to stand out after the manner of Mr. Leutze," elsewhere praising the "softness and the haze of our Florence there."[13] As a result, "I could always lose myself" as soon as he looked at the canvas.[14] Its unity of effect and subordination of details won for it a valued and enduring place in James's memory. Cole's painting did not require any recantation of youthful enthusiasm—although it is true that James did not have to

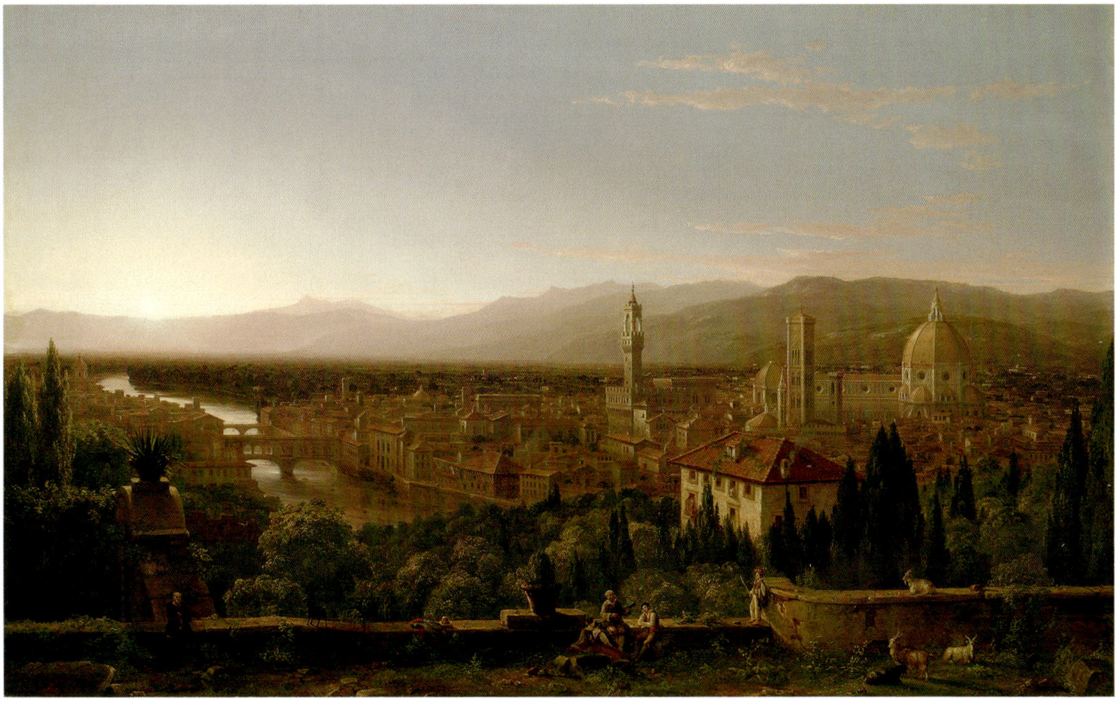

FIG. 1. Thomas Cole (1801–1848), *View of Florence from San Miniato*, 1837, Cleveland Museum of Art.

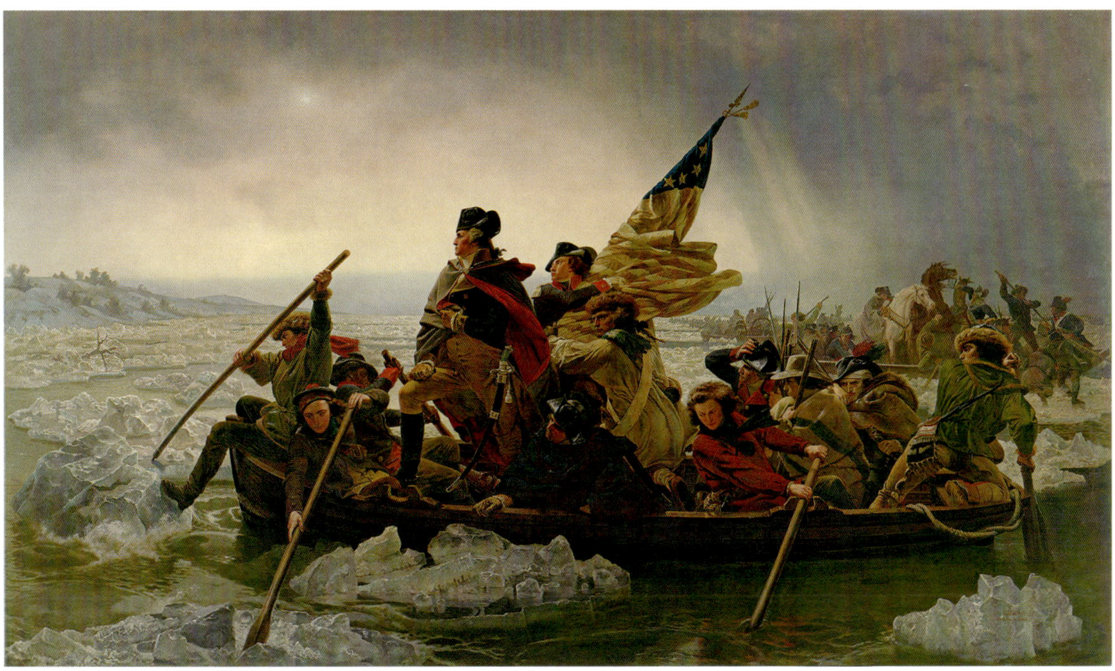

FIG. 2. Emanuel Leutze (1816–1868), *Washington Crossing the Delaware*, 1851, The Metropolitan Museum of Art, New York.

test his memory against the reality of the canvas itself, "the picture being long ago lost to our sight."[15]

With the Cole and the Leutze paintings, James was wringing memory's sponge to write for the first time of pictures seen in the distant past. In other instances late in life, James wrote about recently seen works of American art—as in *The American Scene* of 1907.[16] Here, in graceful asides, he responded to such American artworks as the murals of the Boston Public Library by John Singer Sargent (1856–1925) and Edwin Austin Abbey (1852–1911); portraits by Sargent of the philanthropists Henry Lee Higginson and Henry G. Marquand; the mural and stained glass for the Church of the Ascension in Manhattan by John La Farge (1835–1910); monumental presidential sculptures of Washington by Thomas Crawford (1814–1857) in Richmond and of Lincoln by Augustus Saint-Gaudens (1848–1907) in Chicago; Saint-Gaudens's monuments to the Civil War generals Sherman in New York City's Central Park and Shaw on the Boston Common; and to unspecified pictures by James McNeill Whistler (1834–1903) among the Impressionist paintings in a private collection in Farmington, Connecticut.[17] In these references, however, he moved quickly, being coyly laudatory but giving scant detail concerning his thoughts and responses to specific objects.[18]

More useful for tracking James's pictorial aesthetic are those few instances in which his late writings enter into dialogue with opinions from his published art reviews of earlier decades. These reveal, among other characteristics, the honing of his pictorial taste, lopping off like Occam's Razor those things harmful to a picture's unified impression (those that "stand out"), and the affirmation of this principal virtue from beginning to end of his career as an art critic, albeit with developments and alterations. A survey of James's art criticism as a whole provides a foundation for these comparisons.[19]

In 1868 James, then twenty-four years old, submitted a review of P. G. Hamerton's *Contemporary French Painters* to the *North American Review*, edited by Charles Eliot Norton, a close friend and early mentor in the visual arts. He devoted much of the review's first half to John Ruskin's criticism, bemoaning how few good English-language books there were for the serious student of art and explaining the declaration with which he began one paragraph: "Painters always have a great distrust of those who write about pictures," a point to which he would frequently revert.[20] More important, years before he was to practice the form itself, James articulated precepts for responsible art criticism. Good art critics, he wrote,

> *neither talk pure sentiment (or rather, impure sentiment), like foolish amateurs, nor do they confine their observations to what the French call the technique of art. They examine pictures (or such, at least, is their theory) with an equal regard to the standpoint of the painter and that of the spectator, whom the painter must always be supposed to address,—with an equal regard, in other words, to the material used and to the use made of it.*[21]

Readers of good art criticism, posited James, acquire from the texts "a sense of the great breadth of the province of art, and of its relations with the rest of men's intellectual life."[22] This principle of tying works of art to experience in the world was to animate all his later writing on art.

James's first published art criticism per se was an unsigned essay in the January 1872 *Atlantic Monthly*. The twenty-eight-year-old announced to Norton that William Dean Howells "is a very careful and businesslike editor of the *Atlantic*. As proof of his energy—he has induced me to write a monthly report of the Fine Arts in Boston!!"[23] The double exclamation points signal his excitement. He had just recently returned from fifteen months in Europe, during which he had visited England, France, Switzerland, and Italy. In London—through the interventions of Norton—he had met the much-admired Ruskin, along with the artists Dante Gabriel Rossetti, Edward Burne-Jones, and William Morris, and he had reveled in the treasures of the National Gallery. He summarized his time there in a letter to his brother William: "I have enjoyed the little I have seen in the way of pictures in a manner to suggest that, if I take all I find, I may lay the basis of a serious interest in art & of knowledge which may be of future use to me."[24] During his five months in Italy, he filled his letters home with effusions concerning the art he saw up and down the Apennine peninsula.[25] Primed to share his insights and responses, for the *Atlantic* he wrote first about recent French paintings owned privately in Boston and on view at the Doll & Richards Gallery.[26] Only two other reviews of Boston's art scene, however, and one concerning New York's new Metropolitan Museum of Art—all unsigned—appeared in 1872 because in May James returned to Europe. Two articles on European topics appeared in January 1873 (one on London's Wallace Collection in the *Atlantic*, and a literary review of Henri Regnault's correspondence in *The Nation*). Having returned to the United States in the early fall of 1874, he waited until November before sending another unsigned note from his Boston perch, this one a playfully negative essay dedicated to the old master collection belonging to the duc de Montpensier on view at the Boston Athenaeum.[27] The last but one of James's *Atlantic* reviews appeared in January 1875, telling of works by Americans Hamilton Wilde (1827–1884), George Henry Boughton (1833–1905), J. Appleton Brown (1844–1902), and of a watercolor self-portrait by Marie Spartali Stillman (1844–1927), which "has given us a great deal of pure pleasure, though indeed the pleasure is of a sort which it is hard to refer to definite sources"(sold at Sotheby's, London, 14 July 2016)—all seen at Doll & Richards.[28]

Also in 1875, James had four art-related reviews appear in *The Nation*, one in *The Galaxy* (which is by far his most expansive review of American art), and one that was published on Christmas Day in the *New-York Tribune*, his first newspaper rather than periodical art review. The last of the *Nation* reviews, appearing on 9 September, stands out in at least two ways: it is one of the earliest times that James articulated his prioritization of portraiture over other forms of painting (landscape, genre, still life, or history), and it is his most extended commentary on a historic, rather than contemporary, American work. He had earlier mentioned John Singleton Copley (1738–1815) when, in writing about how the seventeenth-century Spaniard Zurbarán "makes a hard opposition of lights and darks the vehicle of a sort of masculine directness," Copley came "singularly" to mind.[29] Then, in 1875, Copley's *Mrs. Richard Skinner (Dorothy Wendell;* Fig. 3) was on view at Doll & Richards; James took the opportunity to describe and reflect on this "very fine portrait . . . certainly unsurpassable by the artist himself."[30] He marveled at the contemporaneity of her visage, the fact that, but for her costume, she "looks as if she might have stepped out of a Boston street-car." He continued:

For direct, exact reality, Copley almost ranks with the very first, and such a portrait as this satisfies us in so many ways that we are almost puzzled to say what else we demand. When a head is so definite and solid and living as this, we are tempted to believe that it is all it can be. . . . As for suggestiveness, he rendered perfectly and exhaustively all that he saw, and he saw nothing that he could not render. He was definite, as we say; but that adventurous vision of the indefinite which has brushed with its wing all the very greatest works of art is never reflected here. Copley was by no means a Holbein, but he holds a very honourable place in the ranks over which

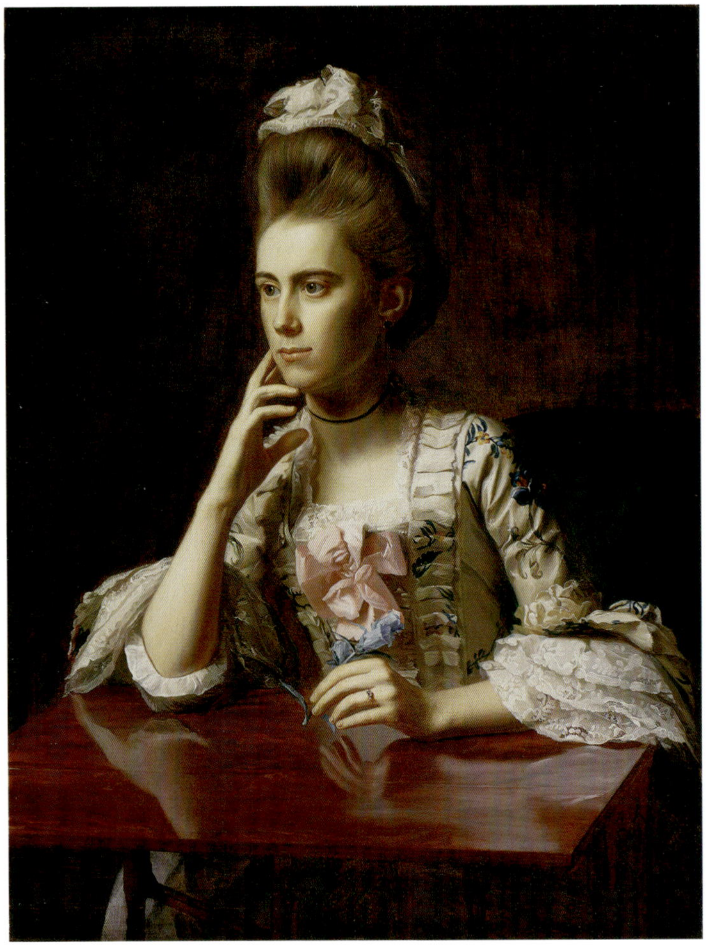

FIG. 3. John Singleton Copley (1738–1815), *Mrs. Richard Skinner (Dorothy Wendell)*, 1772, Museum of Fine Arts, Boston.

Holbein presided as supreme genius. We have called attention to the portrait of Mrs. Skinner because, in these days of complex aims and half-successes, there is something extremely refreshing in the spectacle of a simple aim begetting an absolute triumph.[31]

James would laud both the notion of a simple, unified aim and the value of portraiture in coming decades.

The author sent the Christmas Day *Tribune* article from Paris, where he had moved in November. He served as an occasional correspondent for the *Tribune* from November through August, sending twenty reports touching on aspects of life in Paris and its environs.[32] At least nine of these columns dealt with art topics, including, along with a de rigueur review of the official Salon, dismissals of the second Impressionist show of 1876 and, also at Durand-Ruel's, of the works refused admission to the Salon that year (citing by name only landscapes by the American James Fairman [1826–1904]). Starting in June 1876, four art columns dealing with French art topics appeared in *The Nation,* with focuses on the Salon works of Puvis de Chavannes, Gustave Moreau, Paul Dubois, and on the memorial to Henri Regnault. Late in the year,

James moved to London. It was from that post that he sent virtually all the rest of his art criticism and essays: fourteen articles for *The Nation* (25 January 1877 through 29 May 1879), two for *The Galaxy* (July and August 1877), one for the *International Review* (April 1880), two for the *Century Magazine* (May 1883 and January 1890), and two catalogue prefaces for monographic exhibitions of Englishmen at the Fine Art Society, one on George Du Maurier in 1884 and another devoted to Alfred Parsons in 1891.

Providing an even more regular outlet for James's art writing in the years around 1890 were the publications of Harper & Brothers. For *Harper's Weekly* he published appreciative life-and-works essays on two illustrators who worked often for the firm: Abbey, on 4 December 1886; and Charles S. Reinhart (1844–1896), on 14 June 1890. For *Harper's New Monthly Magazine* in October 1887 he published a long essay on Sargent, following that in June 1889 with an extended article on "Our Artists in Europe"—"our" meaning illustrators who worked for *Harper's* (including the Broadway colony and its artists Millet, Abbey, and Parsons as well as considerations of Boughton, Du Maurier, and Reinhart). All of these, along with his 1890 *Century* essay on Honoré Daumier and a theatrical bagatelle called "After the Play," were lightly reworked and published by Harper's as the book *Picture and Text* (1893)—a volume characterized by one scholar as "a little garland of advertisement for his friends . . . and for the publishers who employed them."[33] This slackening of engagement with new art of a nonillustrational, nonmagazine nature seems to bear witness to James's confession to Norton, in 1892, "*Painting* . . . it is true I have ceased to feel it very much."[34]

Five years later, however, from January through June 1897, *Harper's Weekly* dragged him back into the traces, engaging James to write a column from London; four of the six he completed touched on art topics, among many other things, including notice of American artists. James's last piece of published art writing was another essay on Du Maurier for *Harper's New Monthly Magazine,* which appeared in September 1897. In all, scholars now credit James with sixty art-related reviews, art-book reviews, or critical-biographical essays.

With this overview of James's art writing in place, we can return to the memoirs and the few comparisons they offer, both direct and indirect, with his previously published criticism. One example of the latter is his consideration in *Notes of a Son and Brother* of a painting closely related to one that he had written of at the end of his first piece of criticism, about privately owned French paintings on view at Boston's Doll & Richards Gallery. There, after responding to pictures by Delacroix, Decamps, Troyon, Rousseau, and others, the works of three Americans tempted him to declare, "We should have liked, with more space, to devote a few words to three or four American pictures lately visible in the same rooms," which, in best praeteritio fashion, he then proceeded to do. The subject and handling both of a portrait of a little girl by "R. C. Porter" (probably a typographical error for Benjamin C. Porter [1843/45–1908]) and Elihu Vedder's (1836–1923) small *Girl with Casket* (before 1871; unlocated) charmed him. But it was La Farge's *The Last Valley—Paradise Rocks* (Fig. 4) that sparked his greatest enthusiasm. Calling it the "most important" of the American works, James declared this to be

> *In every way a remarkable picture, full of the most refined intentions and the most beautiful results, of light and atmosphere and of the very poetry of the situation. We have rarely seen a work in which the painter seems to have stored away such a permanent fund of luminosity.*[35]

He ended by pronouncing that "parts of the picture . . . might have been painted by a less sceptical Decamps,"

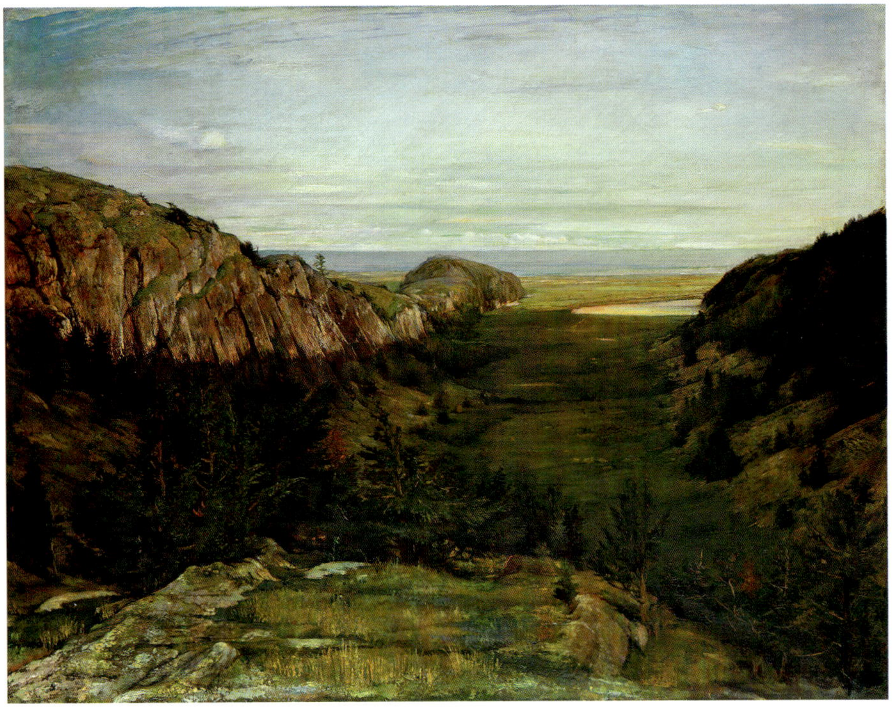

FIG. 4. John La Farge (1835–1910), *The Last Valley—Paradise Rocks*, 1867–68, National Gallery of Art, Washington, DC.

citing the popular French painter of Orientalist scenes whom he had earlier in the review called "factitious" for his privileging of "effect" over "truth."[36] James could certainly avow the truth of both the painter and the site of the Rhode Island scene. He had been acquainted with La Farge from 1859, in a strong and mutually rewarding fashion.[37] La Farge, he later wrote, "opened up to us, though perhaps to me in particular . . . prospects and possibilities that made the future flush and swarm."[38] It was La Farge who, according to his early biographer, proclaimed that James—although not destined to create with a brush—had "the painter's eye," a thing "few writers possessed."[39] The two remained closely enough in touch so that in 1875 James felt able to offer tours of La Farge's New York studio even in the painter's absence.[40] Decades later, La Farge remained for James "one of the most extraordinary and agreeable of men, a remarkable combination of France and America," who provoked wonder "at his combination of social and artistic endowments."[41] La Farge turned that artistry to James's service in 1898, producing a compelling illustration/masthead for the serial publication of *The Turn of the Screw* (see Tóibín, Fig. 5). A dozen years later, on hearing of La Farge's death, James wrote to the painter's daughter, invoking the "old years, when I saw him so much oftener and when the interest and fascination of his wondrous intelligence and rare and distinguished personality were really a feature of my life":

> *I think of him as one of the very small number of* truly *extraordinary men whom I've known. He was that rare thing, a* figure*—which innumerable eminent and endowed men (and particularly in this country) haven't been. And he was the intellectual or temperamental artist as no one else has ever been here. Great, on that score, in the vastly vulgar air, should be his glory, should remain his example.*[42]

More to the point for his response to the picture in 1872, James knew the truth of what was portrayed. He certainly knew the "genius of the scene" and loved it, had even painted side by side with La Farge on at least one Newport morning, "in the bosky open air" outside the town.[43] Late in life he used a sighting not of *The Last Valley—Paradise Rocks* but of the one other major landscape that La Farge made, *Paradise Valley* (1866–68; Terra Foundation for American Art, Chicago), lent to the La Farge Memorial Exhibition in early 1911 at the Museum of Fine Arts, Boston, to reinvoke his affection for the place.[44] He wrote of spending an hour "before a commemorative cluster of La Farge's earlier productions" assembled in the "exquisite array of the Boston 'show'" and of being contentedly beset by questions:

> *I like ambiguities and detest great glares; preferring thus for my critical no less than for my pedestrian progress the cool and the shade to the sun and dust of the way. There was an exquisite effort of which I had been peculiarly sure; the large canvas of the view of the Paradise Rocks over against Newport, but within the island and beyond the "second beach"—such were our thin designations! On the high style and the grand manner of this thing, even though a little uneasy before the absence from it of a certain crânerie* [swagger] *of touch, I would have staked every grain of my grounded sensibility—in spite of which, on second thoughts, I shall let that faded fact, and no other contention at all, be my last word about it.*[45] *For the prevailing force, within the Boston walls, the supreme magic anything was to distil, just melted into another connection which flung a soft mantle as over the whole show. It became, from the question of how even a man of perceptive genius had painted what we then locally regarded as our scenery, a question of how we ourselves had felt and cherished that scenery; which latter of these two memories swept for me everything before it.*[46]

Truth to the complexity of experience is what James valued, and both of La Farge's magnificent pictures, with a "permanent fund of luminosity," conveyed this truth so vividly that the lived experience of being in Newport, rather than that of the painting on the wall, came foremost to his consideration. This was the mark of a wholly successful picture.

James had met La Farge in 1859, when the James family sojourned in Newport, and then solidified the friendship when, in 1860, in a counterintuitive move, they again left Europe in order to allow the eldest of the family's four sons, William, the opportunity to study painting. As James wrote to his friend Thomas Sergeant Perry: "We are going immediately to Newport, which is the place in America we all most care to live in. I'll tell you the reason for this as briefly as I can. Willie has decided to try and study painting seriously, and wished [to] return home to do so, if possible with Mr. Hunt."[47] When settled, both William and Henry studied with William Morris Hunt (1824–1879), who had absorbed the principles of Barbizon art from Jean-François Millet and, on his return to America, had proselytized successfully among collectors in Boston for Millet and his fellow Barbizon artists. La Farge was there for the same purpose. James later wrote:

> *Pupils at that time didn't flock to his* [Hunt's] *gates—though they were to do so in Boston, during years, later on; an earnest lady or two, Boston precursors, hovered and flitted, but I remember for the rest (and I speak of a short period) no thoroughgoing élèves save John La Farge and my brother.*[48]

Henry, surrounded by Hunt's work in the studio, drew after plaster casts while the others, more advanced, painted. This was his true initiation to feelings of sympathy with pictorial artists. "Frankly, intensely—that was the great thing—these were hours of Art, art definitely named, looking me full in the face and accepting my stare in return. . . . I was there, day by day, as much as anyone had ever been, and with a sense of what it 'meant' to be there that the most accredited of pupils couldn't have surpassed."[49] Hunt's studio was the place where James, primed by his experiences of appreciating art in Europe, adopted the sensibilities of a visual artist as a fundamental element of his existence.

So, a dozen years later, in early 1872, James surely felt gratified when, as one of the subjects for his second *Atlantic* art review, he was able to survey a collection of works by Hunt at Boston's Doll & Richards Gallery. Any initial pleasure, however, must have been compromised by the realization that he could not be enthusiastic about the works on view. He wrote that the show "struck us as not fairly representative of the painter. . . . [I]n general, the works present suggested invidious comparisons with various absent companions, which those who have seen them associate with the artist's best powers."[50] He was able to praise a half dozen small canvases, especially two landscapes into which "the very *genius loci* has been cunningly infused." But the exhibit's larger works—*Hamlet* (ca. 1864; Museum of Fine Arts, Boston), *Boy with Butterfly* (1870; private collection), and even the sky of *Marguerite* (1870; Museum of Fine Arts, Boston), who otherwise "stands up in the open air with no small reality and grace"—"vexed" him because of their coarse method. The first of the "absent companions" rued by James, the works that would reveal Hunt's full merits, was *Girl at the Fountain* (Fig. 5).

In his *Notes of a Son and Brother,* written four decades later, he recalled *Girl at the Fountain* and again, through this powers of memory, praised it. Calling to mind Hunt's pictures in the room where he was drawing after plaster casts, James wrote:

> *I believed them great productions—thought in especial endless good of the large canvas of the girl with her back presented while she fills her bucket at the spout in the wall, against which she leans with a tension of young muscle, a general expression of back, beneath her dress, and with the pressure of her raised and extended bare arm and flattened hand: this, to my imagination, could only become the prize of some famous collection, the light of some museum, for all the odd circumstance that it was company just then for muddled* me *and for the queer figures projected by my crayon.*[51]

Although James used the subjunctive voice here, by the time he was writing, the picture had indeed become the prize of a famous collection; Hunt's sister had bequeathed it to the Metropolitan Museum of Art in 1908.

Leutze's picture on second sight, for James, died "lividly"; the power of La Farge's and Hunt's stayed steady. Different from these, a work by Whistler grew in stature over time, and that fact speaks to James's developing aesthetic sensibility. James wrote for the American press of the exhibitions at the avant-garde Grosvenor Gallery in London in 1877, 1878, 1879, and 1882. In those four exhibitions, James had the opportunity of seeing many of the paintings by Whistler that are now among his most respected works. James, however, was not an admirer, in part, one senses, because of the artist's nonconventional, performative self. In 1878, for example, he hesitated to cede him either citizenship or profession: "I may seem to stretch a point, indeed, in speaking of Mr. James Whistler as an American painter, for it is not fair to attach to Mr. Whistler any label that serves for any one else. He is quite sole of his kind."[52] He ignored Whistler's contributions of 1879 entirely. Having observed that Whistler painted "in a manner to make it difficult to attach a high value to individual pieces," he wrote in 1878 without individual notice of any one work, although they included such paintings as *Variations in Flesh-Colour and Green: The Balcony* (1865; Freer Gallery of Art, Washington, DC) and *Nocturne: Grey and Silver*

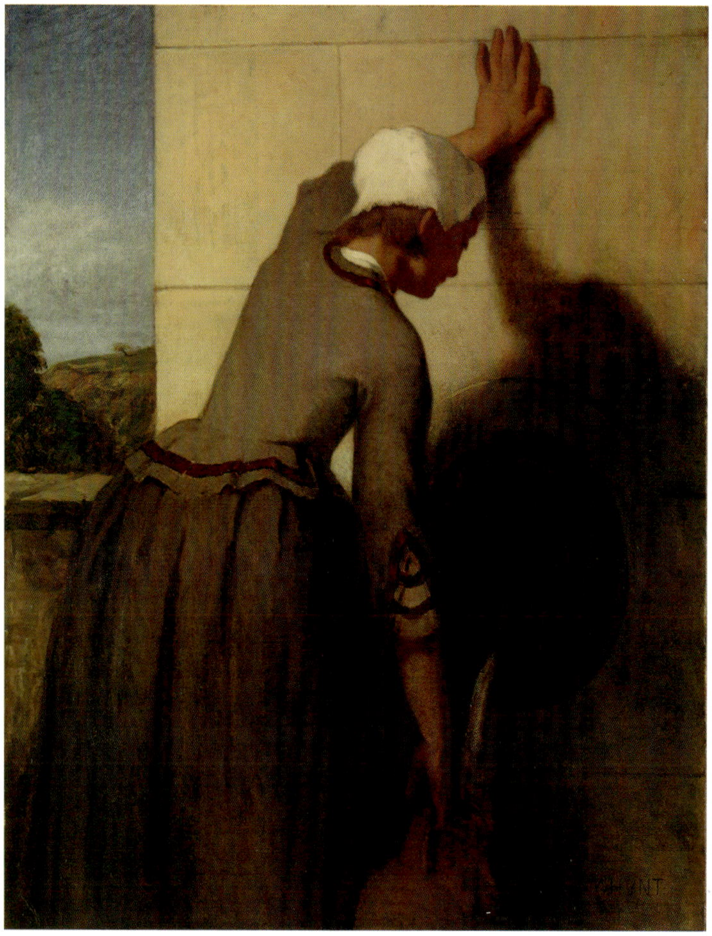

FIG. 5. William Morris Hunt (1824–1879), *Girl at the Fountain*, 1852–54, The Metropolitan Museum of Art, New York.

(1873–75; Philadelphia Museum of Art, Johnson Collection). He did then concede, in as backhanded a fashion as possible, that "Whistler's productions are pleasant things to have about, so long as one regards them as simple objects—as incidents of furniture or decoration. The spectator's quarrel with them begins when he feels it to be expected of him to regard them as pictures."[53] As for the 1877 exhibition—the one that included *Nocturne in Black and Gold: The Falling Rocket* (ca. 1875; Detroit Institute of Art), *Nocturne in Blue and Silver* (1871–72; Harvard University Art Museums, Cambridge, Massachusetts), *Nocturne: Blue and Gold—Old Battersea Bridge* (1872–75; Tate Gallery, London), and five others, he simply declared in *The Galaxy:*

I will not speak of Mr. Whistler's "Nocturnes in Black and Gold" and in "Blue and Silver," of his "Arrangements," "Harmonies," and "Impressions," because I frankly confess they do not amuse me. The mildest judgment I have heard pronounced upon them is that they are like "ghosts of Velasquezes"; with the harshest I will not darken my pages. It may be a narrow point of view, but to be interesting it seems to me that a picture should have some relation to life as well as to painting. Mr.

Whistler's experiments have no relation whatever to life; they have only a relation to painting.[54]

James, however, wrote about this 1877 exhibition twice. The earlier of the reviews, for *The Nation,* did not differ signally in tone. He joked: "Mr. Whistler presents half a dozen canvases which I must take care not to mention as pictures; they are, according to the catalogue, 'nocturnes,' 'arrangements,' and 'harmonies.' Since our business is with pictures, it were better, I suppose, not to speak of these things." He continued, nonetheless, "their material is paint and canvas, and they are framed and hang upon a wall. I have never seen any combination of these ingredients which has struck me as less profitable." As is well known, when Ruskin saw this gathering of pictures, the *Nocturne in Black and Gold: The Falling Rocket* piqued his particular ire, and his printed response accusing Whistler of "Cockney impudence" prompted a famous libel suit.[55] James, on the other hand, who in this instance did take note of individual works, chose to call attention to two of the three portraits on view: "one of his nocturnes is his impression of Mr. Henry Irving, and another his impression of Miss Ellen Terry. It may be good to be an impressionist; but I should say on this evidence that it were vastly better to be an expressionist." He summarized the whole display:

Mr. Whistler's productions are, in the very nature of the case, uninteresting; they belong to the closet, not to the world. They may be good studio-jokes, or even useful studio-experiments, but they illustrate only what one may call the self-complacency of technicality.[56]

Twenty years on, at the Grafton Galleries's *Exhibition of Dramatic and Music Art*, which he wrote about for *Harper's Weekly,* James once again had the chance to see the portrait of Irving (Fig. 6). The intervening decades had transformed James's perception of the work from "studio-joke" to "exquisite image of Henry Irving as the Philip of Tennyson's 'Queen Mary.'" To pause before the work was "to be held to the spot by just the highest operation of the charm one has sought there—the charm of a certain degree of melancholy meditation."[57] Within the limits of Whistler's dim, darkened portrayal of the actor, James perceived a truth and unity of effect that won him over completely.

Consideration of the work transported James from the midst of over three hundred admired works in the exhibition—portraits by Joshua Reynolds, William Hogarth, Thomas Gainsborough, and Johann Zoffany, and the mementos of David Garrick, Sarah Siddons, and other great eighteenth-century actors—to elicit in him a "wonder reintensified" at the dismissive "attitude of a stupid generation" (i.e., his own) toward Whistler's "so rare" art and taste. He then reconsidered his choice of vocabulary:

Wonder is perhaps, after all, not the word to use, for how should *a stupid generation, liking so much what it does like, and with a faculty trained to coarser motions, recognize in Mr. Whistler's work one of the finest of all distillations of the artistic intelligence? To turn from his picture to the rest of the show . . . is to drop from the world of distinction, of perception, of beauty and mystery and perpetuity, into—well, a very ordinary place.*[58]

James proceeded to dream—"hallucination set in," he wrote—that the world would soon recognize Whistler's achievement:

the effect of Whistler at his best is exactly to give to the place he hangs in . . . something of the sense, of the illusion, of a great museum. He isolates himself in a manner all his own; his presence is in itself a sort of implication of a choice corner. Have we, in this, a faint foresight of the

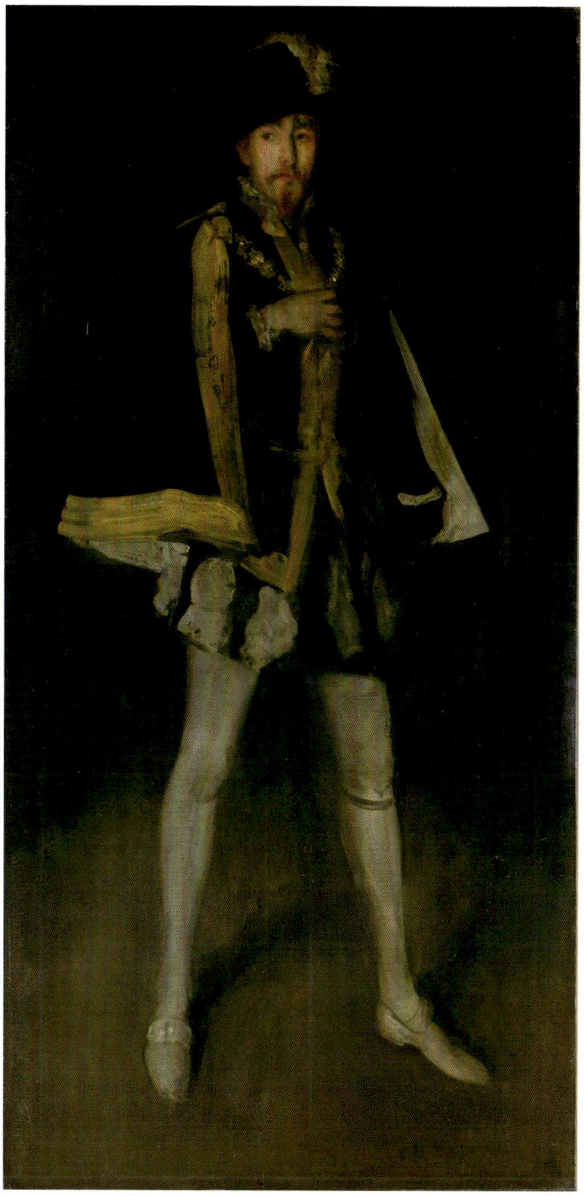

FIG. 6. James McNeill Whistler (1834–1903), *Arrangement in Black, No. 3: Sir Henry Irving as Philip II of Spain,* 1876, The Metropolitan Museum of Art, New York.

eventual turn of the wheel—of one of the nooks of honor, those innermost rooms of great collections, in which our posterity shall find him?[59]

What has changed? In part, the picture. Whistler had repainted it in 1885, so his reworking of the cape, medals, and plumes might account for some of the altered view.[60] Just as likely, however, is the possibility that James had absorbed the lessons of atmosphere and suggestion that so appealed to him in the Cole and La Farge landscapes—ambiguity rather than glare—and was now able to see Whistler's muted gray and ochre portrait as embodying the mystery of both Irving's own personality and the actor's craft—the world of the British theater of which James himself had, just a few years earlier, tried so hard and, with the negative response to his play *Guy Domville,* failed to become a part.

Another difference is that, by 1897, James and Whistler had entered into a respectful friendship. They had been acquaintances when James sniffed at the work of the Grosvenor Gallery twenty years before. In April 1878, just about the time he was to decide that Whistler's canvases were unobjectionable as long as one didn't consider them pictures, James wrote to his father:

I also breakfasted on Sunday last with William [sic—a telling slip] *Whistler the painter, at his queer little house at Chelsea, on the river (near Carlyle's). His Sunday morning breakfasts are somewhat classical. He is a queer little Londonized Southerner, and paints abominably. But his breakfasts are easy and pleasant, and he has tomatoes and buckwheat cakes. I found there Sir Coutts and Lady Lindsay (the Grosvenor Gallery people)—who are very sociable (and Sir Coutts the handsomest man in England); Mrs. Duncan Stewart, Arthur Cecil the actor etc.*[61]

Since the reviews in *The Nation* were unsigned, James could partake of hospitality without awkwardness.

James later reported on the libel trial *Whistler v. Ruskin* at some length, articulating his embarrassment at the whole enterprise:

The case had a two days' hearing, and it was a singular and most regrettable exhibition. If it had taken place in some Western American town, it would have been called provincial and barbarous; it would have been cited as an incident of a low civilisation. Beneath the stately towers of Westminster it hardly wore a higher aspect. . . . [F]ew things, I think, have lately done more to vulgarise the public sense of the character of artistic production.[62]

While he expressed satisfaction that someone had challenged Ruskin's language—"which quite transgresses the decencies of criticism"—still, he did declare that Whistler's "productions" were "very eccentric and imperfect," adding the parenthetical qualification, "I speak here of his paintings only; his etchings are quite another affair, and altogether admirable."[63] When Whistler showed at the Grosvenor in 1882, James was still not convinced about him: "Mr. Whistler, of course, is extremely peculiar; he is supposed to be the buffoon of the Grosvenor, the laughing-stock of the critics. He does the comic business once a year; he turns the somersault in the ring." Yet, James conceded, "for Mr. Whistler this is rather a good year." Of Whistler's seven paintings on view, James wrote only "of the two full-length sketches of female figures"—although calling full-length portraits more than six feet high "sketches" is certainly not meant as praise:

It is a misfortune for Mr. Whistler that he once gave the measure of his talent, and a very high measure it was. The portrait of his mother [1871; Musée d'Orsay, Paris], *painted some years ago and exhibited this year in New York, is so noble and admirable a picture, such a masterpiece of tone, of feeling, of the power to render life, that the fruits of his brush offered to the public more lately have seemed in comparison very crude. . . . One of them, the Harmony in Black and Red* [unlocated], *may or may not be a likeness of the lady who stood for it; but it bears a remarkable resemblance to another person. I conclude from this that it has the appearance of life, which is a good deal, by the way. It may have been painted in three hours. . . . The vague black shadow on Mr. Whistler's canvas lifts its head and poises itself and says something. . . . Mr. Whistler is a votary of "tone;" his manner of painting is to breathe upon the canvas. It is not too much to say that he has, to a certain point, the creative afflatus. His little black and red lady is charming; she looks like some one, as I have said, and if she is a shadow she is the shadow of a graceful personage. Her companion, in flesh-color and pink, is a trifle less graceful, and her hat does n't fit* [*Harmony in Pink and Grey: Portrait of Lady Meux;* 1881; Frick Collection, New York]; *I also contest her flesh-color, which has a light gray tinge, not usually remarked in the human complexion. Still, she does very well on the wall,—which is about all that one is obliged to claim for these light emanations.*[64]

By 1884, however, James's conversion to Whistler's painted work had taken place. He wrote in a letter—a private rather than public communication—that the "best thing" at the Grosvenor Gallery (barring a portrait by Sargent in which he had a personal interest) "is an adorable big Whistler, a portrait of Lady Archibald Campbell. It is almost as good as the portrait of his Mother."[65] Favorably comparing the subtle and shadowed *Arrangement in Black (The Lady in the Yellow Buskin;* ca. 1883; Philadelphia Museum of Art) with the much-admired portrayal of Anna McNeill Whistler signals a marked change indeed.

He was now an enthusiast, and he acted the part. In 1885, serving, at the request of Sargent, as cicerone for Dr. Samuel Pozzi, comte Robert de Montesquiou, and prince Edmond de Polignac—three highly cultured aesthetes visiting London from Paris—James hosted a dinner for them to which he invited Whistler, who was in turn prevailed upon to show them *Harmony in Blue and Gold: The Peacock Room* (1876–77; Freer Gallery, Washington, DC), the dining room he had painted for Frederick Leyland. James undertook to make the arrangements with the Leyland household and to add as guests for the event the wife and daughter of George Boughton. It was a complex affair to organize, for Whistler and Leyland were estranged, and James was not to be in the city when the visit took place. As James wrote to Florence Boughton:

It seems odd that I should be inviting Mrs. Boughton and you to lunch with Whistler!—especially as I shall not be there myself, as I return to the country tomorrow. But on the whole nothing that relates to Whistler is queerer than anything else.[66]

In spite of this amused stance, by the later 1880s their friendship had ripened. In February 1889 Whistler sent James an impression of the etching *Mairie, Loches* (1888; Glasgow 413, K. 382), prompting James to respond:

I take your present of the beautiful etching of the dear old house at the dear old Loches as a most benevolent and graceful act. It is a charming thing with a charming association—or, rather, with many more than one: since I hold it directly from your cunning and liberal hand, with the soft participation, too, as I fondly fancy, of Mrs. Whistler's sympathy. It is already swinging in glory on a poorly-populated wall, where a liberal space has been made for it, and where it is quite the fair high aristocrat of the collection. How much more cachet I now feel that I have![67]

There were visits, too. James reported to Isabella Stewart Gardner about one in 1893: "I went to tea yesterday with the Whistlers in their queer little garden-house off the rue du Bac, where the only furniture is the paint on the walls and the smile on the lady's broad face."[68] There were more gifts and letters: James sent Whistler a copy of *The Spoils of Poynton* in 1897, which elicited a moving exchange from one to the other. Whistler wrote of James's prose being "workmanship itself," "so marvelously cared for and refined in its polish," and praised "the exquisite finish of it all."[69] James responded movingly, articulating again his core belief in the unity of the arts (and with almost the same phrase as he had earlier put in the mouth of Nick Dormer in *The Tragic Muse* [1890]—"All art is one"):

To have pleased you, to have touched you, to have given you something of the impression of the decent little thing one attempted to do—this is for me, my dear Whistler, a rare and peculiar pleasure. For the arts are one, and with the artist the artist communicates. Therefore your good words come to me as from one who knows. You know, above all, better than anyone, how dreadfully few are such. One writes for one's self alone. . . . You have done too much of the exquisite not to have earned more despair than anything else; but don't doubt that something vibrates back when that Exquisite takes the form of recognition of a not utterly indelicate brother.[70]

James had come to recognize in Whistler the careful and delicate artist that a lack of overt finish had, in earlier decades, prevented him from appreciating. Closing the letter, the fifty-four-year-old writer called Whistler "my dear Master." Three months later, as we have seen, he wrote of "Mr. Whistler's work" as "one of the finest of all distillations of the artistic intelligence."[71]

Conversion from scoffer to self-proclaimed acolyte came about both through James's own developing appreciation of pictorial subtleties (matching his own preferred ambiguities rather than glares, as he wrote of La Farge's *Paradise Valley*) but also through personal attachment. Friendship joins a sense of an artwork's truthfulness and wholeness as another motivating criterion in James's criticism of American art—a situation distinct from his reviews of French contemporary painting or Italian Renaissance art. He touched on this when writing of the early-morning painting session shared with La Farge in Newport, hoping that "one's own small daub . . . might incur appreciation by the eye of friendship."[72] It was often with "the eye of friendship, friendship full of character and colour, and full of amusement of its own," that James looked at and appreciated American art of his time.[73] Most of the painters about whom he wrote multiple times for publication—La Farge, Whistler, Abbey, and, above all, Sargent—were, or became, close friends. The much older William Morris Hunt, whose works he reviewed only once but of whom he wrote much in his memoirs, was a formative figure in James's youth. He eventually had strong personal ties even to Frank Duveneck (1848–1919), who, more than a decade after James's writing about him, would marry Elizabeth (Lizzie) Lyman Otis Boott (1846–1888), one of James's closest women friends. It is a question whether James's pictorial taste led him to these men of talent, or whether his social and professional circles were such that they drew men of talent to him. In either case, his interest in them coincided with the high critical appreciation that they shared during their own day. His advocacy of their work thus made him a proponent of a modern art that entwined international subjects and styles with American citizenship, creating at the turn of the twentieth century a truly cosmopolitan American art.

Perhaps the clearest demonstration of friendship as a factor in James's published criticism is his writing on Boughton. By and large, James's public art enthusiasms have been validated over time: Sargent, Whistler, early Duveneck, early La Farge—even Abbey, of late—have, to varying degrees, generated critical and art historical interest and now possess established places in the history of American art. Boughton does not.[74] In his own day, highly respected as both painter and illustrator, the English-born, Albany-raised Boughton was elected to both the National Academy of Design (1871) and the Royal Academy of Arts (ARA 1879; RA 1896). Artists with widely divergent styles admired him: Vincent van Gogh singled him out as particularly praiseworthy (his first sermon was apparently inspired in part by Boughton's work);[75] Whistler maintained a strong and lasting friendship with him (it was Boughton who drew Whistler's attention to Ruskin's criticism of the 1877 Grosvenor Gallery exhibition).[76] James wrote in 1889, and contemporary references bear this out, that "Mr. Boughton is a painter about whom there is little that is new to tell to-day, so conspicuous and incontestable is his achievement."[77] Boughton's current fame is certainly not conspicuous. This in spite of—or perhaps, in part, due to—the onetime ubiquity of reproductions of his *Pilgrims Going to Church* (1867; New-York Historical Society); familiarity breeds contempt.[78] James never wrote of *Pilgrims Going to Church*, but he did mention other works by the artist, sometimes at length, in at least six published reviews. Only Sargent earned so many published exhibition notices from him. Moreover, James's interest was sustained, ranging from 1875 to 1897. A survey of these six entries affirms the priorities that James set for his art criticism.

The earliest was of a "small American winter scene" on view at Doll & Richards in late 1874, which prompted James to offer "a friendly word." He first wrote of Boughton's "rather attenuated, tearful, invalidish sort of grace," and complained that "the artist's figure-pieces always look to us as if some very clever woman had painted them." Yet, in describing the picture's "falling dusk on the edge of a wood, with the pale, smothered gleam of the sunset vaguely touching the thin snow," James came to believe that the canvas was "in its way quite exquisite."

> *The painter who feels and renders the pearly grays of the snow-charged sky and the confusion of desolation along the line where the naked, rusty tree-tops rise against it, the brown, damp depths of leafless woods, and the shuddering chill of the slanting light as it lies down, at length, on the snow, does something which tests the finer edge of his faculty.*

The great proof of the work's effect was simple: "it revived potently a constant taste of ours for all the lurking harmonies of the winter landscape."[79] He would later write that Boughton had "a genius for landscape."[80]

Later in 1875, in an omnium-gatherum review in *The Galaxy,* James turned again to Boughton, "our chief American representative of the fine arts, we believe, in London."[81] At Goupil's, James wrote, the place of honor was held by Boughton's *The Heir-Presumptive* (1874; private collection). Again, he began by writing negative things, wryly and wittily, including that all the figures were "of a fatally meagre execution, and sadly at loss to acquit themselves of their pictorial duties," like a landscape painter's last-minute staffage, "maliciously magnified and trying to play at being real figures." They were "of the cut-paper school." "What misguided friend or insidious enemy," he asked, "is it that is forever prompting Mr. Boughton to meddle with figures? His attempts in this line are painfully amateurish; his drawing, his color, his modelling strike us as almost grotesquely weak." Contrariwise, "Mr. Boughton is a landscape painter of a quite exquisite temper, as this same picture showed; and it was to praise his landscape, and not to criticise his figures, that we mentioned the work."[82]

Then, after moving to London in 1876, James met Boughton, and the two became friends. He began to see "with the eye of friendship"; he characterized him in a letter to his brother William in 1877 as "Boughton, the painter (an American—Londonized), a good plain man."[83] And at the same time, James developed an airy vocabulary that allowed him to write publicly about Boughton's works with irrefutable appreciations of sentiment or color rather than analytical evaluations. In 1877, for example, James wrote that Boughton had "two very charming things . . . touched with ingenious fancy, interesting in sentiment, and peculiarly refined in color" at the Royal Academy, referring to *Homeward Bound* (unlocated) and *Snow in Spring* (1877; private collection).[84] The next year, James declared that, in contrast to Whistler (of whose "impressionist" manner he complained "that a picture is not an impression but an expression—just as a poem or a piece of music is"), Boughton's "results are always charming. More exactly than any one else he preserves the balance between landscape and figures; with him it is always difficult to say whether the group or the background constitutes the subject"—referring to such works as *The Waning of the Honeymoon* (1878; Walters Art Museum, Baltimore), in which the predominance of the figures seems evident. James concluded, "In all Mr. Boughton's work, and especially in his partiality for a certain bright soberness of color, there is something very refined and discreet."[85] To those friends whom he could trust he was more candid. To one in 1883 he wrote that Boughton "is a very good fellow, if a weak painter."[86] As late as 1897, when Boughton was elected academician at the Royal Academy, James would find kind words to allow his friend space in the column without committing any acute judgment to print. Of *Memories* (1897; Royal Academy,

London), he wrote of a "blue subject that derives point from a black figure—a subject blue with the blueness of admirable water, wind and graduated distance."[87] "Bright soberness of color" and "blue with the blueness of admirable water"; such statements are inarguable.

James did, of course, also write about the work of American artists whom he did not know. Living much of his adult life abroad, he necessarily had restrictions on what American exhibitions he reviewed. Moreover, of his eight reviews that respond to events at American venues, seven concern paintings seen in small one-person or dealer-organized exhibitions.[88] The number of major American artists of the time whom James never mentioned in print is thus legion: Cecilia Beaux (1855–1942), Robert Blum (1857–1903), Mary Cassatt (1844–1926), Thomas Wilmer Dewing (1851–1938), George Fuller (1822–1884), Thomas Eakins (1844–1916), William Michael Harnett (1848–1892), Childe Hassam (1859–1935), George Inness (1825–1894), Albert Pinkham Ryder (1847–1917), Henry Ossawa Tanner (1859–1937), J. Alden Weir (1852–1919), Worthington Whittredge (1820–1910), and many, many others. The only time he wrote about large gatherings of contemporary American art, of the same general character as the annual shows at the Salon or Royal Academy, was the 1875 National Academy of Design annual exhibition and, in the same review, the slightly earlier exhibition of the American Water Color Society, along with other pictures seen in galleries or clubs. This review—"On Some Pictures Lately Exhibited," in the *Galaxy* of July 1875—thus merits sustained consideration, since it presents James's sole survey of a broad swath of American art.

Press coverage of the National Academy show was particularly rich in 1875, with eleven newspapers and six magazines covering the exhibition in depth, perhaps because the institution celebrated its fiftieth anniversary that year.[89] One feature of the exhibition that drew attention was the number of exhibiting artists trained or training abroad. Younger men—William Merritt Chase (1849–1916), David Neal (1838–1915), and others from Munich, and Frederick Bridgman (1847–1928) and Edgar Ward (1839–1915) from Paris—all made strong impressions, and James, likewise, took note of them. It was not, however, the first thing in his long review. He began, instead, writing again about how the "standing quarrel between the painters and the *littérateurs* will probably never be healed." In typical Jamesian fashion, he argued that both, in this quarrel, were "in the right," although he complicated the compromise by confessing "it to be our own belief," against the interests of his literary cohort, "that even an indifferent picture is generally worth more than a good criticism."[90] On the other side, however, he concluded that criticism "talks a good deal of nonsense, but even its nonsense is a useful force. It keeps the question of art before the world, insists upon its importance, and makes it always in order."[91] Then, after noting a decidedly literary turn in much recent painting (citing the Hispano-Roman school of Fortuny and the English Pre-Raphaelite Brotherhood in particular), he declared that in Paris, where the cleverest painters and the most vivacious critics were to be found, the painters rightly regarded the critics, "if not as a positive blessing, at least as a necessary evil."[92] After all this, it was with neither a literary nor a demonstrably foreign-trained artist that he opened his discussion of the National Academy show itself, but with Winslow Homer (1836–1910). Indeed, after calling Homer's works "the most striking pictures" in the exhibition, he professed that they presented a critical quandary:

Before Mr. Homer's little barefoot urchins and little girls in calico sun-bonnets, straddling beneath a cloudless sky upon the national rail fence, the whole effort of the critic is instinctively to contract himself, to double himself up, as it were, so that he can creep into the problem and examine it humbly and patiently, if a trifle wonderingly. Mr. Homer's pictures, in other words, imply no explanatory sonnets; the artist turns his back squarely and frankly upon literature.[93]

What was there to say? Later in the long review, he came back to two of Homer's works (the lost *Course of True Love* and *Milking Time*, 1875; formerly in the collection of the Delaware Art Museum) and presented one of the most acute assessments Homer was to receive in the 1870s:

Of Mr. Homer's three pictures we have spoken,[94] *but there would be a good deal more to say about them. . . . Mr. Homer goes in, as the phrase is, for perfect realism, and cares not a jot for such fantastic hairsplitting as the distinction between beauty and ugliness. He is a genuine painter; that is, to see, and to reproduce what he sees, is his only care; to think, to imagine, to select, to refine, to compose, to drop into any of the intellectual tricks with which other people sometimes try to eke out the dull pictorial vision—all this Mr. Homer triumphantly avoids.*[95] *He not only has no imagination, but he contrives to elevate this rather blighting negative into a blooming and honorable positive. He is almost barbarously simple, and, to our eye, he is horribly ugly; but there is nevertheless something one likes about him. What is it? For ourselves, it is not his subjects. We frankly confess that we detest his subjects—his barren plank fences, his glaring, bald, blue skies, his big, dreary, vacant lots of meadows, his freckled, straight-haired Yankee urchins, his flat-breasted maidens, suggestive of a dish of rural doughnuts and pie, his calico sun-bonnets, his flannel shirts, his cowhide boots. He has chosen the least pictorial features of the least pictorial range of scenery and civilization; he has resolutely treated them as if they were pictorial, as if they were every inch as good as Capri or Tangiers; and, to reward his audacity, he has incontestably succeeded. It makes one feel the value of consistency; it is a proof that if you will only be doggedly literal, though you may often be unpleasing, you will at least have a stamp of your own. Mr. Homer has the great merit, moreover, that he naturally sees everything at one with its envelope of light and air. He sees not in lines, but in masses, in gross, broad masses. Things come already modelled to his eye. If his masses were only sometimes a trifle more broken, and his brush a good deal richer—if it had a good many more secrets and mysteries and coquetries, he would be, with his vigorous way of looking and seeing, even if fancy in the matter remained the same dead blank, an almost distinguished painter. In its suggestion of this blankness of fancy the picture of the young farmer flirting with the pie-nurtured maiden in the wheat field [Course of True Love] is really an intellectual curiosity. The want of grace, of intellectual detail, of reflected light, could hardly go further; but the picture was its author's best contribution, and a very honest, and vivid, and manly piece of work. Our only complaint with it is that it is damnably ugly!*[96]

Against his will, he found that he had to admire the works, not least for Homer's ability to see the wholeness of things rather than their details, "everything at one with its envelope of light and air." He closed this discussion with the ironic conclusion that "the best definition of Mr. Homer to the initiated would be, that he is an elaborate contradiction of Mr. La Farge. In the Palace of Art there are many mansions!"[97] By this time James had already taken one of La Farge's exhibited works, *Cupid and Psyche* (1873; Ruth Chandler Williamson Gallery, Claremont, California), to task for the "exceptionally marked" disparity between "the effort and the total achievement." Tempering the negativity with acknowledgment of the "complex and suggestive" painter's subtle and intellectual genius, and calling him one "whose pictures are always a challenge to the imagination and the culture of the critic," James nonetheless pointed out flaws of tone and drawing.[98] Friendship in this case did not prompt avoidance or falsehood.

In his review, James was swayed neither by hanging nor by size. *Birth of Our Flag* (1874; National Academy

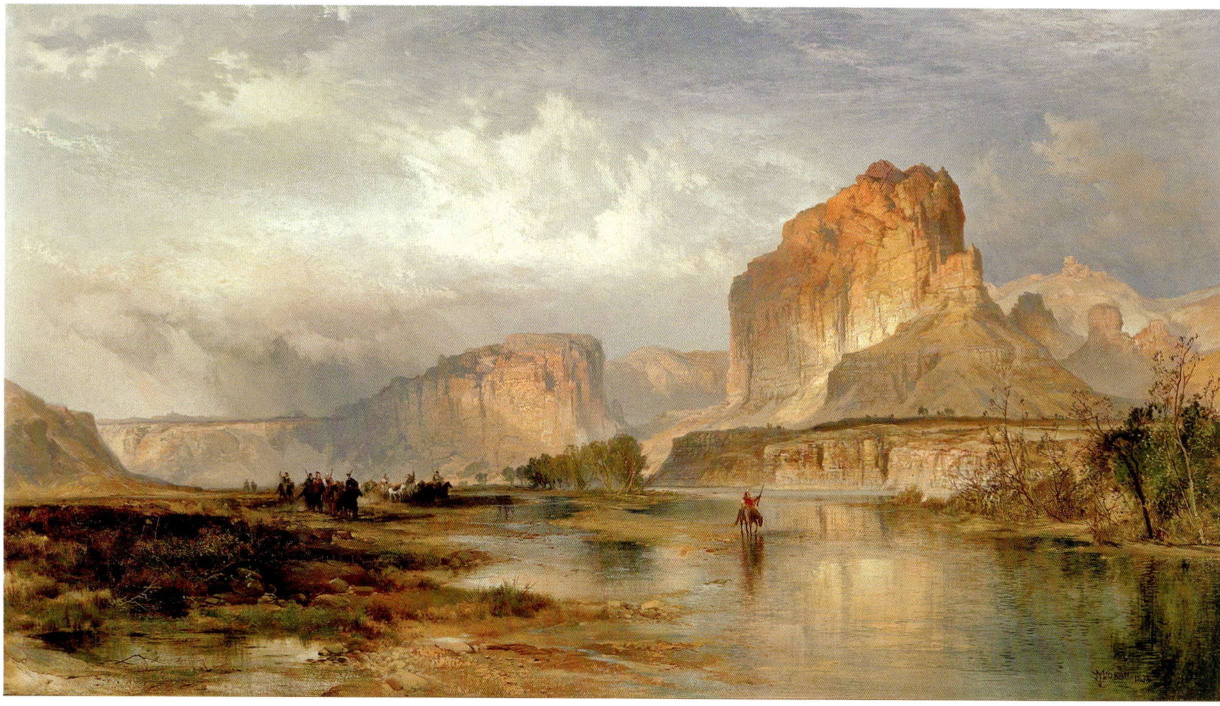

FIG. 7. Thomas Moran (1837–1926), *Cliffs of the Green River (The Overland Train, Green River Utah)*, 1874, Amon Carter Museum, Fort Worth, Texas.

Museum, New York) by Henry Peters Gray (1819–1877) hung in the gallery's position of honor, but James, after noting a certain echo of Titian's coloring, cared little for it. Likewise the large landscapes on view left him cold:

> *It may seem disrespectful, from a certain point of view, to allude to such performances as Mr. Bierstadt's "California in Spring"* [1874; Fine Arts Museums of San Francisco] *and Mr. Cropsey's "Sidney Plains"* [1874; Los Angeles County Museum of Art] *as "details"; they take up much space on the walls; but they have taken little (and even that we grudge them) in our recollections.*[99]

Cliffs of the Green River (The Overland Train, Green River Utah; Fig. 7) by Thomas Moran (1837–1926) escaped a comparably sharp dismissal, but James could not accept the "rather uncomfortable wrench to our prosy preconceptions of the conduct and complexion of rocks, even in their more fantastic moods" that Moran's picture inflicted. He allowed, however, "that all this is in Utah, and that Utah is terribly far away." He ended up wishing Moran "would try his hand at something a little nearer home, so that we might have a chance to congratulate him, with a good conscience, not only upon his brilliancy, but upon his fidelity."[100] He sensed the work was untrue to nature and was unwilling to suspend disbelief so as to enter into the scene. The only Academy landscape to earn James's wholehearted approval was Jervis McEntee's (1828–1891) *Saturday Afternoon* (Fig. 8), "the landscape which most took our own individual fancy." This James considered "excellent in tone," and, more important, he could swear to the fidelity of its gray, autumnal atmosphere. As with La Farge's *Paradise Valley,* the picture transported James to the scene: "it is a genuine piece of melancholy autumn; we felt as if we

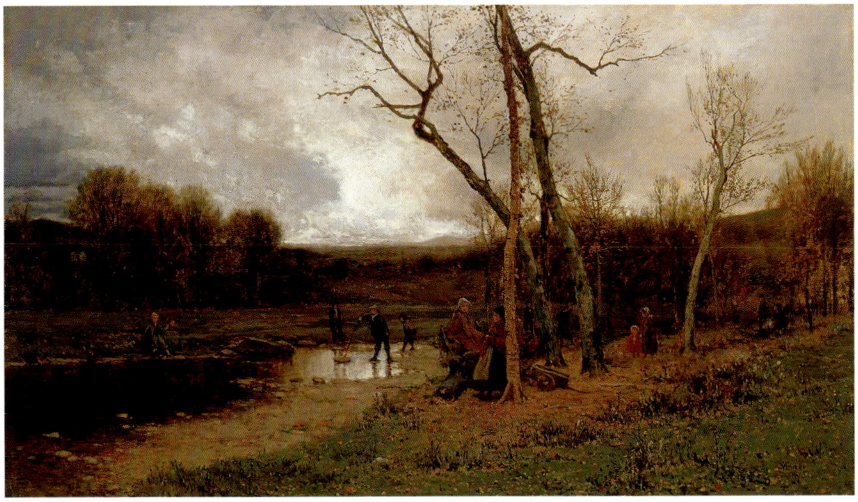

FIG. 8. Jervis McEntee (1828–1891), *Saturday Afternoon*, 1875, The Metropolitan Museum of Art, New York.

were one of the children grubbing un-esthetically in the ugly wood, breaking the lean switches, and kicking the brown leaves."[101]

Of genre paintings, the principal work of Eastman Johnson (1824–1906)—*Milton and His Daughters* (1876; Blanden Memorial Art Museum, Fort Dodge, Iowa)—became acceptable only if one discounted the figure of Milton and, "defilializing these young ladies," turned them into "pretty Americans of the year 1875."[102] He evinced greater enthusiasm for Johnson's two smaller works on view—*The Peddler* (1873; private collection via Nantucket Historical Society) and *The Toilet* (1873; Corcoran Collection, National Gallery of Art, Washington, DC)—finding that Johnson "has the merit of being a real painter—of loving, for itself, the slow, caressing process of rendering an object. Of all our artists, he has most coquetry of manipulation." The brio of Bridgman's *American Circus in France* (1869–70; private collection) also drew his attention, but James expressed disappointment that the young American was showing an older picture that had already been seen in the Salon of 1870.

Of the watercolors, both at the Society show and at Goupil's Gallery, he said little. Homer's "little raw aquarelles" stood out, as did work by Fidelia Bridges (1834–1923). He also extended his admiration, again, to Marie Spartali Stillman, whom he called in all good-heartedness "a spontaneous, sincere, *naïf* pre-Raphaelite." The groups of Roman watercolors, by artists "whose names we forget"—which some would call a dereliction of critical duty—prompted first "impatience and disgust" then amusement and pleasure, "so long as one doesn't talk too much about it."

James specifically mentioned a few other works from the Academy, a portrait of a young girl (present location unknown) by Jeanette Shepherd Loop (1840–1909), which was "in its cool discretion of manner, remarkably good for a woman" (and he noted that he did not mean to be offensive by saying so). He also took note of "two very clever things sent from Munich by American artists"—Chase's *The Dowager* (1874; Melton Park Gallery, Oklahoma City), which was "very picturesquely and yet very soberly painted," and Neal's *Study—Head* (present location unknown), which he judged even cleverer—although not necessarily truer—than Chase's work. "They are evidently very clever in Munich," James concluded, before ending with a mocking, "He must be certain, indeed, to give his lady the ruff; that is an essential point." Finally, there were two or three landscapes, "small for him, and for him, too, rather feeble" by Frederic Church (1826–1900).[103] But the Church, Chase, and Neal pictures prompted James to revert again to recently seen works at the commercial Goupil Galleries in New York and the Boston Art Club.

For earlier at Goupil's, James had been struck by Church's *Valley of Santa Isabel* (Fig. 9). He thought it represented Church's ambitions successfully and so, somewhat unwillingly, he thought well of it. He confessed himself unable, however, to say anything meaningful about it:

> *We know of nothing that is a better proof of the essential impotence of criticism, in the last resort, than Mr. Church's pictures. One can't say what one means about them; the common critical formulas are too inflexible. It would be the part of wisdom perhaps to attempt and to desire to say nothing; simply to leave them to their tranquil destiny, which is apparently very honorable and comfortable. If you praise them very highly, you say more than you mean; if you denounce them, if, in vulgar parlance, you sniff at them, you say less. It is the kind of art which seems perpetually skirting the edge of something worse than itself, like a woman with a taste for florid ornaments who should dress herself in a way to make quiet people stare, and yet who should be really a very reputable person.*

The humor grew broad:

> *As we looked at Mr. Church's velvety vistas and gem-like vegetation, at Goupil's, we felt honestly sorry that there was any necessity in this weary world for taking upon one's self to be a critic, for deeming it essential to a proper self-respect to be analytical. Why not accept this lovely tropic scene as a very pretty picture, and have done with it?*

Yet in pompous overstatement, James revealed much about his taste and the ruling aesthetic that dictated his responses to art over the decades. The sensibility that preferred McEntee's autumn to Moran's Green River was of course unsympathetic to Church's canvas, a picture in which the

> *great, heavy, yellow tropic sun sinks down into the wine-colored mountains as if exhausted and athirst with his own prodigious heat, and his level rays come wandering forward down the mile-long gorges, and floating over the lustrous mountain lake in the middle distance, and flinging themselves in the flower-strewn grass in the foreground, in the most natural fashion in the world—natural, we mean, when nature is in her theatrical, her demonstrative, her exhibitory moods. Certainly if we were able to handle a brush, we should not use it, in some places (especially in our mysterious, deep-toned boskages, and our rich, multitudinous leafage), exactly as Mr. Church does; but his own brush is an extremely accomplished one, and we should be poorly set to work to quarrel with the very numerous persons who admire its brilliant feats.*[104]

It is the theatrical and flashy, narrative elements needing to stand out from one another, as he would come to write of Leutze's *Washington Crossing the Delaware*—the overly overt—that unsettled and disturbed James's aesthetic sensibility.

What did not trouble him was demonstrative, exhibitory technique. He made this clear when, after gently deriding Chase's and Neal's Academy pictures, he

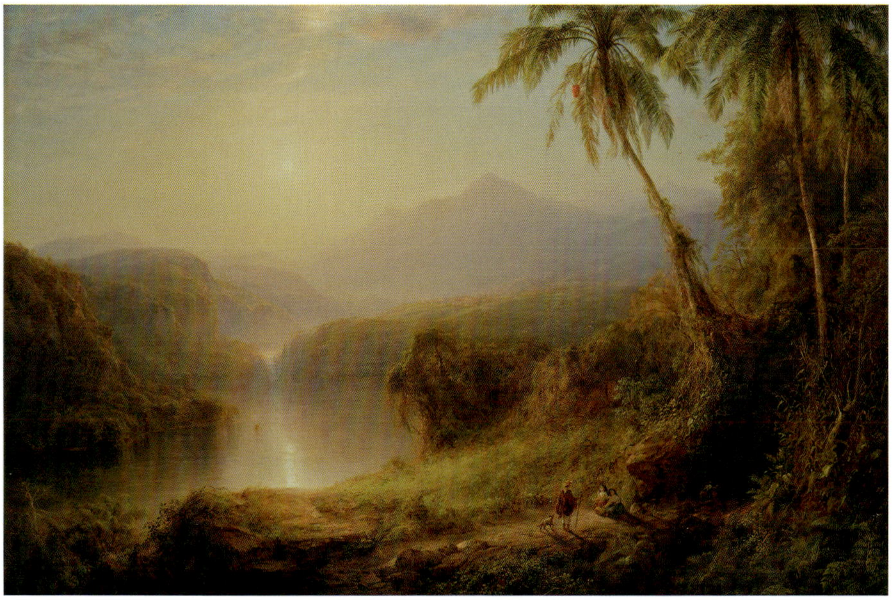

FIG. 9. Frederic Church (1826–1900), *Valley of Santa Isabel*, 1875, Berkshire Museum, Pittsfield, Massachusetts.

referred to an exhibition at the Boston Art Club of works by Duveneck, another Munich-trained painter:

We choose a wrong moment moreover for harboring evil thoughts of the Munich school, for we have lately had evidence that a great talent of the most honorable sort may flourish beneath its maternal wing. The good people of Boston have recently been flattering themselves that they have discovered an American Velasquez.[105]

By comparing Duveneck with the seventeenth-century Spanish master, James paid him the ultimate artist's-artist compliment. The most highly advanced artists of the era were turning their eyes to Velázquez and marveling at what illusions paint could contrive.[106] James apparently realized the rashness of the praise and hastened to add that, given Duveneck's youth, it was "of course of supreme importance" that he "not be talked about intemperately." Nonetheless, he continued, the portraits on display "have an extraordinary interest."

They are all portraits of men—and of very ugly men; they have little grace, little finish, little elegance, none of the relatively superfluous qualities. But they have a most remarkable reality and directness, and Velasquez is in fact the name that rises to your lips as you look at them.

He described three of the five pictures with a line or two each—those portraying mature men, ignoring the pictures of a youth and an infant—and gave their sitters unflattering characterizations. *Portrait of William Adams* (1874; Milwaukee Art Museum) showed "a plain old agricultural character, we should say, of Quakerish rigidity and of an extremely plebeian type."[107] *Portrait of Ludwig Loefftz* (1873; Cincinnati Art Museum) was "a young man in a shabby coat and a slouched hat, holding a stump of a cigar." *The Old Professor* (1871; Museum of Fine Arts, Boston), according to James, was "most grotesquely hideous in feature and physiognomy, looking a good deal, as to his complexion and eyeballs, as if he had just been cut down after an unpractical attempt to hang himself." These were not attractive subjects; it was the technique, the artistic approach combined with a true and frank vision that appealed to James:

There is little color in these things save a vigorous opposition of black and white, or of shaded fleshtints and heavy browns; yet they are strikingly solid and definite. Their great quality, we repeat, is their extreme naturalness, their unmixed, unredeemed reality. They are brutal, hard, indelicate, and as the maximum of the artist's effort they would be almost melancholy; but they contain the material of an excellent foundation. . . . We frankly confess that we shall take it hard if he fails to do something of the first degree of importance.[108]

If, by chance, readers of James's "On Some Pictures Lately Exhibited" in *The Galaxy* also subscribed to *The Nation*, they might have thought they were experiencing an episode of déjà vu. For James had already written, in an unattributed "Note," much the same thing:

The discovery of an unsuspected man of genius is always an interesting event and nowhere perhaps could such an event excite a higher relish than in the aesthetic city of Boston. Many people just now in the New England capital are talking of Mr. Frank Duveneck, and incidentally of Velasquez. . . . Mr. Duveneck is a painter of the rigidly natural school; unadorned reality is as yet his exclusive theme. These five portraits are indeed singularly real and natural. They are all male portraits—one at least is a head of a baby, whose sex is not yet apparent—and they are also thoroughly masculine in execution. Mr. Duveneck's models happen to have been very ill-favored persons, and he has reproduced them without a hint of compromise or arrangement.[109]

In this earlier notice, he had described the same three pictures, largely ignored the other two, and concluded that, although the color was extremely spare, "the relief, the vigor, the frankness, the comprehensive simplicity, are most striking." He had worried whether Duveneck, whose youth he had pointed out, might have his head turned by all the praise the works had generated, and applauded his decision to return to Europe instead of settling in Boston, as some had hoped he would. "He is now about to return to Europe. This, doubtless, is the wisest course, and it would be a serious pity that he should adopt any but the wisest. We confess that, as things stand with us at present, almost any young artist of promise is likely to do better out of America than in it." Of course, the Europhile James—in common with many but by no means all commentators on American art life—would think this; he himself would, within the next few months, be on his way to settle there.

At the end of the review, James, by considering these pictures of Duveneck's, tells his readers what makes up the important equipment for a painter:

we repeat that these five portraits are, in quality, of signal interest. They lack, certainly, a dozen things—most of which the painter is probably quite conscious of; but they possess the great, the all-important quality—the air of the artist's having the temperament, the natural instinct, of his business; of the whole man infusing himself, without a scruple, into his effort. This is what makes (after years of labor) the work that is supreme in its kind.[110]

Then, almost before the reader has put down this issue of the *The Nation*, James again wrote about Duveneck. Three different Duveneck portraits were on display in Boston for at least the month of August, and James responded to them with renewed enthusiasm. They removed, he wrote, any doubts about "the very high

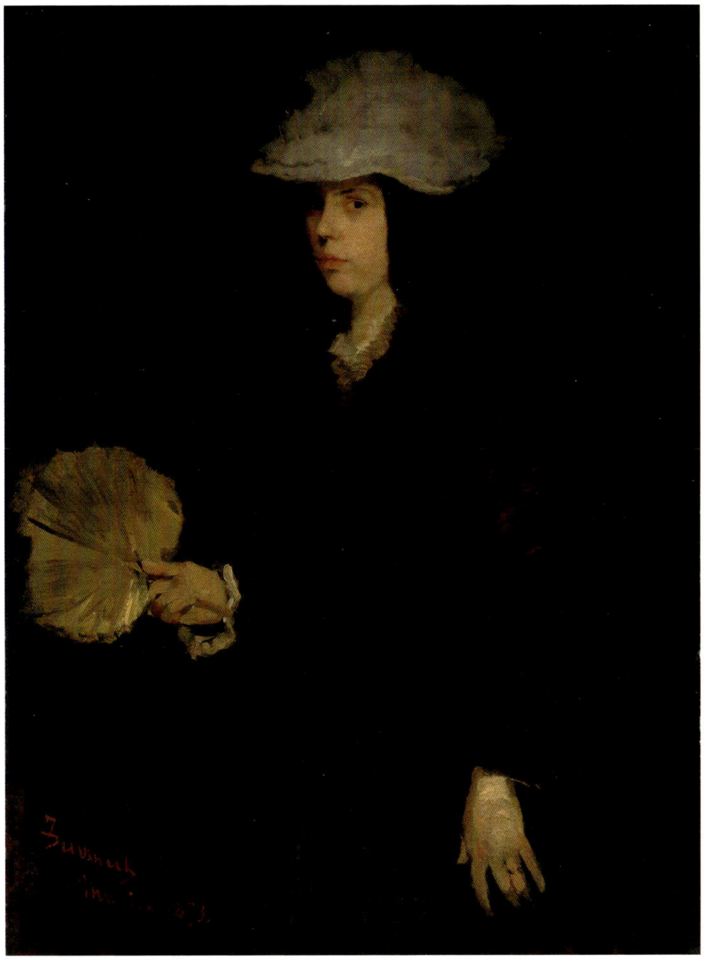

FIG. 10. Frank Duveneck (1848–1919), *Lady with a Fan,* 1873, The Metropolitan Museum of Art, New York.

opinion we had formed of his talent."[111] One, *Head of an Old Man in a Fur Cap* (1870; Cincinnati Art Museum), showed a "forlorn, grotesque personage, very strikingly rendered," and was "skillful and forcible," but it did not break new ground in James's sense of the artist. The other two he judged to be "extremely remarkable" and superior to any he had seen before. One, of a young man in a broad, black hat, is currently unidentified, although James lauded its truth to the "essence" of the sitter and freedom of handling; it gave him, he wrote, "the excitement of adventure and the certitude of repose."[112] The third work, *Lady with a Fan* (Fig. 10), earned the writer's unalloyed enthusiasm:

> *This was the first female subject by Mr. Duveneck we had seen, and it is quite the finest of his portraits; this, too, in spite of the fact that only the face is finished. . . . The consummate expressiveness of the eyes, the magnificent rendering of flush and bloom, warmth and relief, pulpy, blood-tinted, carnal substance in the cheeks and brow, are something of which a more famous master than Mr. Duveneck might be proud. The figure is, moreover, full of*

James maintained that his first impressions of Duveneck's work had been apt ones. Nothing from the intervening years, however, marked growth or progress, a lapse of responsibility to one's talent that offended the writer; being an excellent teacher was, it seems, a highly compromised compliment.

Three decades earlier, just a few years after declaring Duveneck to be "much the most highly-developed phenomenon in the way of a painter the U.S.A. has given birth to," James found another young American painter, trained in Europe, who merited superlatives, and this time he could admire paintings and personality both. Writing from Paris to a friend in early 1884, James declared Sargent to be the "only Franco-American product of importance," who had, moreover, "high talent, a charming nature, artistic and personal, and is civilized to his finger-tips. . . . I like him extremely; and the best of his work seems to me to have in it something exquisite."[130]

James had earlier, more than a year before their introduction,[131] noted a Venetian genre scene by Sargent that was part of the 1882 exhibition at London's Grosvenor Gallery, writing of it in the same review in which he ascribed to Whistler the "creative afflatus." He closed a paragraph devoted to "several American talents which are exemplified there"—referring to Boughton, Julian Story (1857–1919), and Sargent—noting that the latter, "whose only defect is a certain papery texture, contributes a charming little gray Venetian interior, with figures," probably referring to *Venetian Women in the Palazzo Rezzonico* (Fig. 12).[132] It was 1887, however, before he published another word on the man.

It was not that James did not see Sargent or his works during the intervening years. On the contrary, from at least February 1884 they were in frequent touch. As one example, later that spring, James welcomed and played host to Sargent, who was on a three-week visit to London. They dined together, visited studios and galleries, and attended the theater; on one day alone, James arranged a visit to the studios of ten of London's most important painters, including John Everett Millais and Frederic Leighton, then hosted a dinner for Sargent at the Reform Club, which included, among other guests, Edward Burne-Jones.[133] More actively still, he worked on Sargent's public profile behind the scenes. He wrote:

> *We are in the midst of the explosion of exhibitions; most of which are plentifully stocked with "rot." The Academy is "filthy." The Grosvenor Gallery is better only in possessing a beautiful Burne-Jones. . . . A young friend of mine of whom I am very fond, & whose talent I think rare, (John Sargent) has sent over from Paris, through my mediation, a portrait which is universally gibed and jeered at* [*Mrs. T. W. Legh*, 1883; private collection]—*so that it is almost a personal discomfiture to me.*[134]

During this visit, James also introduced Sargent to Abbey—and from that connection there emerged ties to Frank Millet (1846–1912) and the circle of Anglo-American artists, writers, and actors who in subsequent years worked and played together in the Worcestershire village of Broadway, where Sargent was to paint *Carnation, Lily, Lily, Rose* (1885–86; Tate Britain, London), with James in occasional attendance.[135] So it was a very productive stint of hosting on James's part. At the end of it, he wrote to Lizzie Boott:

> *I saw and shall probably see again a great deal of him; I was able, I think, to make things pleasant and easy for him. I like him extremely (he is more intelligent about artistic things than all the painters here rolled together) and in short we are excellent friends.*[136]

By late 1886, partly in response to repeated urgings by James, Sargent left Paris and settled in London.

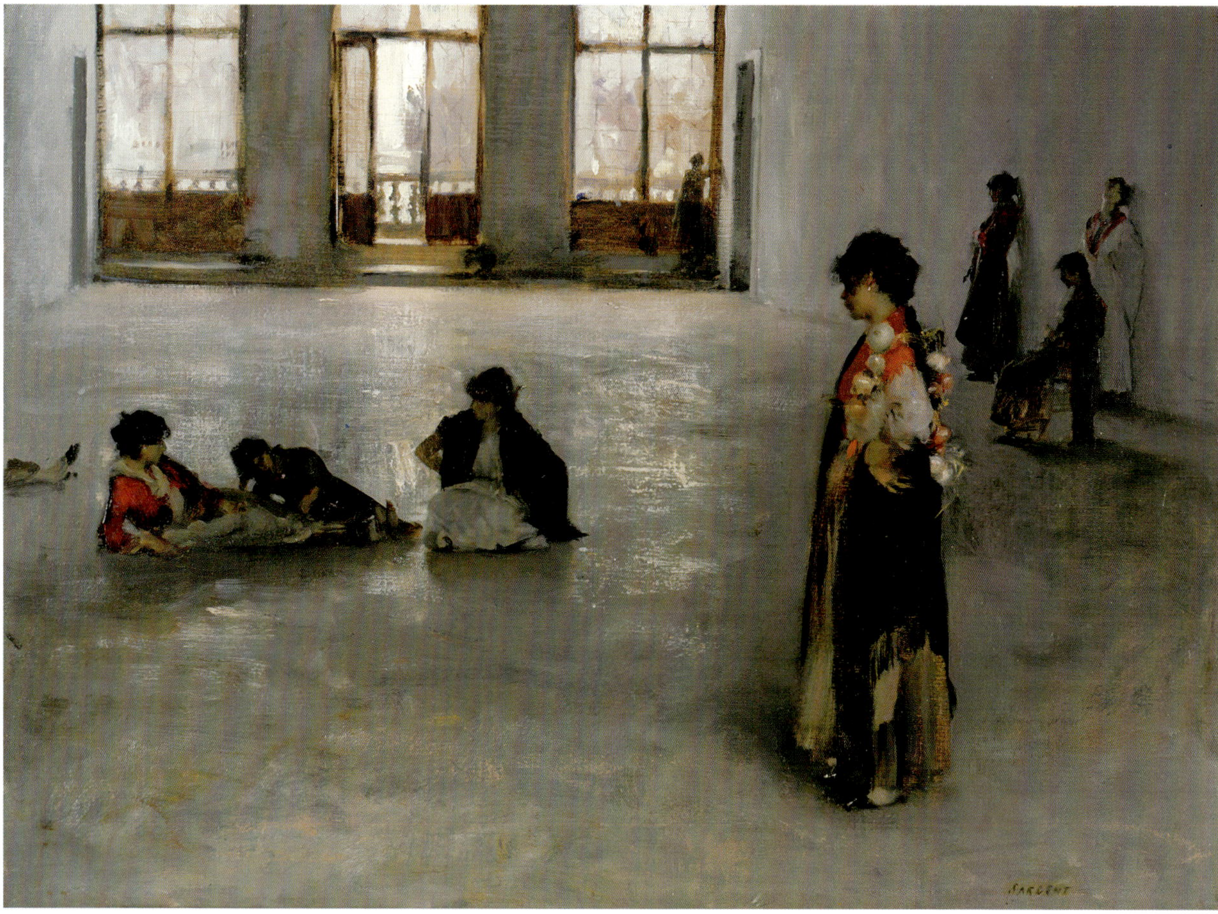

FIG. 12. John Singer Sargent (1856–1925), *Venetian Women in the Palazzo Rezzonico,* ca. 1880, private collection, courtesy of David Nisinson.

Throughout later years, continuing until James's death in 1916, the two saw much of one another and shared a growing and close-knit circle of friends. Their apparently abundant correspondence has not survived.[137] James wrote about Sargent and his work to others, however, frequently throughout the 1880s and 1890s—arguably more often and in more detail than about the work of any other painter. So, for just a few of many possible examples, we know that he thought Sargent's portrait of Margaret Rutherfurd (Mrs. Henry) White (1883; Corcoran Collection, National Gallery of Art, Washington, DC) was "splendid and delightful," "a masterpiece (*selon moi*) of style and tone," whereas he only "half liked" the portrait of Virginie Amélie (Mme Pierre) Gautreau (Fig. 13).[138] Of the White portrait at the Royal Academy in 1884, in fact, he wrote the playfully erotic lines: "*I* think [it] far and away, in style, tone, etc., the 1st portrait there & the only thing which touches a woman (with the brush) as a woman should be touched."[139] The double portrait of Mr. and Mrs. Robert Louis Stevenson (with him "shuffling about his room & pulling his moustache") was "very sure and charming" (see Tóibín, Fig. 17).[140] *The Misses Vickers* (1884; Sheffield City Art Galleries), when at the Royal

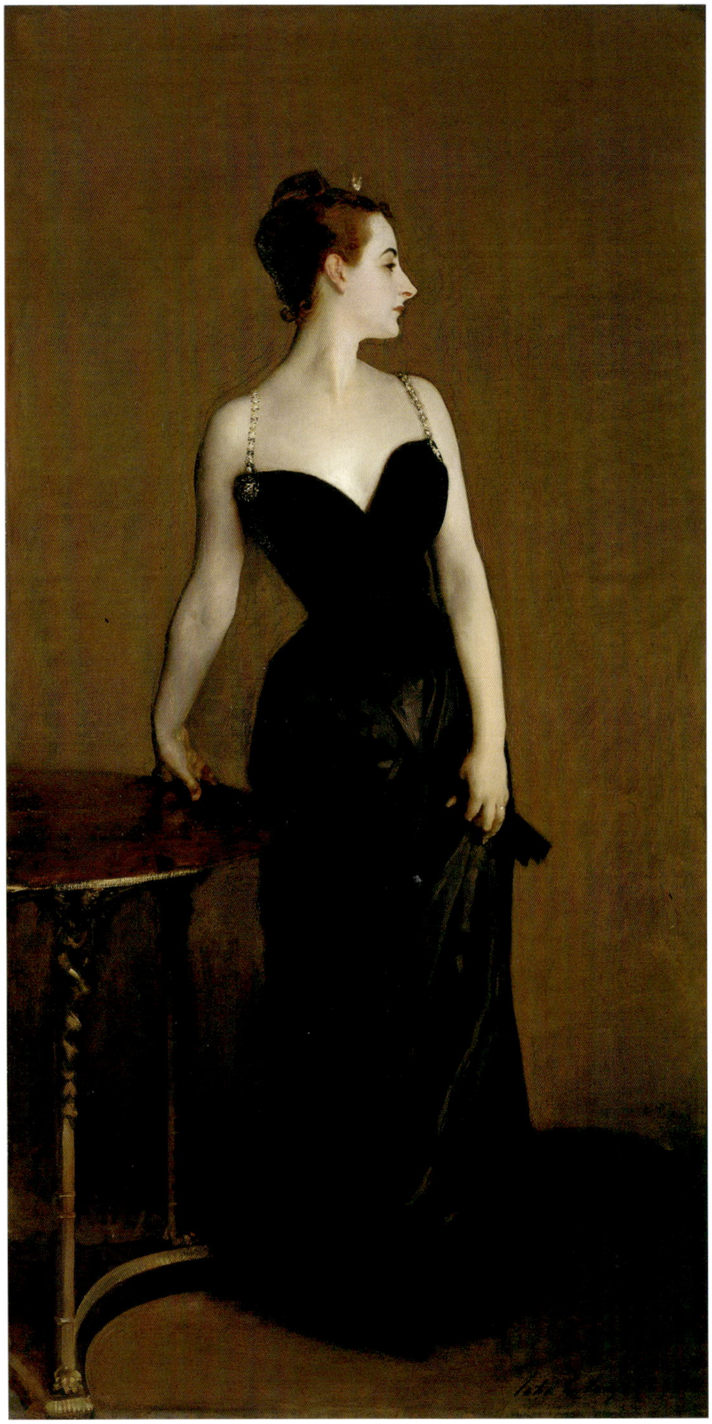

FIG. 13. John Singer Sargent (1856–1925), *Madame X (Madame Pierre Gautreau)*, 1883, The Metropolitan Museum of Art, New York.

Academy in 1886, was "perfectly hung . . . , & strikes me as a magnificent thing. I have the greatest admiration for it—& so haven't a great herd of stupidities here. But those who know what they are talking about—such a deplorable minority anywhere—have."[141]

Yet while James's private correspondents could glean his feelings about various pictures by Sargent when they first appeared in public, the general readership could not. As noted above, between August 1882 and October 1887, James published only three articles devoted to any publicly accessible art: two essays on the English caricaturist and writer George Du Maurier (1883 and 1884) and one on the illustrations and watercolors of Abbey in *Harper's Weekly* (December 1886). Each was more a reflection on the artists and their art in general (and in the case of the 1883 Du Maurier article, on nineteenth-century British comic illustration) than a response to specific works.

James's long essay on Sargent that appeared in the October 1887 issue of *Harper's New Monthly Magazine* was of the same ilk: a retrospective consideration of many pictures rather than a response to paintings at a specific exhibition.[142] In the laudatory article, James made points that have served as foundations for writers on Sargent ever since. First, he questioned whether or not the painter could be called American, a point close to his own expatriated heart. He decided in favor of the question by declaring, in one of his most often-quoted lines about American art, that Sargent:

has even on the face of it this great symptom of an American origin, that in the line of his art he might easily be mistaken for a Frenchman. It sounds like a paradox, but it is a very simple truth, that when to-day we look for "American art" we find it mainly in Paris. When we find it out of Paris, we at least find a great deal of Paris in it.[143]

He then marveled at Sargent's fluent technique, the apparently easy way that "an intention and the art of carrying it out are for him one and the same thing." So struck was James in this regard that he repeated the point three times more in subsequent sentences: "perception with him is already by itself a kind of execution"; "in Mr. Sargent's case the process by which the object seen resolves itself into the object pictured is extraordinarily immediate"; closing the paragraph with the summary that Sargent's work made it seem "as if painting were pure tact of vision, a simple manner of feeling."[144] James next turned to the troublesomely modern issue of Impressionism, a then loosely defined movement with which he had little sympathy at the time.[145] Recognizing the futility of fighting it, however, since "to-day he is for many people most conveniently pigeon-holed under that head," he reconciled the term and Sargent with a qualification: "It is not necessary to protest against this classification if this addition always be made to it, that Mr. Sargent's impressions happen to be interesting." He was also struck by the artist's precocity: Sargent's work "offers the slightly 'uncanny' spectacle which on the very threshold of its career has nothing more to learn."[146]

James then surveyed fourteen works—three genre scenes and eleven portraits—that had been seen in London and Paris exhibitions from 1879 to 1886. In turning to the largest of the genre scenes, *El Jaleo* (1882; Isabella Stewart Gardner Museum, Boston), he recognized its verity, its seeming to be "an actual scene, with its accidents and peculiarities caught, as distinguished from a composition where arrangement and invention have played their part." In this case, however, verity did not please him:

It looks like life, but it looks also, to my view, rather like a perversion of life, and has the quality of an enormous "note" or memorandum, rather than of a representation. . . . The merit of this production is that the air of reality is given in it with remarkable breadth and boldness; its defect it is difficult to express, save by saying that it makes the spectator vaguely uneasy and even unhappy. . . . "El Jaleo" sins, in my opinion, in the direction of ugliness, and, independently of the fact that the heroine is circling round incommoded by her petticoats, has a want of serenity.[147]

Fumée d'ambre gris (Fig. 14), by contrast, portrayed a subject who was "charming" and "mysterious," in a picture that was "exquisite, a radiant effect of white upon white."[148] Later in the essay, he wrote of a Venetian interior seen at the Grosvenor Gallery, "a pure gem," of which he retained "a grateful memory." He described it mostly in terms of light effects: a "big, dim hall of a shabby old palazzo"; "a chink of light"; "the scagliola pavement gleams faintly"; "the whole place . . . bathed in a kind of transparent shade"; "the tone of the picture . . . dark and cool." Since he described the women as "counting turnips or stringing onions," and that "these small vegetables, enchantingly painted, look as valuable as magnified pearls," it seems that he is remembering *Venetian Women in the Palazzo Rezzonico* (Fig. 12); this, then, is likely the "charming little gray Venetian interior, with figures" that he wrote of in 1882—the first and last word he published about Sargent before this extended article.

James had submitted the article for publication on 1 December 1886 (apparently having promised it long before that).[149] When it did not appear in any of the next seven or eight issues, in August 1887 he wrote to the journal's London agent asking him "to use your influence with the Harpers to induce them to publish without more delay (in the Magazine) an article on Sargent (the painter) that I wrote for them many months ago?"[150] James's sense of urgency was sparked by knowledge that another author—R. A. M. Stevenson, cousin of Robert Louis

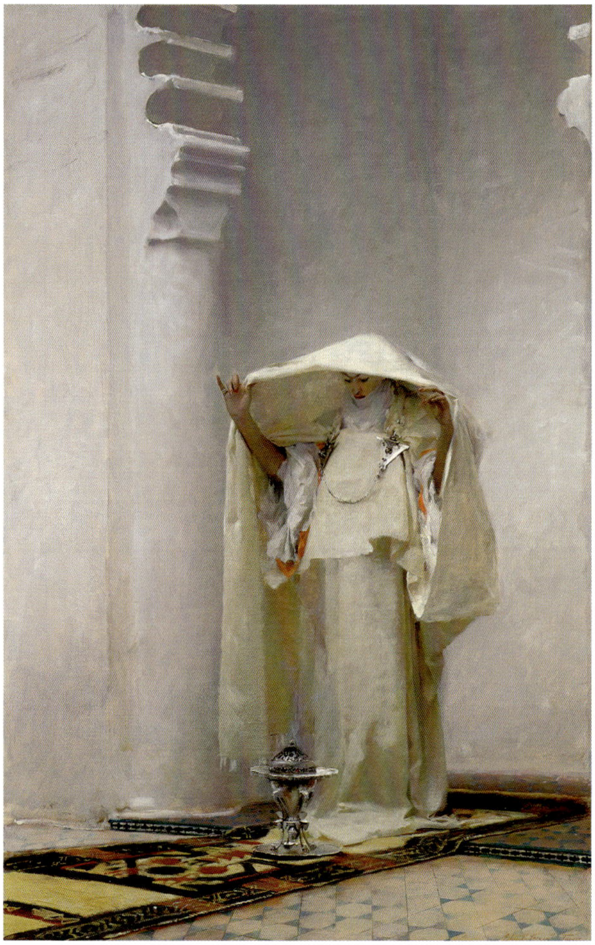

FIG. 14. John Singer Sargent (1856–1925), *Fumée d'ambre gris,* 1880, Clark Art Institute, Williamstown, Massachusetts.

Stevenson—was in the process of writing a detailed consideration of Sargent's work; Stevenson, a popular art critic, an academic art historian, and an exhibited painter having trained in the same Parisian atelier as Sargent, was in a position to scoop him.[151] In the event, *Harper's* published the article just as Sargent was arriving in the

United States on his first professional portrait-painting trip to his native land (albeit, born in Italy, he had not set foot outside Europe until he was twenty years old), and it could not have served him better.

In his article, James privileged Sargent's work in portraiture over the genre pictures. Sargent, in his exhibition practice, had given almost equal weight to the two types of painting, but James virtually ignored the scenes of daily life: "His work has been almost exclusively in portraiture," he wrote. For him, moreover, there was no comparison of the two categories in terms of ambition or achievement. He gave unstinting praise to all but one of the eleven portraits he wrote about directly in the article. The one that he treated most circumspectly, that of Madame Gautreau (Fig. 13)—which is now Sargent's most famous work and was certainly, when Sargent sold it to the Metropolitan Museum of Art in 1916, the work he valued most highly[152]—prompted James to employ oratorical devices ranging from rhetorical questions ("What shall I say of the remarkable canvas?") to invocations of John Ruskin.[153] One senses that he willed himself to find good to say of it:

It is a work to take or to leave, as the phrase is, and one in regard to which the question of liking or disliking comes promptly to be settled. It is full of audacity of experiment and science of execution; it has singular beauty of line, and certainly in the body and arms we feel the pulse of life as strongly as the brush can give it.[154]

Of the others, about which he felt no qualms, two were portraits of men—Sargent's teacher Carolus-Duran (1879; Clark Art Institute, Williamstown, Massachusetts) and the sophisticated aesthete-gynecologist Dr. Samuel Pozzi (1881; Armand Hammer Museum, Los Angeles). He found these to be "fine" and "splendid" pictures of "gallant pictorial" types—"types," continued the appreciative James, "which strike us as made for portraiture."[155] He mentioned, further, portraits of the French sitters Madame Édouard Pailleron (1879; Corcoran Collection, National Gallery of Art, Washington, DC) and her children (1881; Des Moines Art Center), and of Madame Allouard-Jouan (ca. 1882; Musée du Petit Palais, Paris), whose portrait, James wrote:

remains in my mind as a masterly rendering of the look of experience—such experience as may be attributed to a woman slightly faded and eminently sensitive and distinguished. Subject and treatment in this valuable piece are of an equal interest, and in the latter there is an element of positive sympathy which is not always in a high degree the sign of Mr. Sargent's work.[156]

James opined that painting the two American subjects—Mrs. Henry White and Edith, Lady Playfair (1884; Museum of Fine Arts, Boston)—"must have been a delight to paint." James thought that these two pictures in particular

possess, largely, the quality which makes Mr. Sargent so happy as a painter of women—a quality which can best be expressed by a reference to what it is not, to the curiously literal, prosaic, Philistine treatment to which, in the commonplace work that looks down at us from the walls of almost all exhibitions, delicate feminine elements have evidently so often been sacrificed. Mr. Sargent handles these elements with a special feeling for them, and they borrow something of nobleness from his brush.[157]

James dismissed the scandalized "prodigies of purblind criticism" that greeted the portrait of the Misses Vickers, the only portrait of British-born sitters James wrote of, and the picture with which he closed his discussion of individual works:

Works of this character are a genuine service; after the short-lived gibes of the profane have subsided, they are found to have cleared the air. They remind people that the faculty of taking a fresh, direct, independent, unborrowed impression is not altogether lost.[158]

The two paintings mentioned in the essay that most excited James's admiration were *Lady with the Rose (Charlotte Louise Burckhardt;* Fig. 15) and *The Daughters of Edward Darley Boit* (Fig. 16), two of the three he advocated *Harper's* use as illustrations.[159] He devoted multiple full paragraphs to them and called up significant resources to justify his enthusiasm. The former was the "most brilliant of all Mr. Sargent's productions."

My admiration for this deeply distinguished work is such that I am perhaps in danger of overstating its merits; but it is worth taking into account that to-day, after several years of acquaintance with them, these merits seem to me more and more to justify enthusiasm. . . . It is not only a portrait, but a picture, and it arouses even in the profane spectator something of the painter's sense, the joy of engaging also, by sympathy, in the solution of the artistic problem.[160]

He described it at length: pose, posture, dress (which "has an old-fashioned air, as if it had been worn by some demure princess who might have sat for Velasquez"), hair, silken drapery background. The whole's "most striking characteristic," he enunciated, "is its simplicity, and yet . . . [it] overflows with perfection." He continued:

I know not why this representation of a young girl in black, engaged in the casual gesture of holding up a flower, should make so ineffaceable an impression, and tempt one to become almost lyrical in its praise; but I well remember that, encountering the picture unexpectedly in New York a year or two after it had been exhibited in Paris, it seemed to me to have acquired an extraordinary general value, to stand for more artistic truth than it would be easy to declare, to be a masterpiece of color as well as of composition, to possess much in common with a Velasquez of the first order.[161]

Of the Boit daughters' portrait, James marveled especially at the composition:

The artist has done nothing more felicitous and interesting than this view of a rich, dim, rather generalized French interior (the perspective of a hall with a shining floor, where screens and tall Japanese vases shimmer and loom), which encloses the life and seems to form the happy play-world of a family of charming children. The treatment is eminently unconventional, and there is none of the usual symmetrical balancing of the figures in the foreground. The place is regarded as a whole; it is a scene, a comprehensive impression; yet none the less do the little figures in their white pinafores (when was the pinafore ever painted with that power and made so poetic?) detach themselves, and live with a personal life.[162]

These two pictures together presented the "uncanny spectacle" that James wrote of: not mere precocity but "the freshness of youth combined with the artistic experience, really felt and assimilated, of generations." And, in James's eye, these two most dramatically revealed Sargent's love of Spain and things Spanish, especially Velázquez, who "became the god of his idolatry."[163]

James wrote his article for the readers of *Harper's New Monthly Magazine,* but its last paragraph was written pointedly for the artist. Rather than updating the essay with news of the great triumph that Sargent had just experienced at the Royal Academy summer exhibition—the purchase for the British nation by the Chantrey Bequest of his genre scene *Carnation, Lily, Lily, Rose*—James proselytized Sargent to forgo genre and to concentrate on portraiture: "There is no greater work of art than a great portrait—a truth to be constantly taken to heart by a painter holding in his hands the weapon that Mr. Sargent wields."[164] In his nearly contemporary novel *The Tragic Muse,* James wrote explicitly of the "greatness of the art of the portraitist," putting into the mouth of his

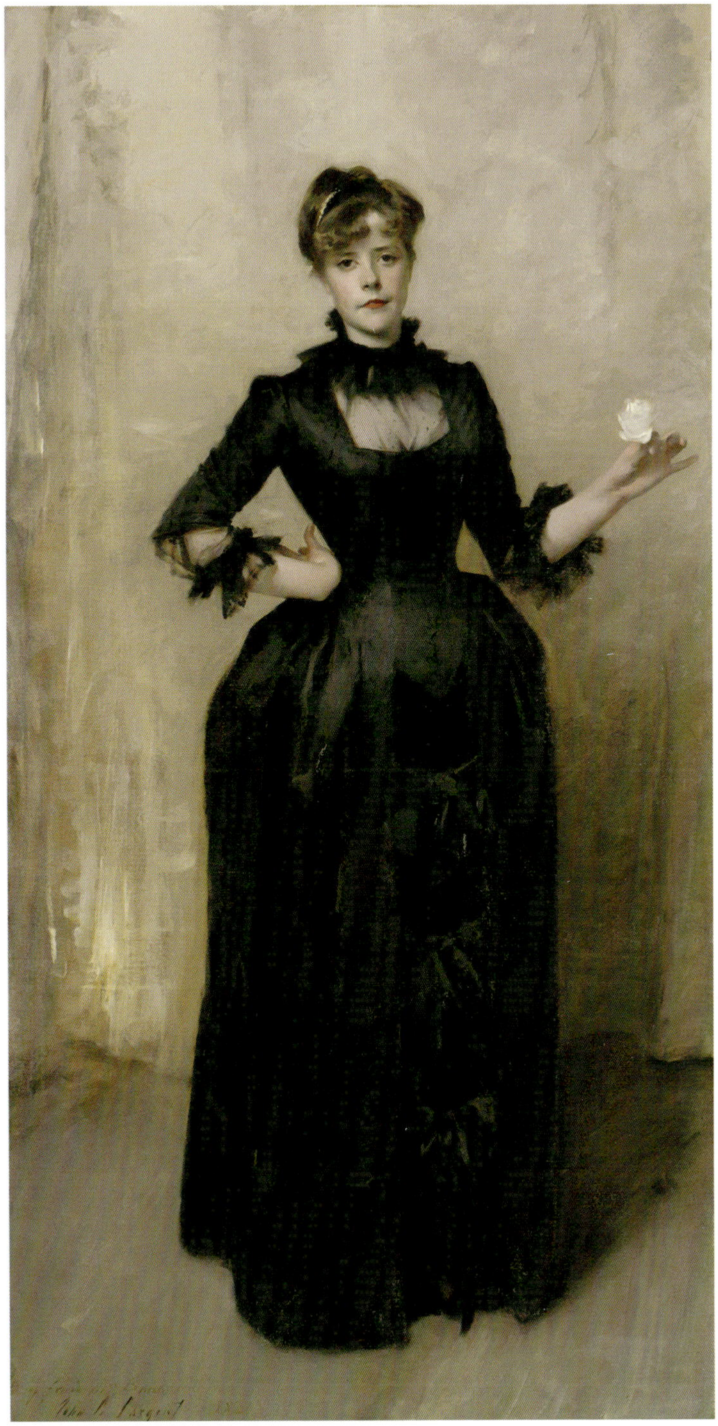

FIG. 15. John Singer Sargent (1856–1925), *Lady with the Rose (Charlotte Louise Burckhardt)*, 1882, The Metropolitan Museum of Art, New York.

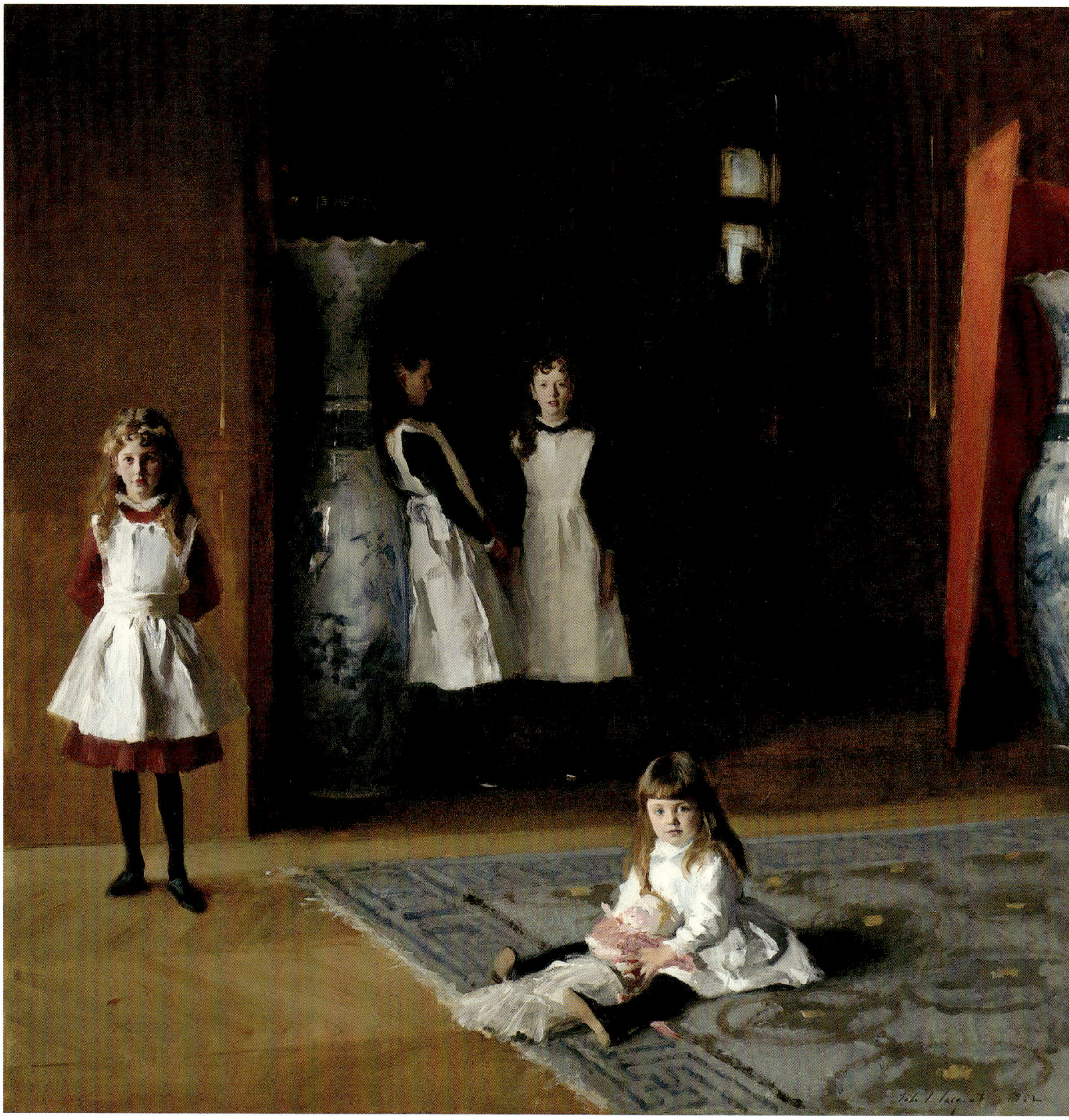

FIG. 16. John Singer Sargent (1856–1925), *The Daughters of Edward Darley Boit,* 1882, Museum of Fine Arts, Boston.

character Gabriel Nash (whom James labeled as "an ambiguous character but an excellent touchstone"[165]) praise for portraiture's

> *reach, its range, its fascination, the magnificent examples it had left us in the past: windows open into history, into psychology, things that were among the most precious possessions of the human race. He insisted, above all, on the interest, the richness arising from this great peculiarity of it: that, unlike most other forms, it was a revelation of two realities, the man whom it was the artist's conscious effort to reveal and the man (the interpreter) expressed in the very quality and temper of that effort. It offered a double vision, the strongest dose of life that art could give, the strongest dose of art that life could give.*[166]

James, the supreme prose portraitist, found in Sargent a potential pictorial match. Commentators of the day agreed. As one negatively inclined critic wrote in response to Sargent's works in the Royal Academy exhibition of 1886, "He is the Henry James of portraiture; and I can't help wishing he were not—as I can't help wishing that Henry James were not the Sargent of the novel."[167]

Whether it was James's urging or the incredible financial and social success of his season's portrait-painting campaign in the United States, from September 1887 to May 1888, Sargent did thereafter alter his strategy of public presentation, undoing the careful balance between portrait and genre works that he had fostered from the late 1870s.[168] For the next two decades, with the exception of his American mural projects, Sargent appeared before the public mostly as a painter of portraits, those works that, as James wrote, "when they joined hands . . . made the indestructible thread on which the pearls of history were strung."[169] His visions of landscape and genre, on the contrary, although no less ambitious or accomplished than before, populated a more private realm.[170]

James did not publish anything further on Sargent's art until 1897. His private letters from the years in between, however, are filled with news of the painter's comings and goings and with commentaries on his works. Several times, for example, he unstintingly praised *Elizabeth Allen (Mrs. Henry G.) Marquand* (Fig. 17) while offering more restrained appreciation of *Louisa "Iza" (Mrs. Edward Darley) Boit* (1887; Museum of Fine Arts, Boston), two of the three pictures Sargent showed at the 1888 Royal Academy. To art writer Theodore Child, he was circumspect about his feeling, letting silence imply less regard: "Sargent has sent from America two big female portraits to the academy, admirable, almost incomparable (to my sense), for talent and life. One of them is a really noble picture of Mrs. Marquand."[171] He was more open to an intimate friend:

> *I have seen the two great portraits which Sargent has sent over to go into the Academy—a month hence: Mrs. Marquand and Mrs. Boit. They are both full of talent life and style and as he only could have painted them, but very different from each other. Mrs. M. will do him great good with the public—they will want to be painted like that—respectfully honourably, dignement. It is a noble portrait of an old lady. Our dear Iza won't do him good—though she is wonderful and of a living! But she not only speaks—she winks—and the philistine will find her vulgar. Poor dear Iza!*[172]

The conflicting feelings about these two pictures, in fact, provided the occasion for James's most overt articulation of disappointment in Sargent. He wrote to this same mutual friend in Paris, updating her on Sargent's activities after the painter's long professional stay in the United States:

> *I believe Sargent arrives from one day to the other, but starts immediately for Florence. . . . His Mrs. Boit is admirable for life & impudence & talent,*

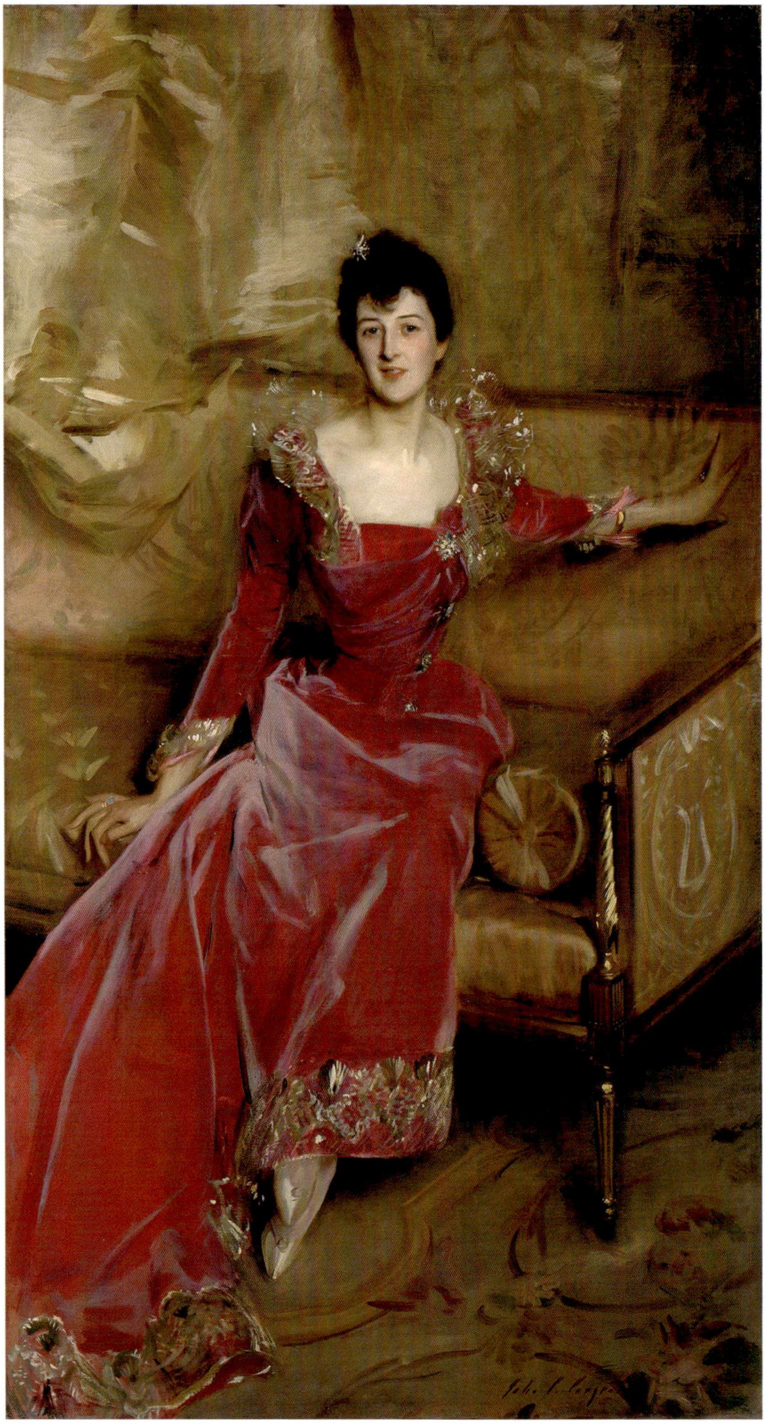

FIG. 18. John Singer Sargent (1856–1925), *Mrs. Hugh Hammersley*, 1892, The Metropolitan Museum of Art, New York.

tioned other Americans—Abbey (with particular notice of *The Play Scene from Hamlet* (1897; Yale University Art Gallery, New Haven, Connecticut) and James Jebusa Shannon (1862–1923)—noting how, at the Royal Academy, "the new Americans, in 1897, have it much their own way." Although he did not write more of Shannon, of Abbey he acknowledged the triumphant picture of the previous year (*Richard, Duke of Gloucester, and the Lady Anne,* 1896, Yale University Art Gallery, New Haven, Connecticut), noted the astonishing rapidity with which Abbey had transformed himself from an illustrator in black and white into a successful painter, and applauded his "picture of to-day, noble in color and strongly composed," which

> *shows him as one of the first of dramatic painters. I apply that term not because he takes subjects from plays, but because he has in any subject so rare a sense for the dramatic moment. In his version of the play-scene in Hamlet he holds it with the firmness of a master. The "story-picture" is an affliction whenever it is not a joy; when Mr. Abbey paints it, at all events, I lose myself in it for long—I lose myself in that deep within where, on their painted, parti-colored bench, his king and queen, like a couple behind a runaway, draw long, pale faces, hesitate between sitting tight and taking the jump, and instinctively add, on the royal seat, to the space that separates them. I lose myself not less in the white beauty of Ophelia—all whiteness in a sombre field—whose expression, as strange, almost, and as rendered, as Lady Anne's, last year, shows, as germs of her doom and with an admirable unbearded Polonius at her back, a slow wonder and terror at what is before her.*[184]

At the end of the month, James's final art review appeared. It was devoted to the Grafton Galleries exhibition of the Dramatic and Musical Arts, wherein he wrote so movingly of Whistler's portrait of Henry Irving, with asides about Sargent's portrait of Ellen Terry as Lady Macbeth (1889; Tate Britain, London) in the same show and, at the National Portrait Gallery, London, the portrait of Coventry Patmore.

James did not stop looking at American art in 1897 or writing about it in his personal and professional correspondence. Indeed, even after ceasing to publish his thoughts and reflections, he would continue to have a dramatic effect on American visual arts. One signal fashion in which this occurred was his decision to have photographic frontispieces for the volumes of the New York Edition (his own selection of his works, issued in twenty-four volumes, revised and with new prefaces, published between 1907 and 1909). Earlier than this, James had relatively little say in how various illustrators of his tales and novels approached their tasks. He had strong views, especially relating to the fiction as opposed to the travel writing, but little control.[185]

With the New York Edition, however, James wrote frequently to the photographer, Alvin Langdon Coburn (1882–1966), and consulted, advised, scouted locations, and in every way involved himself in the sites to be photographed: "I was provided with the most detailed instructions concerning my pictures," Coburn later wrote.

> *Although not literally a photographer, I believe Henry James must have had sensitive plates in his brain on which to record his impressions! He always knew exactly what he wanted, although many of his pictures were but images in his mind and imagination, and what we did was browse diligently until we found such a subject.*[186]

The resulting photographs are marvels as both art objects and frontispieces.

Coburn first approached James seeking to photograph him, and the initial exercise was pleasant enough for both men that the collaboration continued. Coburn

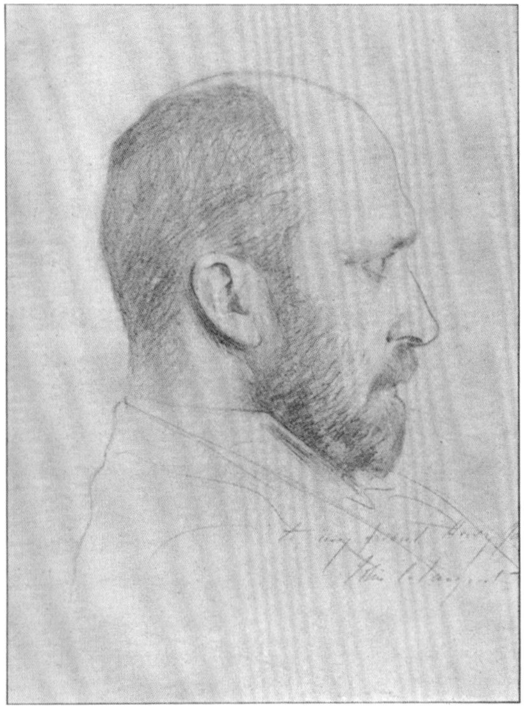

FIG. 19. James Singer Sargent (1856–1925), *Portrait of Henry James, The Yellow Book*, vol. 2, July 1894.

notion that James here declared that his visage and two of his late novels represent the "difficult, perverse, obscure" reveals the challenges Sargent and James both faced. The next—the third and, it proved, final—sitting was more than a month later. On the eve of the event James again wrote to Wharton:

I am to sit to-morrow to Sargent for the third time (and I surmise, and hope, [Mary Hunter] will be there—for she really helps the sitter).[206] *I have a certain amount of impression that he may sacrifice the work of the two other sittings and make a fresh start. If he does he will probably, over the known, the learnt, ground go much straighter. But he may pick himself—or me—up, and dash along as is.*[207]

The third sitting did, indeed, prove the charm—at least for a while. James wrote a strikingly short note to Wharton announcing the project's fruition.

I have sat again to Sargent with complete success, and he has made an admirable drawing. He kept on with the work of the two previous séances—and brought it round, beautifully developed, and redeemed and completed. It's a regular first class living, resembling, enduring thing.[208]

James wrote approvingly of the drawing elsewhere, citing "Sargent's admirable charmed head of me—just done (for Mrs. Wharton!)."[209] Sargent, however, felt otherwise. He wrote to Wharton: "The photograph [of the drawing] that has reached me proves that I am right in considering H. J. drawing a failure—I will try again if his patience holds out—at any rate I consider your commission unfulfilled." Sargent retained the drawing and never completed the commission.[210]

The next year, however, Sargent did once again have the opportunity to test James's patience and to portray his old friend. James was to turn seventy on 15 April 1913.

Many sought to honor and celebrate him. British admirers organized a consortium of almost three hundred people, each contributing no more than £5, to acquire for James a silver-gilt Charles II porringer and dish, apt for the author of *The Golden Bowl*, and to commission an oil portrait from Sargent (see Tóibín, Fig. 16).[211] The first sitting took place on 13 May, and James wrote of it to his artist nephew:

I must mention, however, that I gave Sargent this a.m. my first sitting for the portrait—the *portrait; and that nothing has been of such promise since that first a.m.—April 1911—that I sat to you in Mt. Vernon Street. It struck me that he could say to me—even* he—*after all his record—that in consequence of his having now stopped portraiture for these last three or four years, he had quite "lost his nerve" about it; this he said the other day when we were arranging to begin, and that he therefore felt he must reserve the faculty of destroying or not delivering the picture if he didn't succeed in pleasing himself. I seem this a.m., however, to see that this* wouldn't—*or won't—be the case. He got at it and placed it within the first half hour (more or less full face). It is an auspicious start in fact, and* looks *as if it were going to go. . . . He has in this year's Academy—a deplorable show—a portrait of his own niece (Rose-Marie) which is a most exquisite and lovely image of a young girl of seventeen (of* any *young girl) that there can be in the world—an absolutely perfect thing* [1912; private collection].[212]

Over the next month or so, James reported on the sittings to various friends, often noting how "I have myself greatly enjoyed the process and his company—and I judge he will really have done a fine and characteristic thing."[213] The letters to his nephew William are the most detailed:

much the most interesting thing . . . has been, during the last three weeks, my regular sittings for my portrait to Sargent; which have numbered now some seven or eight, I forget which, and with but a couple more to come. So the thing is, I make out, very nearly finished, and the head apparently (as I much hope) to have almost nothing more done to it. It is, I infer, a very great success; a number of the competent and intelligent have seen it, and so pronounce it in the strongest terms. . . . In short it seems likely to be one of S.'s very fine things. One is almost full-face, with one's left arm over the corner of one's chair-back and the hand brought round so that the thumb is caught in the arm-hole of one's waistcoat, and said hand therefore, with the fingers a bit folded, entirely visible and "treated." Of course I'm sitting a little askance in the chair. The canvas comes down to just where my watch-chain (such as it is, poor thing!) is hung across the waistcoat: which latter, in itself, is found to be splendidly (poor thing though it also be) and most interestingly treated. Sargent can *make such things so interesting—such things as my coat-lappet and shoulder and sleeve too! But what is most interesting, every one is agreed, is the mouth—than which even he has never painted a more living and, as I am told, "expressive"! In fact I can quite see that myself; and really, I seem to feel, the thing will be all that can at the best (the best with such a subject!) have been expected of it. I only wish you and Alice*[214] *had assisted at some of the sittings—as Sargent likes animated, sympathetic, beautiful, talkative friends to do, in order to correct by their presence too lugubrious expressions.*[215]

James wrote as sitter, as keen-eyed (if, by this date, somewhat out-of-practice) art critic, and as a guide desiring to be helpful to his artist nephew. The canvas's virtues and priorities are clear to him. While many commentaries on portraits focus on the eyes, here the speaking mouth is the portrait's foremost feature in James's view, akin to what La Farge had effected in the profile portrait of fifty-plus years earlier. He also noted that the pose is a complex one, with a subtle twist torquing the whole body, thus animating the manifold patches and strokes of blacks and grays that cover the majority of the canvas. James also appreciated that one hand—his left, not his writing hand, and, of course, he had long been dictating most things—was fully worked up, which is a notoriously difficult challenge for many painters.[216] Nor

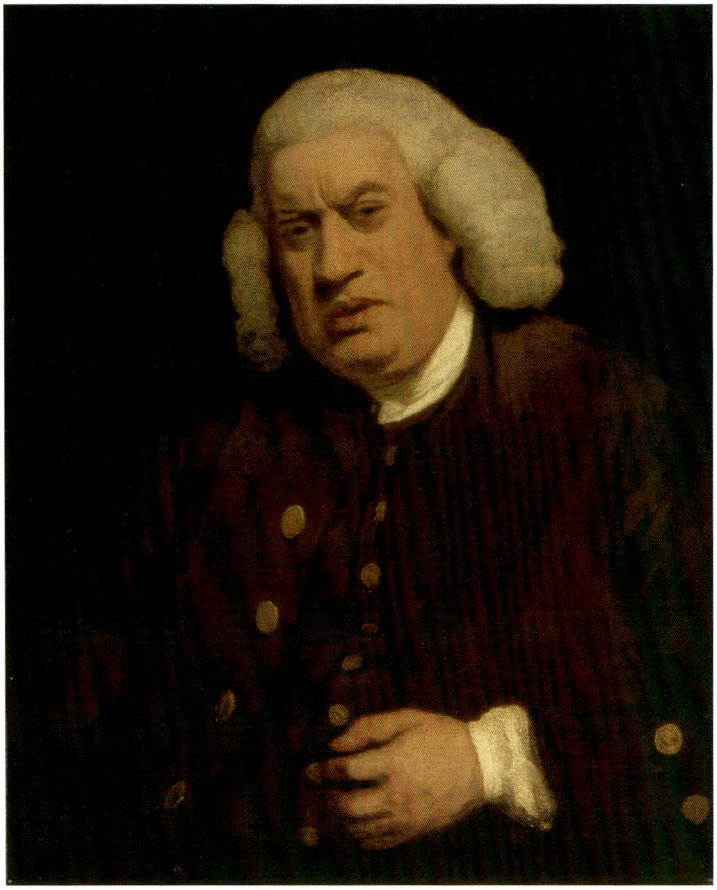

FIG. 20. Sir Joshua Reynolds (1723–1792), *Dr. Samuel Johnson*, ca. 1772, Tate Britain, London.

did he ignore the understated but dynamic elements of vest and watch chain and their contribution to the whole.

On 24 June it was finished.[217] He wrote to a friend:

> *It is now finished,* parachevé *(I sat for the last time a couple of days ago;) and is nothing less evidently, than a very fine thing indeed, Sargent at his very best and poor H. J. not at his worst; in short a living breathing likeness and a masterpiece of painting. I am really quite ashamed to admire it so much and so loudly—it's so much as if I were calling attention to my own fine points. . . . And I am sorry to have ceased to sit, in spite of the repeated big holes it made in my precious mornings: J. S. S. being so genial and delightful a* nature de grand maître *to have to do with. . . . He liked always a friend or two to be in to break the spell of a settled gloom in my countenance by their prattle; though you will doubtless think this effect but little achieved when I tell you that, having myself found the thing, as it grew, more and more like Sir Joshua's Dr. Johnson* [Fig. 20], *and said so, a perceptive friend reinforced me a couple of sittings later by breaking out irrepressibly with the same judgment.*[218]

Note the fine and perceptive reference to an eighteenth-century precedent, one that surely had some role in Sargent's initial set-up.

James adored the portrait: "I do really rejoice so that I have been able to be the occasion of such a supreme manifestation of Sargent's genius."[219] Presumably the invited guests who crowded into Sargent's studio for several days in December, with James in attendance, all praised the work as well. James wrote to the artist's sister Emily: "Such a carnival of glory as I have been seeing enacted in the studio of 33 [Tite Street—Sargent's home and studio]. Such a multitudinous jig-dance round & round the Portrait! Sitting for it was a bliss, but this standing *by* it has been an even richer experience."[220] To Gosse he proclaimed the "exhibition of the Portrait" a "great and charming success," and the work itself

> *acclaimed with unanimity of admiration and, literally, of* intelligence, *that I can intimately attest to. For I really put myself on exhibition beside it, each of the days, morning and afternoon, and the translation (a perfect Omar Khayyam,* quoi!) *visibly left the original nowhere.*[221]

These are close to the last words that James wrote about a specific picture, and they aptly circle back to his principal concern of joining inextricably the experience of art and of life: the one is the other.

Early in his writing on pictorial art, James declared that, "There is only one rule of general application, we fear, for appreciating a picture—namely, to enjoy it. The greatest painter cannot ask more than that."[222] This is a modernist statement, parallel to what Charles Demuth asserted half a century later:

> *Paintings must be looked and looked at and looked at—they, I think, the good ones, like it. They must be understood, and that's not the word, either, through the eyes. No writing, no talking, no singing, no dancing will explain them. They are the final, the 'nth whooppee of sight. . . . "Look at that!" is all that can be said before a great painting, at least, by those who really see it.*[223]

James did "really see" a number of great paintings. Yet a writer will write (he wrote once to La Farge: "Properly to see things you need to talk about them," and writing is close to talking.[224]) Across the decades, he wrote about American art in ways that conveyed his admiration and appreciation of those who made drawings, sculptures, photographs, and, especially, paintings. His tone was often amused and lofty. Even when condemnatory, as he was early on about Whistler and the French Impressionists, James recognized and valued almost all efforts involved in the making of art; he mostly lived by the tenet, "Criticism is appreciation or it is nothing."[225] One has the sense of him wandering through galleries in much the same way as a character in an Iris Murdoch novel does:

> *Dora did not need to peer. She could look, as one can at last when one knows a great thing very well, confronting it with a dignity which it has itself conferred. . . .*
>
> *Dora was always moved by the pictures. . . . She marvelled, with a kind of gratitude, that they were all still here, and her heart was filled with love for the pictures, their authority, their marvellous generosity, their splendour. It occurred to her that here at last was something real and something perfect. Who had said that, about perfection and reality being in the same place? . . . [T]he pictures were something real outside herself, which spoke to her kindly and yet in sovereign tones. . . . When the world had seemed to be subjective it had seemed to be without interest or value. But now there was something else in it after all.*[226]

From beginning to end of his looking at pictures, from boyhood's Cole through to mature master's Abbey, the picture that allowed James "to lose himself," to forget for an instant his own quivering subjectivity, was a good and effective one.

The works James most admired shared several other characteristics, and the conveying of a felt truth, sharing an experience of the real world, was perhaps the core feature. While James was perhaps not quite one with Spinoza concerning reality and perfection, his admiration for conveying a perceived reality was deep and enduring. The goal recurs continually as key in the theory of his own art:

I may therefore venture to say that the air of reality (solidity of specification) seems to me to be the supreme virtue of a novel—the merit on which all its other merits . . . helplessly and submissively depend. If it be not there, they are all as nothing, and if these be there, they owe their effect to the success with which the author has produced the illusion of life. The cultivation of this success, the study of this exquisite process, form, to my taste, the beginning and the end of the art of the novelist.[227]

This was required of not only the writer but also the painter:

It is here, in very truth, that [the writer] competes with life; it is here that he competes with his brother the painter in his *attempt to render the look of things, the look that conveys their meaning, to catch the colour, the relief, the expression, the surface, the substance of the human spectacle.*[228]

Later, writing of both the literary and pictorial arts, James generalized on "the immense field of contemporary life observed for an artistic purpose":

There is nothing so interesting as that, because it is ourselves; and no artistic problem is so charming as to arrive, either in a literary or a plastic norm, at a close and direct notation of what we observe.[229]

By convincingly representing the observed thing, the artist could prompt parallel recognitions, or sympathetic memories, in others.

So for James, landscape paintings—whether a modest scene by McEntee or an expansive vista by La Farge—were successful to the extent that they aroused memories of comparable places and appropriate sensations. When Abbey re-created literary scenes, or Johnson portrayed a Yankee peddler, it was the complex truths of emotions beneath the costumes and fictional situations, brought to life with sufficient technical finesse so as to leave the fiction uninterrupted, that rang true. The complement to this was that, for breadth of appeal, in American pictures at least, he preferred the quotidian to the sensational, the broader truth to the dramatic flourish. Church's tropical views and Moran's vistas of Utah might well be accurate, but their drama could gain no traction for James. As his friend La Farge said, in reference to his *Paradise Valley*: "My programme was to paint from nature a portrait, and yet to make distinctly a work of art which should remain as a type of the sort of subject I undertook, a subject both novel and absolutely 'everydayish.'"[230]

Closely related to this is James's favoring, as he wrote, of ambiguities over great glares. Given how he constructed his stories, James's predilection for things that slowly reveal themselves and reward attentive looking is not surprising. As in the world, things in good pictures are often more involved than first meet the eye.

A further characteristic that James articulated about admired pictures was their projection of a unified and integrated effect. Cole's Italian landscape and Whistler's portrayal of Henry Irving in the character of Philip II, as different as they are in subject and facture, nonetheless keep their various components in place—unlike the "lividly dead" Leutze picture that was such an excitement to the young boy. James seems to have understood the truth spoken years later by his friend La Farge: "In nature nothing sticks out."[231]

Unity of expression was a quality that James not only appreciated in pictures but also strove for in his writing. Ruminating in 1894 on his plan for a short story, James observed:

> *The formula for the presentation of it in 20,000 words is to make it an* Impression*—as one of Sargent's pictures is an impression. That is, I must do it from my own point of view—that of an imagined observer, participator, chronicler. I must picture it, summarize it, impressionize it, in a word—compress and confine it by making it the picture of what I see. . . . A strong subject, a rich subject* summarized*—that is my indispensable formula and memento.*[232]

It should come as no surprise that James draws upon the example of an American painter friend as one possible model in the creation of this story, for James felt, as he wrote in his guise as literary theorist:

> *the analogy between the art of the painter and the art of the novelist is, so far as I am able to see, complete. Their inspiration is the same, their process (allowing for the different quality of the vehicle) is the same, their success is the same. They may learn from each other, they may explain and sustain each other. Their cause is the same, and the honour of one is the honour of another. . . . [I] insist on the fact that as the picture is reality, so the novel is history.*[233]

Elsewhere—as but one of many examples—he wrote of the two arts: "The forms are different, though with analogies; but the field is the same."[234] Late in life, he summarized this in his memoirs, writing of his Newport days and "that dawning perception that the arts were after all essentially one."[235]

Nor is it a surprise that he would specify Sargent, a portraitist, as this pictorial exemplar. For James also stressed consistently the priority of portraiture in his hierarchy of the visual arts. His enthusiasm for early Duveneck (who was "essentially a portraitist"), the impassioned closing of the essay on Sargent ("there is no greater work of art than a great portrait"), the advocacy of *The Tragic Muse*'s Gabriel Nash (who called the portrait "the strongest dose of life that art could give, the strongest dose of art that life could give"), the simple fact that he titled volumes of diverse writings—literary essays, travel accounts, and a novel—as *Partial Portraits, Portraits of Places,* and *The Portrait of a Lady* all testify to his regard for that form above all others. It is surely no coincidence that Hans Holbein—one the greatest of European portrait-ists—was the sole artist to find his way into the title of a tale with "The Beldonald Holbein" (1899).

Henry James grew up with a Thomas Cole landscape on the wall of his family's New York parlor and died in possession of one of John Singer Sargent's last great portraits. As American art framed his life, American painters provided key experiences and milestones over its course. James, in his turn, looked closely at selected pictures, wrote about them shrewdly and openheartedly, and provided insights that art historians almost 150 years later turn to when thinking about work by artists as diverse as Sargent and Winslow Homer. Henry James and the subject of American art are well entwined.

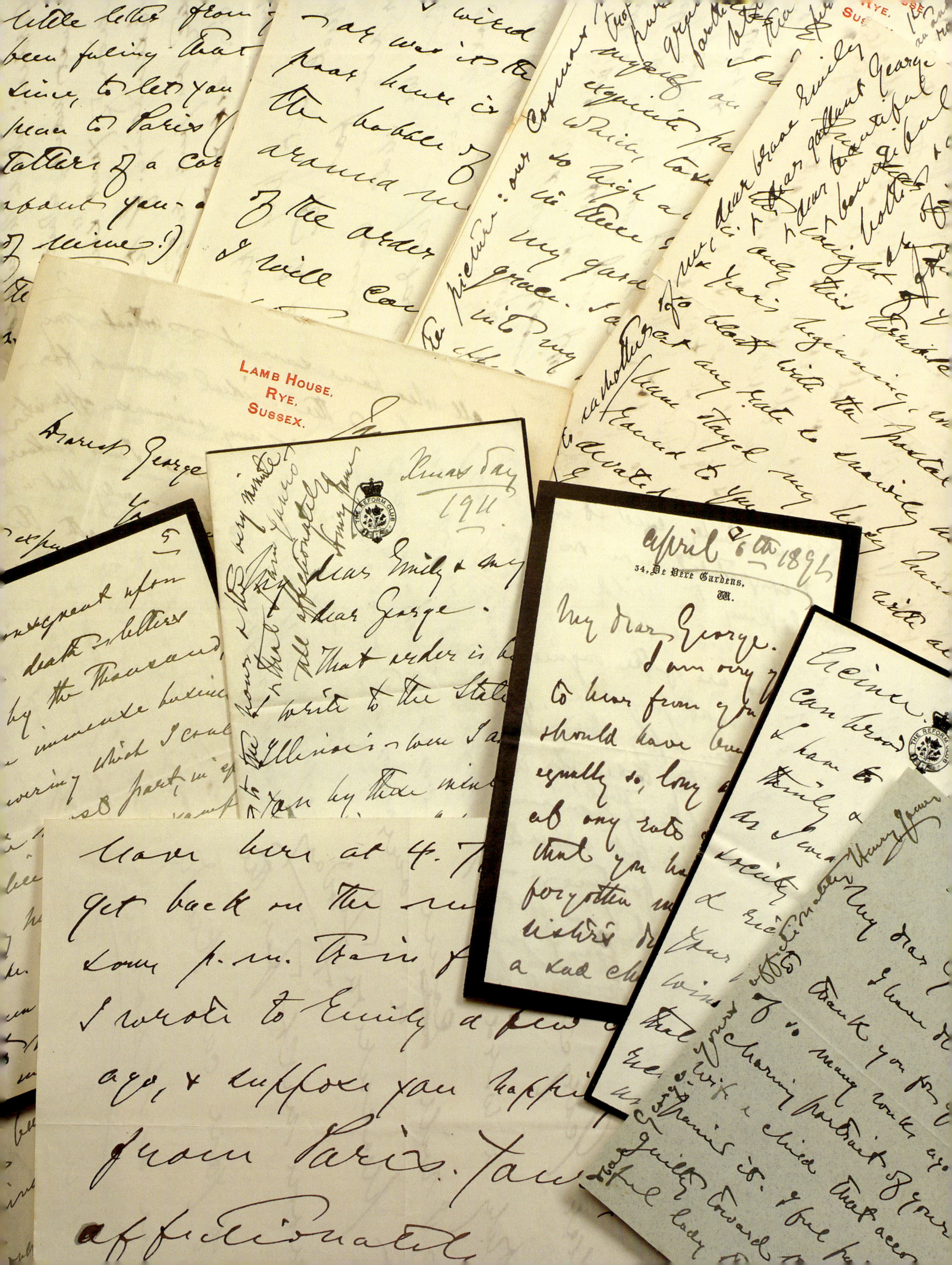
LAMB HOUSE,
RYE,
SUSSEX.
THE REFORM CLUB
34, De Vere Gardens,
W.

DECLAN KIELY

"Pardon my too many words"
Henry James Manuscripts and Letters at the Morgan Library & Museum

"A trustful guardian"

In regard to manuscripts and letters, it could be said that writers generally fall into two categories—they are either preservers or destroyers. Henry James was the latter. As the final volumes of the New York Edition of *The Novels and Tales of Henry James* appeared in 1909, James, having recently recovered from a protracted and distressing illness, set about the destruction of his vast hoard of personal papers, including his incoming correspondence accumulated over the preceding decades. In the garden of Lamb House, his Georgian home in Rye, East Sussex, James made a "gigantic bonfire" in pursuance of "the law that I have made tolerably absolute these last years . . . of not leaving personal and private documents at the mercy of any accidents, or even of my executors!"[1] As Nathaniel Hawthorne recorded in his journal in June 1853, after destroying the letters his wife, Sophia, had written him during their courtship and marriage: "What a trustful guardian of secret matters fire is! What should we do without Fire and Death?"[2]

What, indeed! James completed his self-appointed task with another conflagration in 1915, the year before his death.[3] In doing so he was following—consciously or not, we do not know—the practice of Charles Dickens, another great destroyer of personal papers. Although Dickens sensibly gave most of the original manuscripts of his fictional work to his friend and executor John Forster, the novelist consigned a huge amount of personal correspondence to the

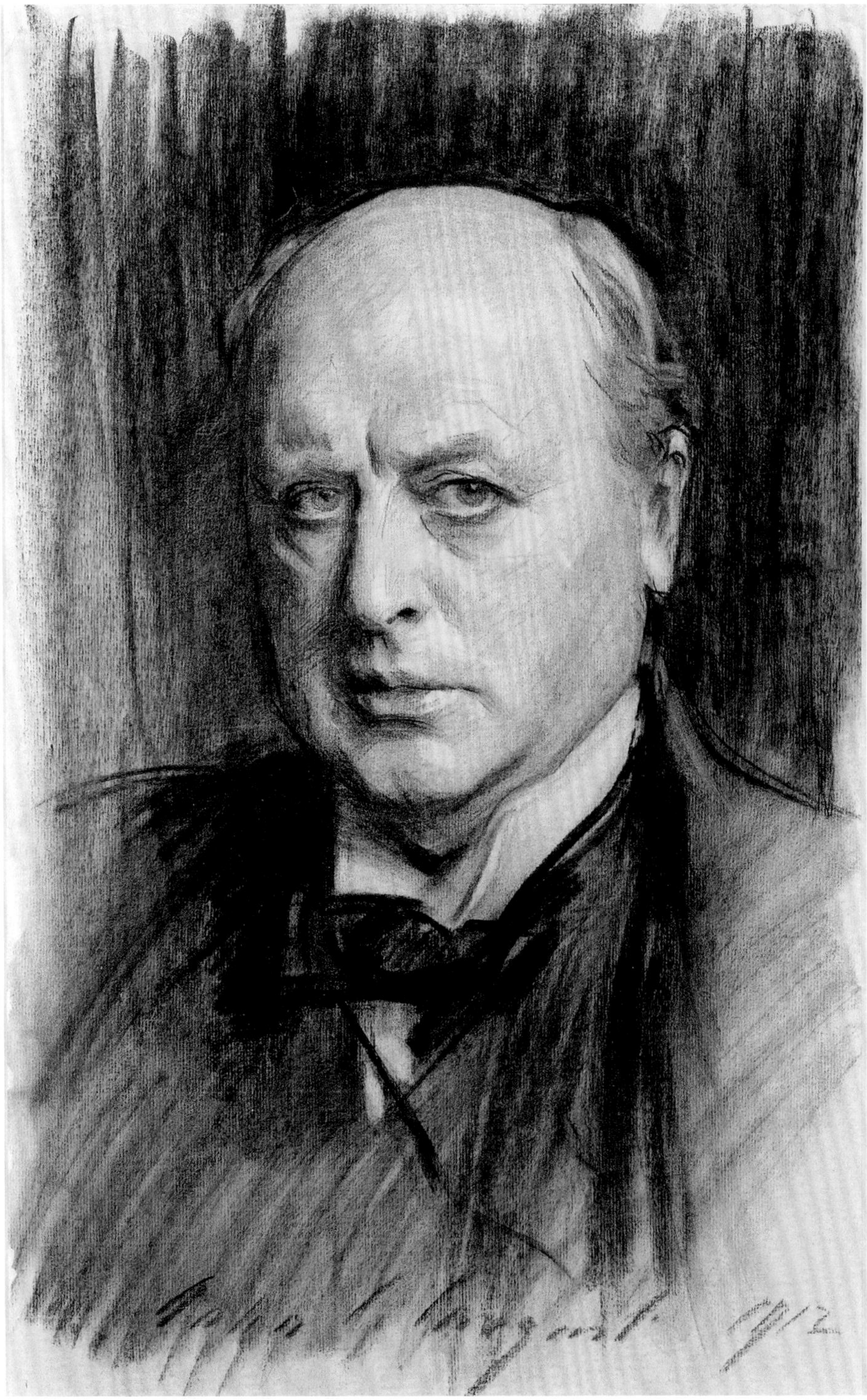

FIG. 1. John Singer Sargent (1856–1925), *Henry James,* 1912, Royal Collection Trust, London.

fire. This makes Dickens's correspondence "largely a one-sided survival" because, while recipients invariably retained and, subsequently, treasured his letters, from early in his career he systematically destroyed the letters that he received.[4] Dickens expressed horror at the notion of private correspondence being published and read, and his motivation in burning his incoming correspondence seems to have been to protect his privacy and that of others. On 3 September 1860, in the garden of his Gad's Hill home, Dickens made a huge bonfire and burned "the accumulated letters and papers of twenty years."[5] Afterward, he is reported to have said: "Would to God every letter I had ever written was on that pile."[6] Dickens committed another tranche of his papers to the fire in 1869, the year before his death.

According to Michael Millgate, before James died he destroyed "the vast bulk not only of his personal papers but also of such working papers as manuscripts, typescripts, proofs, and corrected copies of his own books."[7] What survive are the thousands of letters James wrote to family, friends, acquaintances, editors, and publishers who—not following James's express instructions to destroy—retained them. Other survivals include only a small number of manuscripts that were no longer in the author's possession as well as nine notebooks that James used between 1879 and 1911. The notebooks were discovered in 1937 by the biographer Leon Edel "in what looked like an old sea chest or footlocker sequestered in the basement of Harvard's Widener Library, where the James family papers had been deposited for safekeeping before they would be finally presented to Harvard."[8]

"The rights of privacy" and "the tower of art"

So, why did James decide to destroy so much of what we would now consider his literary archive? Some biographers have attributed the decision to illness and depression, but it is apparent that the novelist was concerned about the final disposition of letters and manuscripts for most of his writing life. As early as 1872, in his review of *Passages from the French and Italian Note-Books of Nathaniel Hawthorne*,[9] James began to express his uneasiness with the practice of setting before the reading public texts culled from unpublished papers whose author never intended them to see the light of day. While Hawthorne had burned personal letters, he had not taken the step of placing his own journals beyond the reach of a curious public. James began his review with an acerbic observation that took aim at this increasingly common publishing activity: "Mr. Hawthorne is having a posthumous productivity almost as active as that of his lifetime." James went on to assert that "these liberal excisions from the privacy of so reserved and shade-seeking a genius suggest forcibly the general question of the proper limits of curiosity as to that passive personality of an artist of which the elements are scattered in portfolios and table-drawers." Although he allowed that "there is much that is very worthy and signally serviceable to art itself in this curiosity," he felt that there was also "much that is idle and grossly defiant of the artist's presumptive desire to limit and define the ground of his appeal to fame." Insofar as James assessed the value—or otherwise—of publishing extracts from Hawthorne's journals, he noted that "they deepen our sense of that genius, while they singularly diminish our impression of his general intellectual power."[10] And, adumbrating his own, much later, decision to leave relatively little for posterity, he predicted that "artists, of course, as time goes on, will be likely to take the alarm, empty their table-drawers, and level the approaches to their privacy. The critics, psychologists, and gossip-mongers may then glean amid the stubble."[11]

Five years later, writing about the *Correspondance de H. de Balzac, 1819–1850,* for the February 1877 issue of *The Galaxy,* James went even further, relating the strong feeling of uneasiness—amounting to a sense of personal guilt—he experienced when reading Balzac's letters under review: "The first feeling of the reader . . . is that he has almost done wrong to read them. He reproaches himself with having taken a shabby advantage of a person who is unable to defend himself. He feels as one who has broken open a cabinet or rummaged an old desk. The contents of Balzac's letters are so private, so personal, so exclusively his own affairs and those of no one else, that the generous critic constantly lays them down with a sort of dismay and asks himself in virtue of what peculiar privilege or what newly discovered principle it is that he is thus burying his nose in them."[12] In review after review, over nearly three decades, James was unable to consider editions of authorial correspondence without worrying about the ethical issues related to its publication—the invasion of privacy that it implied, and the cultural and literary consequences.[13] For James, it "is always a question whether we have the right to investigate a man's life for the sake of anything but his official utterances—his results."[14] In 1900, reviewing *The Letters of Robert Louis Stevenson to His Family and Friends*—and this was personally significant because Stevenson had been a friend and correspondent—James reminded his readers that "Nothing comes up oftener today than the question of the rights of privacy; of our warrant, or want of warrant, for getting behind, by the aid of editors or other retailers, certain appearances of distinction."[15] The word *retailers* is instructive here: James was well aware of the commercially driven nature of such publications—he had, after all, witnessed the advent of mass communication.[16] This was an issue that fascinated James because he was a fierce protector of his own privacy and that of his friends, while cognizant of the scholarly benefit and aesthetic pleasure derived from reading personal correspondence.[17] He balanced his wariness about the publication of Balzac's letters by saying "we are thankful for it." In January 1897, writing in *The Yellow Book* about the recent publication of George Sand's letters to Alfred Musset, James identified "the greatest of all literary quarrels" as the "eternal dispute between the public and the private, between curiosity and delicacy." Looking into an increasingly anxiety-ridden future for those in the public eye, he signaled his own later course of action:

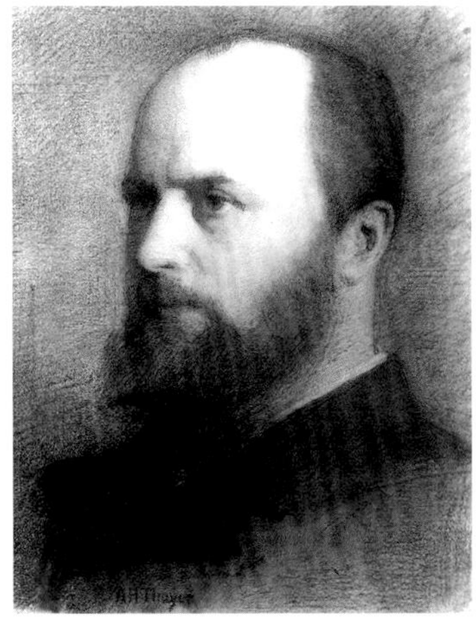

FIG. 2. Abbott Handerson Thayer (1849–1921), *Henry James,* ca. 1881, Courtesy of the American Academy of Arts and Letters, New York.

> *The reporter and the reported have duly and equally to understand that they carry their life in their hands. There are secrets for privacy and silence; . . . Then the cunning of the inquirer, envenomed with resistance, will exceed in subtlety and ferocity anything we to-day conceive, and the pale forewarned victim, with every track covered, every paper burnt and every letter unanswered, will, in the tower of art, the invulnerable granite, stand, without a sally, the siege of all the years.*[18]

"Ah, you publishing scoundrel!"

Subsequently, James was able to redirect his own disquiet about the potential exploitation of personal correspondence by turning it to literary account in his fiction, especially in short stories that appealed to his dedication to dramatic revelation. This was a fruitful subject for James, possessing what he would call significant "emotional capacity."[19] The subject was still very much on his mind in the fall of 1887, when he mused in his notebook that "one sketches one's age but imperfectly if one doesn't touch on that particular matter: the invasion, the impudence and shamelessness, of the newspaper and the interviewer, the devouring *publicity* of life, the extinction of all sense between public and private."[20] It is, without question, dramatized most famously in his novella *The Aspern Papers* (1888), in which an unscrupulous and ambitious—even predatory—editor (in the story the narrator refers to himself as a "critic") employs devious means to obtain the letters of Jeffrey Aspern, a deceased American poet.[21] In the guise of a disinterested man of letters who has come to Venice "having some literary work, some reading and writing to do," the editor takes up lodgings in the Venetian palazzo of Juliana Bordereau, an old lady who was, many years earlier, Aspern's lover and the inspiration for some of his finest lyrics and is believed to be in possession of the poet's love letters and other papers. The narrator grows increasingly anxious about the fate of the letters, observing in chapter 6: "The worst of it was that she looked terribly like an old woman who at a pinch would burn her papers."[22] In order to carry through his plan, the biographer ingratiates himself with Miss Bordereau's dowdy spinster niece, Miss Tita, eventually divulging his real motive to her. Realizing that the biographer's affection for her is entirely dependent upon his "literary concupiscence"—as James characterized it in the first published version of the story in 1888—Miss Tita agrees to help the biographer obtain Aspern's letters by thwarting her aunt "before she commits that horrible sacrilege" of burning them.

But when Miss Bordereau becomes ill, the biographer, through sheer sophistry, convinces himself to seize the opportunity to examine the letters. As he is about to rifle the secretary in which the papers are stored, he is discovered by an outraged Miss Bordereau, who "hissed out passionately, furiously: 'Ah, you publishing scoundrel!'" We can see that James is here reusing, in his fiction, the image of the unwelcome snooper who "[rummages] an old desk," that he first imagined in his review of Balzac's letters over ten years before. Feeling "horribly ashamed," the biographer flees the scene but later returns to the palazzo to find that Miss Bordereau has died. Miss Tita now offers to relinquish the Aspern papers on condition that the biographer will agree to marry her. After first refusing, the biographer changes his mind, but by that point he discovers that Miss Tita has burned, one by one, all of Jeffrey Aspern's letters to Miss Juliana Bordereau.

The novella's devastating second climax ultimately leaves the reader in no doubt about the powerful mystique surrounding unpublished personal papers and the lengths that pertinacious and unscrupulous editors or publishers will go to obtain them.[23] The power of James's story derives in large part from the ambiguous depiction of the narrator, with whose higher, literary motives the clement reader may be inclined to sympathize even while disapproving of his actions. As Lyndall Gordon observed, James "rejected the prospect of biography, not only to protect his privacy, but also, we might guess, because he was so much a biographer himself—he well knew the excitements and dangers of biographic power."[24] The reader is never in doubt about the high stakes for which the narrator is playing, and there is no question as to the plausibility and conviction of his arguments in favor of saving Aspern's papers in the interests of literary scholarship and general appreciation. The interplay between the narrator and the wily Miss Bordereau, whom the reader comes to suspect is fully aware of the narrator's true motives, is wickedly comical. James brilliantly created and sustained tension between the narrator's increasingly desperate desire to preserve and Miss Bordereau's legitimate power—and possible propensity—to destroy. The reader is inclined to believe that the author's own mixed feelings are being played out in the choreography of his characters' motives and actions.

"A collection of literary remains"

James's exploration of this theme—the fate of what he referred to as "literary remains"—can also be traced in *The Abasement of the Northmores,* a somewhat neglected short story he wrote in the winter of 1899–1900. This deeply ambivalent and ironic tale concerns the imprudence of publishing, posthumously, the letters of Lord Northmore, a highly regarded public figure. This story and *The Aspern Papers* are a thematic diptych.[25] James thought highly enough of *The Abasement of the Northmores* to include it in the New York Edition of his work, published in 1909, from which he excluded almost half of his other stories or tales.[26]

In the nineteenth century, almost as an extension of the customary obsequies performed for famous men, it was common for a close friend or descendant to write a (usually hagiographic or at least well-disposed) biography. John Forster performed this service for Dickens, devoting the final years of his life to a three-volume biography of his friend, published between 1871 and 1874. Lord Tennyson's biography was written by his son Hallam in 1897. Sir Winston Churchill, despite having limited firsthand knowledge of his father, wrote a two-volume biography of Lord Randolph Churchill in 1906. Sometimes the biography would be preceded, or followed, by an edition of letters or a collection of miscellaneous writings. Henry James participated in just such an exercise of filial devotion by assisting his brother, William, when they edited *The Literary Remains of the Late Henry James* (1884) two years after the death of their father, Henry James, Sr.[27]

After the death of William James in 1910, Henry began to write a memoir of his brother. Ultimately the memoir metamorphosed into *A Small Boy and Others* (1913) and in doing so became almost exclusively autobiographical. It was followed by *Notes of a Son and Brother* (1914). Originally conceived as the "Family Book," this intended publication was to be an account of William and Henry's youth based on his brother's early letters. For *Notes of a Son and Brother* James relied upon what had become a standard form of nineteenth-century biography—authorial commentary organized around the subject's letters. But his animated correspondence with his sister-in-law, Alice James, and his nephew Henry James III, reveal that his brother's family was furious and outraged by the manner in which James had edited William's letters for his own purposes.[28] In publishing the autobiography and memoir that constitute his final works it is, then, ironic that James found himself embroiled in the very issues of privacy—and the concomitant sensitivities of the family of the deceased—that had engaged his own critical judgments and provided such rich subject matter for his short fiction.

In the spring of 1899, James went to Rome to examine the papers of William Wetmore Story (1819–1895)—meeting the sculptor Hendrik Andersen (1872–1940) for the first time while in the city—in order to prepare himself to write the biography that Story's family had asked him to undertake.[29] But, as James confided in a letter to his friend William Dean Howells, he felt considerable ambivalence about the request because he had never really taken Story seriously as an artist: "there is no *subject*—there is nothing in the man himself to write about. There is nothing for me but to do a *tour de force*, or try to—leave poor dear W. W. S. *out*, practically, and make a little volume on the old Roman, Americo-Roman, Hawthornesque and other bygone days."[30] The result was *William Wetmore Story and His Friends: From Letters, Diaries, and Recollections*. Published in two volumes in 1903 and drawing heavily upon letters written to Story by far better known figures such as Nathaniel Hawthorne, Robert and Elizabeth Barrett Browning, Charles Eliot Norton, Henry and Marian Adams, and James Russell Lowell, it re-created the social and artistic milieu of the expatriate Anglo-American painters and sculptors of the preceding generation. James's deep misgivings about writing Story's biography—as he contemplated his task in the fall of 1899—shaped and inflected the narrative of *The Abasement of the Northmores*.[31]

The issue at stake at the heart of James's dark comedy is the role of posthumously published letters in shaping the writer's reputation. Lord Northmore's reputation suffers irreversible damage when his letters are published. Mrs. Hope entertains the possibility that the reason her husband so carefully retained all of Northmore's letters is because he was aware that an edition of the peer's letters would inevitably be published after his death.

In order to secure her own husband's reputation as a man of genius, Mrs. Hope painstakingly transcribes his letters to her—the only letters of his that survive—and has a single copy "struck off and the type, under her eyes, dispersed." She puts the sheets, "which, she was pleased to find, would form a volume of three hundred pages, carefully away" and leaves instructions in her will that this edition of Warren Hope's letters be published after her death.

"The fat little bundle"

Readers may find in this story a telling indication of James's own sense of personal letters as hostages to fortune, fraught with potential consequentiality. This particular work of fiction reflects not only the wider public debate at this time about kinds of biographical publications but also James's own anxiety about the fate of his personal correspondence.[32] In the first section, the reader is told that "John Northmore had known her [Mrs. Hope] first, and how he had wanted to marry her the fat little bundle of his love-letters *still survived to tell*" [emphasis added]. This group of letters is referred to no fewer than five times in the story, and is invariably described by the narrator as "fat"—an ambiguous adjective that nicely conveys a sense of their physical bulk and, perhaps, the rotundity of the packet of letters (or their writer), enabling the reader to see them perfectly in the mind's eye. But the word *fat* is also unavoidably morbid, connoting fleshly appetite and corpulence, or the possibility that the letters are rich in some important constituent, or might be turned to some potentially profitable use in the future. Repetition adds a sense of increasing discomfort with each successive appearance of the word and also reminds the reader of the overinflated reputation of Northmore.

The second mention of these letters also raises another unresolved question: "The faded fat packet lurked still where it had lurked for years; but she could no more to-day have said why she had kept it than why—though he knew of the early episode—she had never

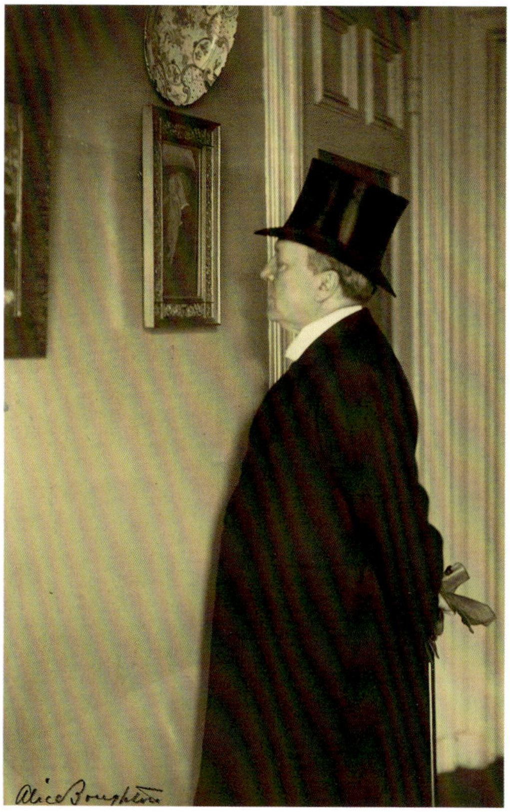

FIG. 3. Alice Boughton, *Henry James,* 1906, National Portrait Gallery, Smithsonian Institution, Washington, DC.

mentioned her preservation of it to Warren." There is more than a hint of menace or danger in James's use of the verb *lurked.* Anticipating the reader's inquiry—why had Mrs. Hope kept these letters throughout her long and happy marriage?—the narrator continues: "The odd part of the matter was, at any rate, that her retention of these documents had not been an accident. She had obeyed a dim instinct or a vague calculation. A calculation of what? She couldn't have told: it had operated, at the back of her head, simply as a sense that, not destroyed, the complete little collection made for safety. But for whose, just heaven?" The impulse to retain and save competes with the impulse to destroy.

The existence of a cache of personal letters poses, always for James, a sense of immanent threat—of publication and exposure of the inner self. In the aftermath of the publication of Lord Northmore's letters, Mrs. Hope "fished out of their nook, after long years, the packet of John Northmore's epistles to herself, and, reading them over in the light of his later style" comes to see that "they constituted her supreme treasure." She contemplates publication of the letters. The reader is told that "The vision closed round her and she lingered on the idea—fed, as she handled again her faded fat packet, by re-perusals more richly convinced." Mrs. Hope goes so far as to obtain legal opinion regarding the viability of publication of Northmore's letters and, contemplating a visit to solicit Lady Northmore's permission to publish them, regards the prospect "as supreme as the treasure of the fat packet." But it is during this visit that pity overcomes Mrs. Hope, and she abandons her vindictive plan: "They were suddenly, on the spot, transformed for her by the depth of their misfortune, and she saw them, the great Northmores, as—of all things—consciously weak and flat." When Mrs. Hope returns to her home she "took out for the last time the faded fat packet. Sitting down by a receptacle daily emptied for the benefit of the dustman, she destroyed, one by one, the gems of the collection in which each piece had been a gem. She tore up, to the last scrap, Lord Northmore's letters. It would never be known now, as regards this series, either that they had been hoarded or that they had been sacrificed. And she was content so to let it rest." Ultimately, it is her sympathy for the abased Northmores that leads Mrs. Hope to destroy the letters of her former suitor—a recognition that in addition to the damage to personal reputation, there are the larger issues of how letters may subsequently reflect upon the family of the letter writer. As we shall see, this dual concern was very much on the minds of James's own family members when the time came to determine the disposition of his correspondence.

"My sole wish is to frustrate"

After James's death in 1916, his family discussed how best to remember and represent him. He had given his nephew Harry (Henry James III, the son of William James), explicit instructions in 1914:

> *My sole wish is to frustrate as utterly as possible the post-mortem exploiter—which, I know, is but so imperfectly possible. Still, one can do something, & I have long thought of launching, by a provision in my will, a curse not less explicit than Shakespeare's own on any such as try to move my bones. Your question determines me definitely to advert to the matter in my will—that is to declare my utter & absolute abhorrence of any attempted biography or the giving to the world by "the family," or by any person for whom my disapproval has any sanctity, of any part or parts of my private correspondence. One can discredit & dishonour such enterprises even if one can't prevent them, & as you are my sole & exclusive literary heir & executor you will doubtless be able to serve in some degree as a check & frustrator.*[33]

Continuing, however, the tradition of publishing a postmortem edition of letters as a sort of family memorial to the deceased relative, the James family chose Percy Lubbock, a young friend of Henry James, as editor. The family, led by Harry, proceeded with great caution and discretion, reviewing letters and deciding among themselves which ones were appropriate for inclusion in the edition. Their overall approach might best be characterized as highly selective and protective.

The First World War intervened to delay the publication of Lubbock's two-volume *Letters of Henry James*, which appeared in 1920. That edition included 403 letters, carefully selected by Lubbock with family approval, and sometimes with family editorial intervention—as the scholar Greg W. Zacharias notes, "many of the Henry James letters in the Houghton Library at Harvard, for example, show the blue-pencil marks probably made by a family member marking out some passages with brackets or parentheses and a direction to 'omit'." Portions of many of James's letters were, unbeknownst even to Lubbock, silently resected. The result was an edition that presented a particular version of James, one that most closely accorded with the James family's sense of the novelist and, presumably, one that they considered would not have greatly discontented their late uncle. As Leon Edel wrote in the introduction to his edition of James's letters, published over half a century later, "Lubbock's image of James was set for fifty years, the figure of the fictional lawgiver, as well as the gregarious expatriate. But James was never seen in these volumes as relaxed and unbuttoned: he is always in a top hat."[34]

Members of the James family and their descendants remained closely involved in the construction of the image of Henry James presented to later generations of readers. Beginning in the late 1930s, Harry James gave Leon Edel "all possible assistance and access to family papers."[35] Edel continued to work with Harry's brother, William (Billy), and later Billy's son John, as he worked on a biography and edition of James's letters. Later, Edel "allied himself to John's cousin, Alexander R. James."[36] Edel enjoyed an unrivaled and largely unchallenged monopoly of access to James's papers.[37] His edition of James's letters, published in four volumes between 1974 and 1984 and entitled *Henry James Letters*, contains 1,069 letters, over twice as many as published in Lubbock's 1920 edition. Just as Lubbock's edition of letters presented a family-sanctioned image of James, so Edel's edition and biography sought to present the author as the Master. As Zacharias noted, "Edel's version of James is just that—a version that stresses certain elements of his life and deemphasizes others" and his "particular selection of letters themselves might have been made in order to protect the family's sense of their relative's privacy."[38]

In some respects, Edel's hands were tied. He had made a somewhat Faustian bargain—free access to the letters brought with it a concomitant obligation to preserve and protect the James family's preferred image of their famous relative. He seems to have been realistic about the ultimate limitations of his edition of James's letters, acknowledging in his introduction that "the large James archives in many libraries will provide opportunities for amplification and further collections in the years to come."[39] Greg W. Zacharias has estimated that there are more than 10,400 extant James letters, and in 2006 a new edition of James's letters was begun.[40] *The Complete Letters of Henry James* is edited by a team of Jamesians led by Greg W. Zacharias and Michael Anesko. This ambitious edition, the early volumes of which are now in print, aims to provide transcriptions of all "known letters, notes and telegrams . . . in a way that helps readers read them more like the letters James's correspondents would have read."[41] The editors have drawn upon the Morgan's collection of James letters for this edition and recent acquisitions will, eventually, appear in print within its pages. As Philip Horne noted, "even relatively minor letters contribute to the jigsaw, refresh our sense of the endless interest of his life and career" and, in this regard, "the canon of James's published writings is still expanding."[42]

It is within this larger context of authorial self-erasure—brought about by James's decision to destroy much of what we would now regard as his literary archive—that the Morgan's collection of Henry James manuscripts and letters should be assessed.

Henry James Comes to Pierpont Morgan's Library

In the Morgan archives there is a book bearing the gilt-stamped arms of John Pierpont Morgan. It is ornately bound in brown leather—elaborately gold-tooled and inlaid with lighter brown leather—the work of the binder Marguerite Duprez Lahey. This book, titled *J. P. Morgan et Amicorum,* is the manuscript guest book of visitors to Pierpont Morgan's library, spanning the years 1908 through 1996 (Fig. 4).[43] This guest book was kept for many years in the North Room of the library, which is currently used as exhibition space. The North Room was the office of Belle Greene, Pierpont Morgan's librarian and, later, the first director of the Morgan. She began to keep the visitors' book in 1908, on behalf of her employer, and it records the names of all the notable individuals who visited the library over the course of the twentieth century. Under the date *January 18, 1911,* the reader's eye falls upon the distinctive signature of Henry James (Fig. 5).

There is no evidence that James ever met Pierpont Morgan, either during his visit to the great financier's library in January 1911, or when, in 1907, he visited the art galleries at Princes Gate, Morgan's family home in London.[44] James was, however, quite familiar with Pierpont Morgan's father, Junius Spencer Morgan, having been a guest at Dover House, London, in the 1880s, sometimes with Alice Mason, at other times with his close friend Jonathan Sturges, or occasionally alone.[45] Jean Strouse noted that Junius S. Morgan "entertained legions of guests—among them Henry James, John Singer Sargent, the William Wetmore Storys."[46] James can scarcely have imagined, when he visited the library on that cold Wednesday in January 1911, that a

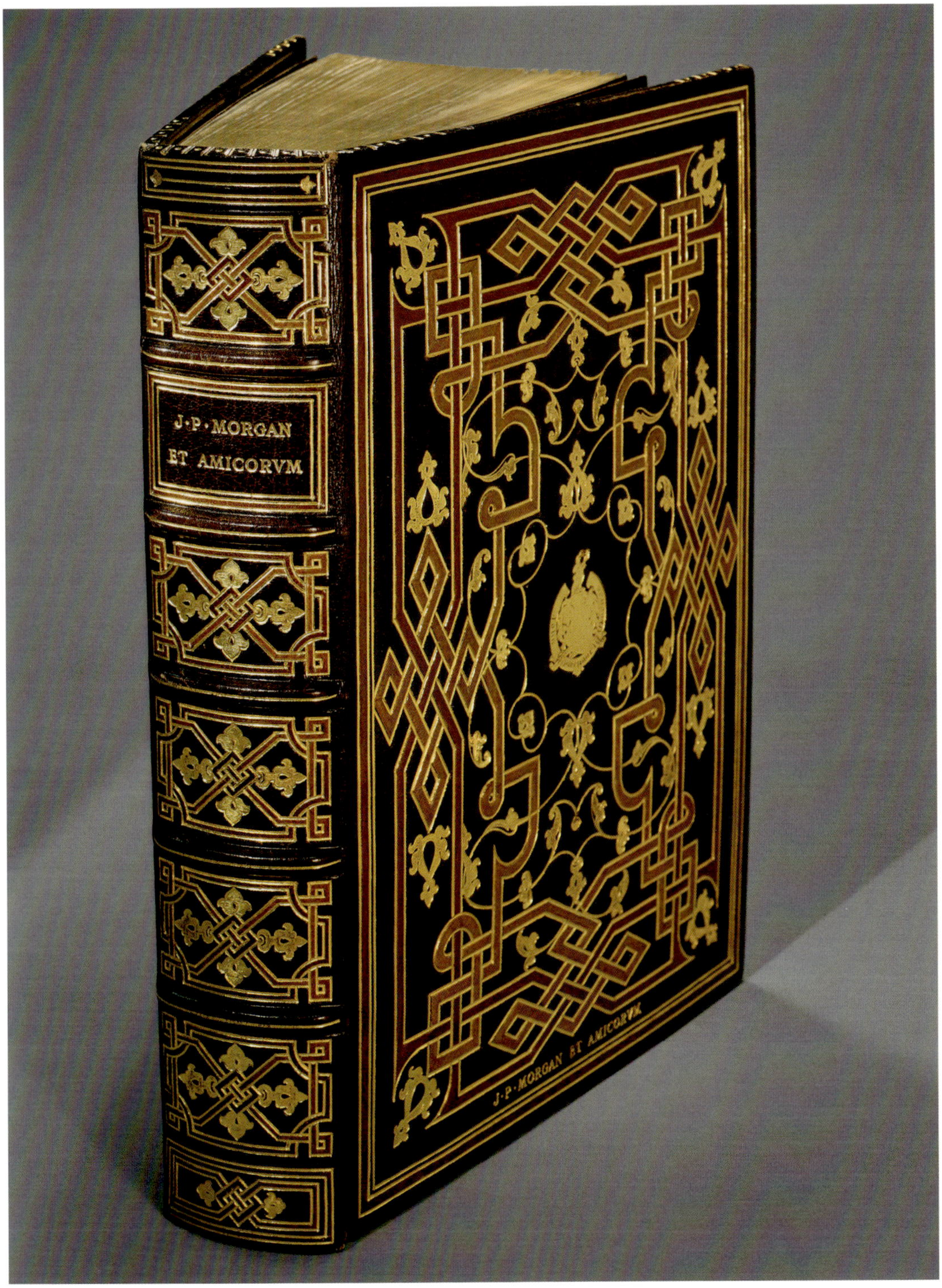

FIG. 4. *J. P. Morgan et Amicorum,* 1908–96, The Morgan Library & Museum, New York.

was "'seeing' my native country with a vengeance & hearing it too & feeling & tasting it in a hundred interesting and extraordinary ways." On traveling to Boston, he "gave [himself] up to 4 or 5 days to the dental drill & other refinements of torture" before returning to his public engagements. Writing about the success of his lecture tour, he reported that he had been particularly well-received in St. Louis, where he said he was "positively & preposterously caressed by the people." He found the people of St. Louis "much more cordial & demonstrative than we of the fishy east." Continuing his letter on 16 March from "this unspeakable Chicago," he told Mrs. Sullivan that he had traveled "to strange places, have 'lectured', feasted (all but fatally), speak [*sic*] last night at the Catholic University of Notre Dame," and that "a deluge of hospitality has floated me as if I were a second Noah, stored with animal & vegetable food. Again I seem to swagger—but I don't—I only stagger." He concluded his letter by asking Mrs. Sullivan to "Give my love, please, to Mr. [Frederick] Sturges, & tell him how I wish there were again something in my life as sweetly irresponsible as those morning strolls down to that pier of soft breezes & agitated female spectators to see the sharks, or whatever, landed by the amateur anglers." As is the case with so much of James's correspondence in the Morgan's collection, this letter conveys a vivid sense of time and place through the master novelist's eye for memorable details. The amused disinterest of "the sharks, or whatever" is a reminder of James's humor and alerts us to how fresh and contemporary his epistolary voice often is.

Henry James in the Gordon N. Ray Collection

In 1991 the Morgan acquired the typescript of two chapters (17 and 18) of *What Maisie Knew,* which—with the exception of seven pages—is all that survives of James's draft of this novel (Fig. 7).[50] In 1897, after experiencing prolonged pain in his right wrist, James purchased a typewriter and began to dictate his fiction and parts of his correspondence and fiction to a stenographer.[51] Whether or not this change in compositional method was a significant factor in the evolution of the author's complex late style, as some critics have argued, it introduced new rhythms into his prose. This typescript provides insights into his construction and revision of the narrative. Purchased with funds endowed by the collector Gordon N. Ray, it represents a significant addition to the Gordon N. Ray collection of English and French literature and illustrated books, which was bequeathed to the Morgan in 1987.

Ray's library—which comprised thousands of books, typescripts, corrected proofs and other materials, as well as approximately ten thousand letters by various authors—included the revised typescript of *Notes of a Son and Brother* (MA 7319), which, at 523 pages, is the most extensive James manuscript in the Morgan's collection (Fig. 8). This typescript has autograph corrections in ink as well as directions to the printer in red and blue pencil throughout (Figs. 9 and 10). James was a special interest of Gordon N. Ray; he had published, in 1958, *Henry James and H. G. Wells,* written with Leon Edel. In addition to the typescript of *Notes of a Son and Brother,* Ray's collection also included hundreds of first editions of James's fiction, published in England and the United States, as well as seven autograph letters to various recipients.

Since the bequest, in addition to the acquisition of the typescript of *What Maisie Knew,* numerous unpublished autograph letters have also been added to the Ray collection. These include two letters written at moments of particular historical significance. In 1989 the Morgan acquired a letter from James to Alice Runnells James, the wife of James's nephew William James, Jr. Written on 20

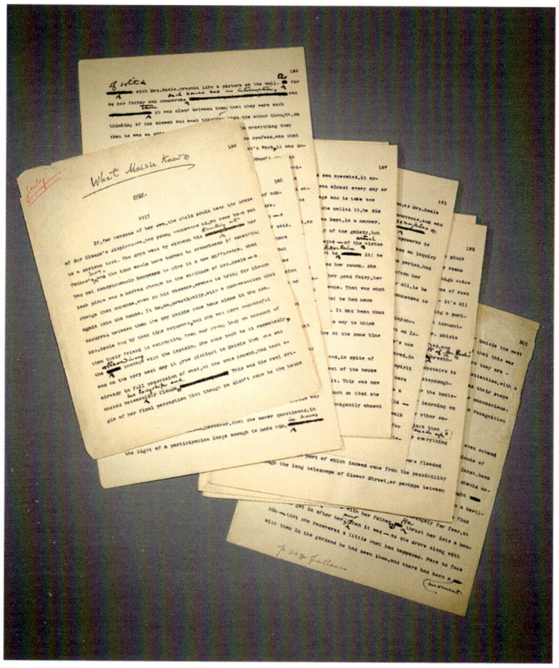

FIG. 7. Henry James, typed manuscript of *What Maisie Knew*, [1897], The Morgan Library & Museum, New York.

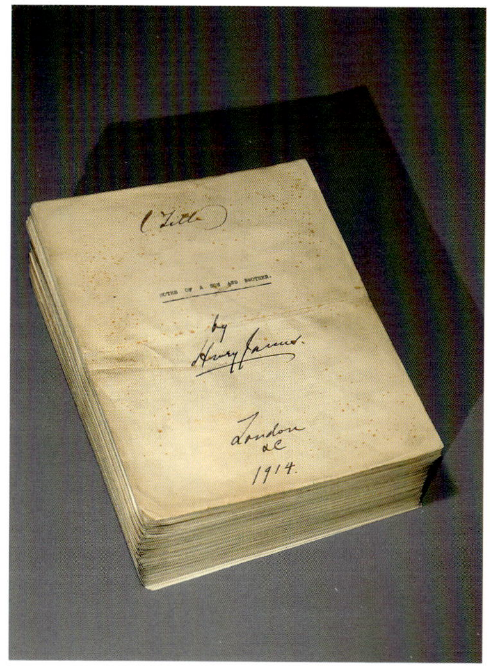

FIG. 8. Henry James, typed manuscript of *Notes of a Son and Brother*, 1914, The Morgan Library & Museum, New York.

August 1914, this letter (MA 4640; Figs. 11 and 12) records James's anguished reaction to the outbreak of the First World War. It is one of his most heartfelt and orthographically expressive letters, its handwriting, syntax, and punctuation conveying to the reader how severely shocked James had been by recent events. Explaining to his American relative the war's impact on him and his friends in Britain, he wrote:

It defies all description, it beggars all comment, I mean the horrible violence & shock of the change of consciousness that overtook us in a single night at the end of July—only 3 weeks ago—does; with the formidably, the terrifically altered world that we have been living in ever since, & that we are evidently to live in more & more. The sudden break with the past, the sudden unspeakable tension & earthshake, at once, of the present, are overwhelming, & we live along from day to day & hour to hour as in face of an enormous series of interrogation-points ??????—the most formidable that could be thought of.

A further addition to the Ray Collection was made in 2004 when the Morgan acquired an important unpublished letter from James to Émile Zola.[52] Written (in French) on 24 February 1898, at the height of the Dreyfus scandal, James praised his fellow novelist for his "rare and

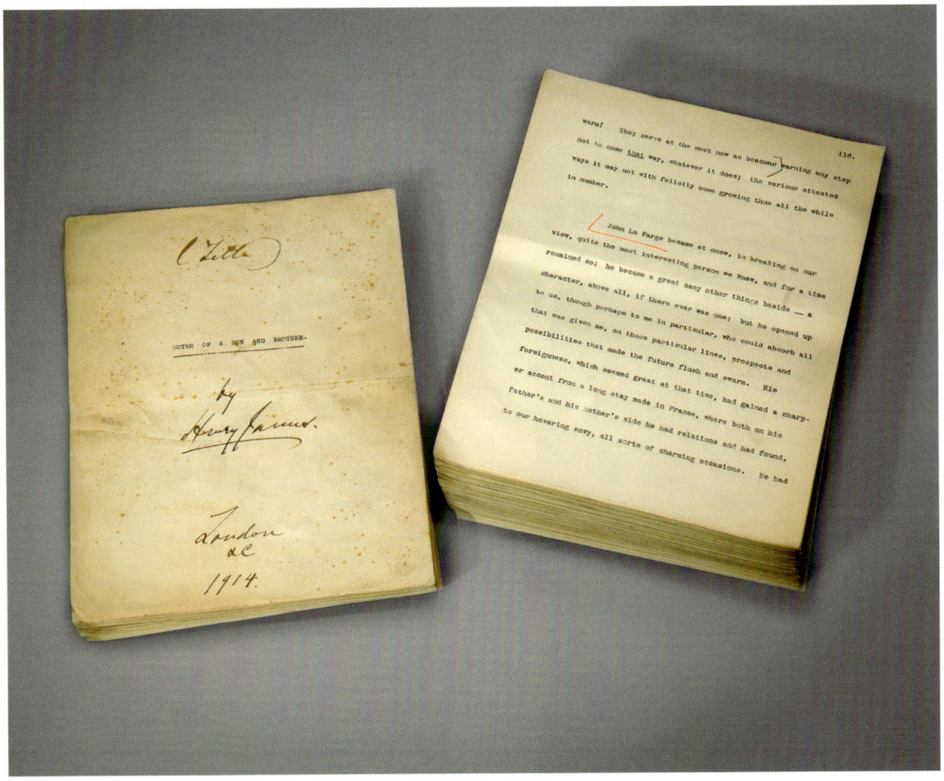

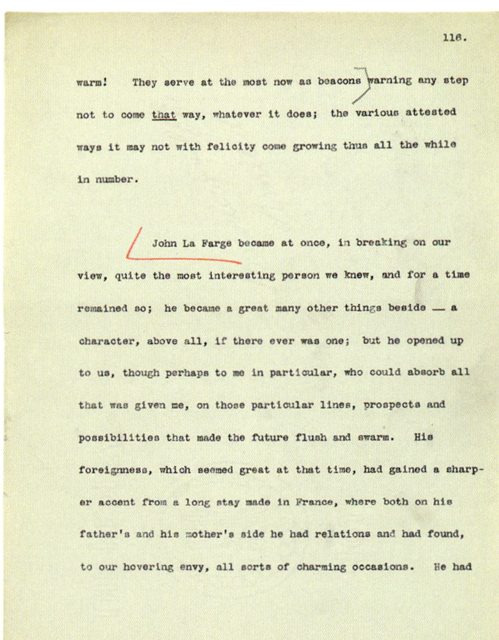
116.

warm! They serve at the most now as beacons warning any step not to come that way, whatever it does; the various attested ways it may not with felicity come growing thus all the while in number.

John La Farge became at once, in breaking on our view, quite the most interesting person we knew, and for a time remained so; he became a great many other things beside — a character, above all, if there ever was one; but he opened up to us, though perhaps to me in particular, who could absorb all that was given me, on those particular lines, prospects and possibilities that made the future flush and swarm. His foreignness, which seemed great at that time, had gained a sharper accent from a long stay made in France, where both on his father's and his mother's side he had relations and had found, to our hovering envy, all sorts of charming occasions. He had

FIG. 9. Henry James, title page and page 116 of the typed manuscript of *Notes of a Son and Brother,* 1914, The Morgan Library & Museum, New York.

FIG. 10. Henry James, page 116 of the typed manuscript of *Notes of a Son and Brother,* 1914, The Morgan Library & Museum, New York.

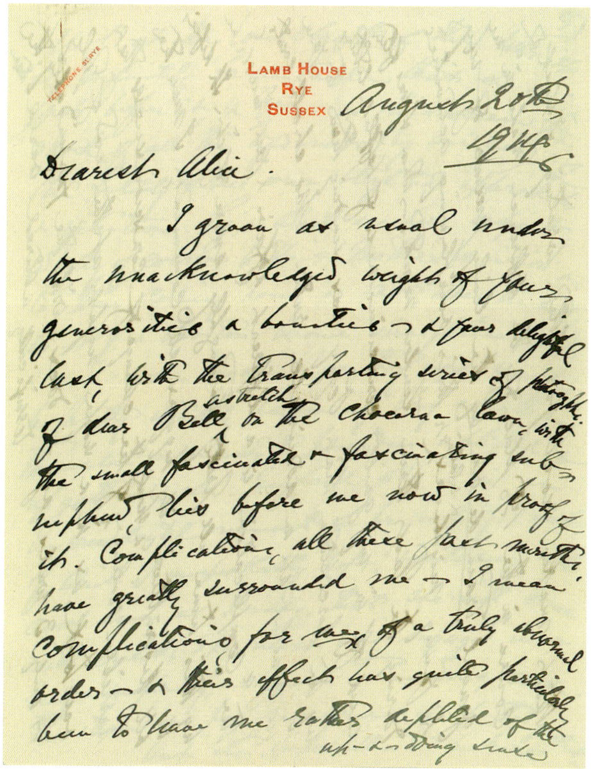

Lamb House
Rye
Sussex

August 20th 1914

Dearest Alice.

I groan as usual under the unacknowledged weight of your generosities & bounties - & your delightful last, with the transporting series of photographs of dear Bill astretch on the Chocorua lawn, with the small fascinated & fascinating sub-nephew, lies before me now in proof of it. Complications, all these past months, have greatly surrounded me - I mean complications for us of a truly abnormal order - & their effect has quite particularly been to leave me rather [illegible] of the [illegible]

FIG. 11. Henry James, page 1 of autograph letter, signed, to Alice Runnells James, 20 August 1914, The Morgan Library & Museum, New York.

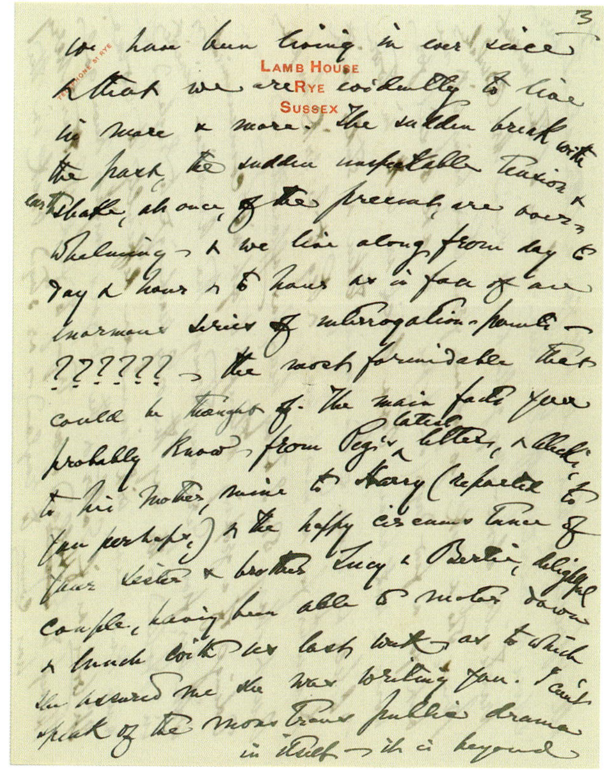

3

Lamb House
Rye
Sussex

we have been living in ever since & that we are constantly to live in more & more. The sudden break with the past, the sudden unspeakable tension, at once, of the present, are overwhelming, & we live along from day to day & hour to hour as in face of an enormous series of interrogation-points - ?????? - the most formidable that could be thought of. The main facts you probably know, from Peggy's latest letter, & Alec's to his mother, mine to Harry (repeated to you perhaps) & the happy circumstance of your sister & brother Lucy & Bertie, delightful couple, having been able to motor down & lunch with us last week, as to which she assured me she was writing you. I can't speak of the monstrous public drama in itself - it is beyond

FIG. 12. Henry James, page 3 of autograph letter, signed, to Alice Runnells James, 20 August 1914, The Morgan Library & Museum, New York.

solitary courage" in exposing the Dreyfus affair and told him that "all our colleagues of the pen . . . and of the soul" are joined in a "communal outcry," and all of England and America are "inflamed and indignant" about Dreyfus's treatment.

The largest tranche of unpublished letters to be added to the Ray collection was acquired in 1996 and relates to the composition of James's novella *The Lesson of the Master.* These fifteen autograph letters and notes (MA 5004) are addressed to Harry Quilter, editor of *The Universal Review,* an ambitious and short-lived periodical that Quilter had founded in January 1888. The letters were written between 29 May 1888 and 17 May 1892 and provide an informative snapshot of the author's negotiations with the editor, who published the novella in the July and August 1888 issues. When James sent the first installment on 28 June, he cautioned Quilter: "Please don't be frightened at the apparent length: it will make but a little more than twenty pages of print." He promised the second half "in a week or two." The letters reveal that James requested several deadline extensions in order to complete this work. In his note of 17 July 1888, he explained: "I am a little delayed by my having undertaken to tell rather a complicated story in a small compass—& am condensing, condensing." On 20 July, he sought a further extension because of illness: "I lost a couple of days work through having been shockingly, though fortunately not fatally, poisoned, by some vile unknown

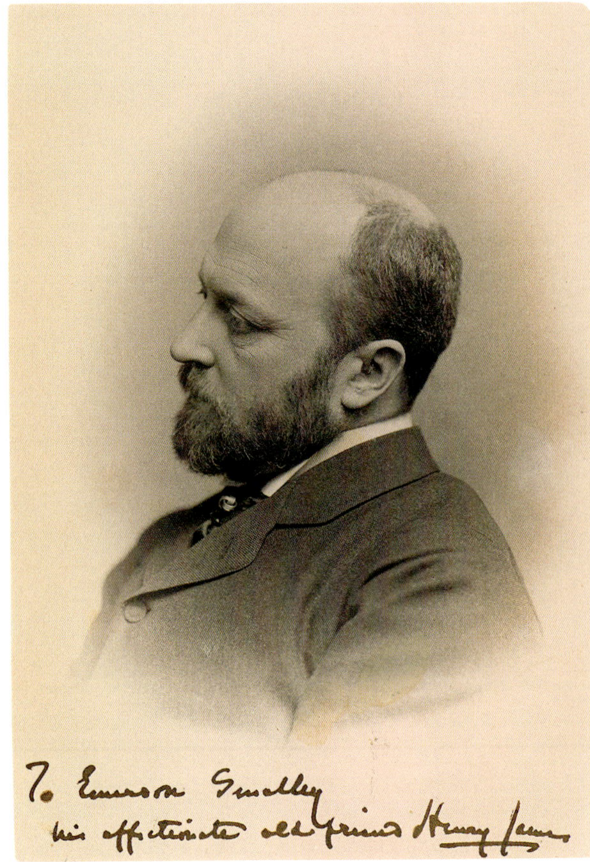

FIG. 13. Cabinet photograph of Henry James, inscribed to Emerson Smalley, [1890s], The Morgan Library & Museum, New York.

substance that I ate at a dinner party. In other words I have been beastly sick & incompetent." He promised Quilter "You shall have, positively and absolutely have, my copy by the 25th so help me God!"

When James submitted the second installment of the story on July 24th, he cautioned the editor in what by then must have been familiar terms: "don't be scared at its apparent bulk—it is long—considerably longer than the 1st part; but by no means as long as it looks." James ascribed its "apparent bulk" to his "thick paper and sprawling hand" and told the editor that he had made "heroic sacrifices to cut out thirty pages this blessed day. Therefore the number on the last sheet doesn't represent the real quantity. So far as it does take up space I hope you will consider that it occupies it creditably—that is that the thing is good enough to be a little indulged." The psychological insight and devastating wit of *The Lesson of the Master* has led it to be regarded by many critics as among James's finest work.

The later letters in the group are concerned with other writing projects and the reprinting of the novella. On 25 February 1890, James wrote to Quilter turning down the offer of a journalistic assignment. He explained: "I am much obliged to you for the 'chance,' but, frankly speaking, it doesn't irresistibly appeal to me. I am engaged with other work & of a different kind which commands all my limited resources." He concluded his letter: "Lastly, my love of literature is so jealous a passion that, despicably perhaps, I dislike more & more to write illustrated articles—people never regard—seriously—the text." James subsequently denied Quilter permission to reprint *The Lesson of the Master* in an anthology. On 11 May 1892, he wrote: "I am very sorry to say that I don't see my way to assenting to your proposal in regard to your republishing 'The Lesson of the Master.' The tale forms the principal feature of a volume lately published, to which it gives its title and to which it would be no benefit that this story should be known to form part of another volume.[53] Moreover, frankly speaking, I greatly prefer that my stories, when reprinted, should not form part of any volume but my own. In short the request does not, to my regret, commend itself—in my view—to an enlightened conception of my interests, literary and commercial." Quilter seems to have written in an attempt to persuade him otherwise, but James's last letter (of this group) to the editor, written on 17 May 1892, restates his decision to decline the request.

Henry James in the Carter Burden Collection of American Literature

The most recent acquisition of a significant number of books, manuscripts, and letters by Henry James came with the gift of the Carter Burden Collection of American Literature. Between 1973 and 1996, Carter Burden, a cultural benefactor and former New York City councilman, assembled the greatest collection of modern American literature in private hands. Burden regarded James—alongside Hemingway and Faulkner—as a foundational figure in his collection. As Burden once wrote, "I'm happy to tell you that my collection of these three gentlemen are [*sic*] also the richest, most extensive, and certainly the most valuable parts [*sic*] of my entire collection." In 1997, among the many treasures in the first installment of the collection donated by Burden's family, the Morgan received the typed manuscript draft of "The Novel in *The Ring and the Book*," (MA 6092) with James's autograph revisions. This working draft of a 1912 essay on Robert Browning's poem is also something of a chance survival; it was salvaged from a wastepaper basket by James's typist, Theodora Bosanquet (Fig. 14).

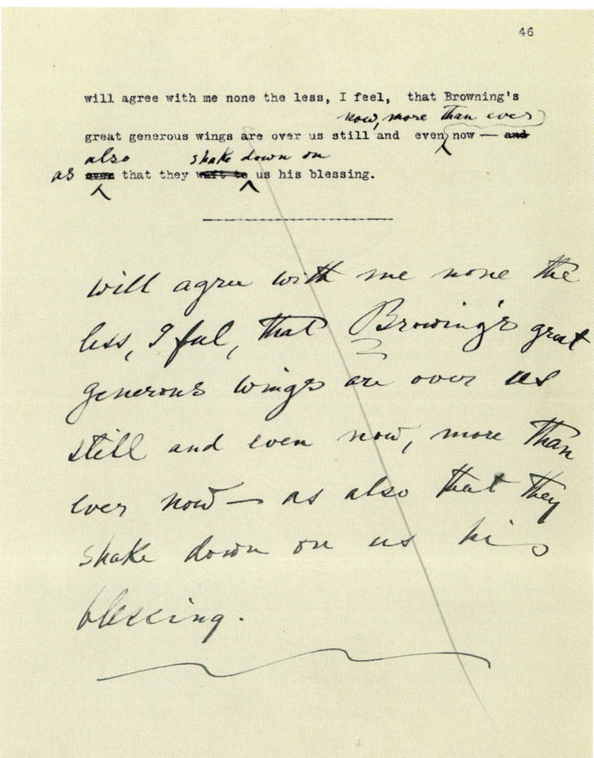

46

will agree with me none the less, I feel, that Browning's great generous wings are over us still and even now, more than ever now — as also that they shake down on us his blessing.

will agree with me none the less, I feel, that Browning's great generous wings are over us still and even now, more than ever now — as also that they shake down on us his blessing.

FIG. 14. Henry James, page 46 of the revised typescript of "The Novel in *The Ring and the Book*," undated, The Morgan Library & Museum, New York.

The Carter Burden Collection includes important copies of books by James. Among the most important is James's personal copy of *The American: A Comedy in Four Acts*. This stage adaptation of his 1877 novel, in original wrappers, is the first impression of an edition of fewer than ten copies published by William Heinemann in 1891. James signed the front cover and recorded his annotations, corrections, and final revisions throughout the text as he prepared for the second impression. Only eight copies are known to survive—Edel suspected that perhaps only fifteen copies of the first impression and perhaps twenty copies of the second impression were issued.

Among association copies, two others stand out: James's two-volume set of his short story selection *The Madonna of the Future and Other Tales* that he presented to his sister Alice in September 1879, in advance of its official publication in October 1879, and an inscribed copy of *The Golden Bowl* (1904) that he gave to Walter Berry, a lifelong friend of Edith Wharton. Berry kept this inscribed copy with a postcard that James and Wharton had written to him as they motored through France in 1907 (Fig. 15).

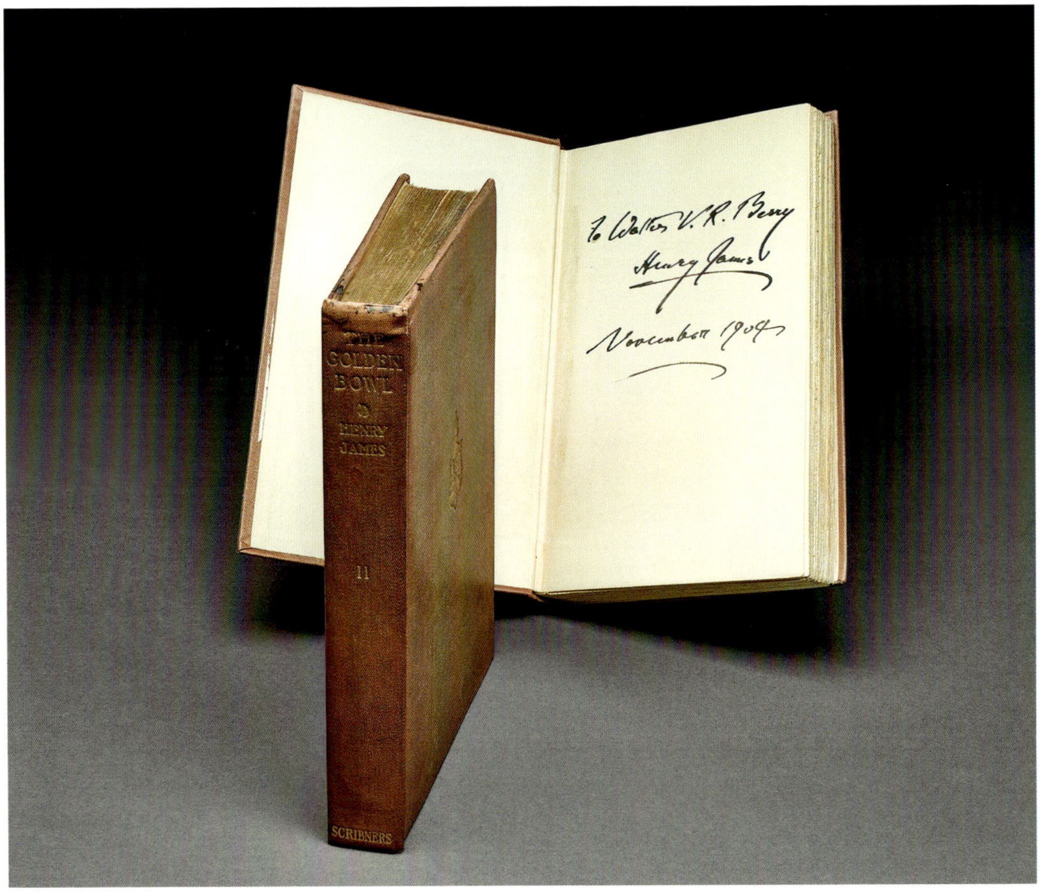

FIG. 15. Henry James, *The Golden Bowl*, New York, 1904, The Morgan Library & Museum, New York.

The Carter Burden Collection also includes fourteen unpublished Henry James autograph letters. The earliest is written to Madame Helena Modjeska, dated 17 November 1891 (MA 5459). James wrote this long letter to the actress, who had expressed interest in the starring role in *The American* if there were to be a New York production of the play. James identified numerous problems with the London production and led her away from this play toward the role of Mrs. Vibert in another three-act play titled *Mrs. Vibert* that he was writing at the time. It was later retitled *Tenants* but was never produced. Of his new play he told Modjeska that, "I am going—in the light of some later experience that I have had—to subject it to a minute revision." He concluded his long letter by saying that "I should particularly like my information to be surrounded with inviolate secresy [*sic*]."

Burden also acquired two small groups of unpublished letters to augment his extensive collection of first editions of James's work. The larger of these two groups (MA 6091.1–8) comprises eight letters written between 24 February 1896 and 8 November 1900 from James to Clement K. Shorter, editor of *The Illustrated London News*. The chief interest of these letters, most of which date from the spring and summer of 1896, is the insight they offer into the publication of the novel *The Other House*, which James was writing at that time and was serialized in the weekly magazine in thirteen installments from 4 July to 26 September 1896. The letters offer a glimpse of the kind of negotiations James engaged in with journal editors, as he sought the most beneficial terms for his work, accounted for his writing process, and reported on its progress.

In the earliest letter to Shorter, James agreed "to meet [Shorter's] requirement of a 'love-story'" but noted that the sum offered in payment is "less than [he was] in the habit of receiving." Nevertheless, James offered to give Shorter "the English serial rights of the work in question for £300." The subsequent letters reveal something of James's attitudes toward mass market publication and again voice his distrust of illustration: when he sent Shorter the first installment on 6 May, he wrote that "I like so little to be illustrated (I resent it so, amiably speaking, on behalf of good prose and real writing)." He also commented on the title of the story, and promised to send Shorter another batch of writing quickly so that "the whole thing shall practically be in your hands by the time the beginning appears." Six of the letters span the period during which the novel was written and published, but in a somewhat later letter, written on 5 April 1898, James asked Shorter if *The Illustrated London News* would be interested in purchasing, for "£300 on delivery of the complete work," the English serial rights to *The Awkward Age,* which he was publishing in the United States in *Harper's Weekly.*

The second, smaller group (MA 5460–64) consists of five letters written to the English novelist Marie Belloc Lowndes, sister of Hilaire Belloc, between 6 February and 17 August 1915. The most significant unpublished letter in this group (MA 5462; Figs. 16 and 17) was written on 27 April 1915 and concerns the death of Rupert Brooke, whom Belloc Lowndes had first met at a lunch at James's house when the poet was still largely unknown. Brooke was commissioned into the Royal Naval Volunteer Reserves and died of sepsis en route to Gallipoli. James poured out his sorrow in this letter, thanking Belloc Lowndes "for feeling with me about the deplorable, the infinitely detestable extinction of our splendid young Rupert Brooke. I knew him enough exceedingly to prize him and I find in his death an unmitigated pang. I confess that I have no philosophy, nor piety nor patience, no art of reflection nor theory of compensation, to meet things so hideous, so cruel and so bête; they are just unspeakably horrible and irremediable to me, and I stare at them with angry and with almost blighted eyes. He was of an exquisite poetic value and personal charm. It's purely black!"[54]

After the outbreak of the First World War, in a declaration of loyalty to his adopted country and to protest President Wilson's refusal to enter the war on behalf of Britain and France, James applied for British citizenship. Having lived in Britain for the past forty years, his request was granted on 28 July 1915. Writing to Belloc Lowndes a few weeks afterward—his 17 August 1915 letter is, chronologically, the latest by James in the Morgan's collection—he commented on all of the good wishes he had received on gaining British citizenship, telling her that "though I pretty well thought I should like doing what I have done, I find it agrees with me still better than I have imagined."[55]

"A mine of gold, a precious independent work"

Perhaps the best example of adventitious survival is the typescript of the scenario for *The Ambassadors,* modestly titled "Project of a Novel" (MA 3140.1; Fig. 18). In terms of its literary significance, this is the most important James manuscript in the Morgan's collection. Philip Horne's

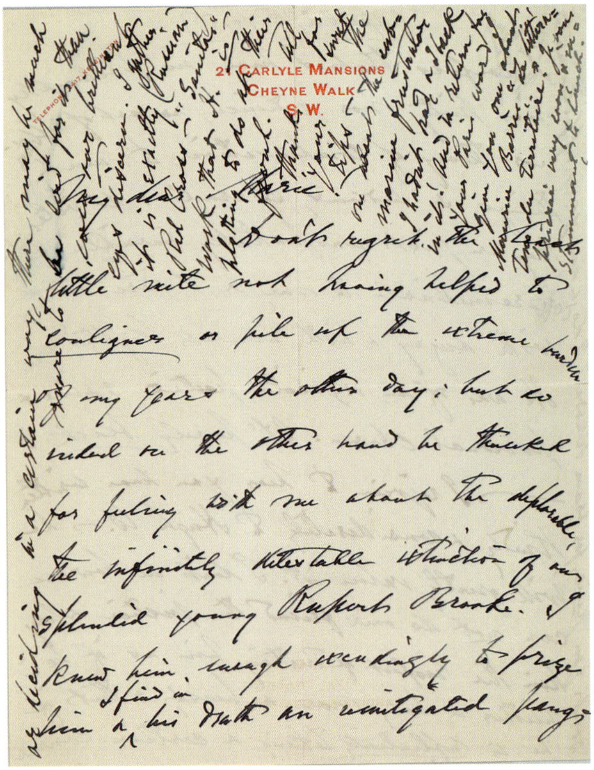

FIG. 16. Henry James, page 1 of autograph letter, signed, to Marie Belloc Lowndes, 27 April 1915, The Morgan Library & Museum, New York.

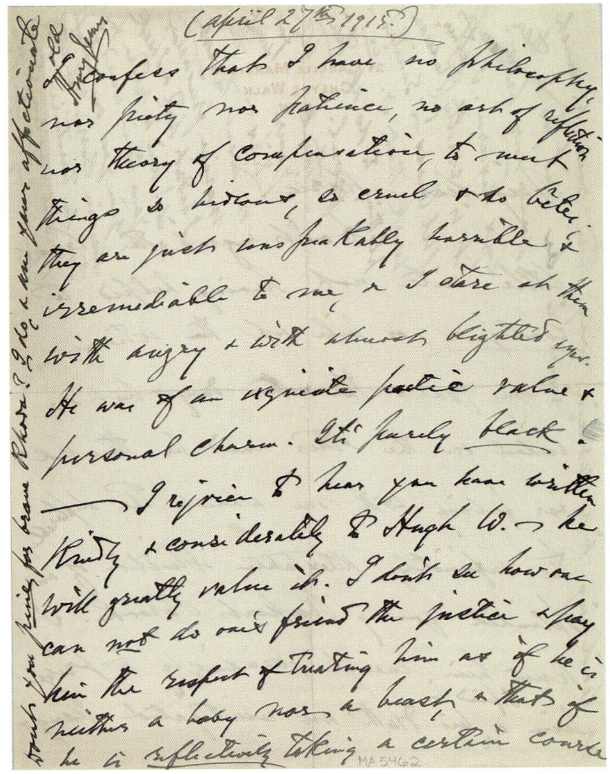

FIG. 17. Henry James, page 2 of autograph letter, signed, to Marie Belloc Lowndes, 27 April 1915, The Morgan Library & Museum, New York.

assessment of James's notebooks is equally applicable to the scenario for *The Ambassadors* because it, too, constitutes "a treasury of insights into the workings of James's imagination" and contains "passages of such extraordinary brilliance and suggestiveness" that it amounts to "a masterwork in [its] own right."[56]

In *The Death of the Lion*, Neil Paraday, the fictitious author in James's short story, speaks of a scenario he has written for the new novel he is contemplating. This synopsis, "full . . . of fine maturities," he asserts, is "really in summarised splendour a mine of gold, a precious independent work." James's disappointment as a dramatist—which culminated in the humiliating failure of his play *Guy Domville* when it was produced in the West End in 1895—taught him the usefulness of drafting a scenario and, accordingly, he incorporated the lessons of that failure into his creative process. Thus, from the late 1890s, it was James's practice to dictate an elaborate outline sketch prior to writing a novel that subsequently assisted him with the construction of the work. This scenario would also serve to provide a synopsis for his agent as well as any editor who might need to acquire a clear impression of the work when considering it for magazine serialization or book publication.

In a candid letter about his writing process that he sent to H. G. Wells on 15 November 1902, James revealed that he would invariably draw up "a plan for *myself*, as copious and developed as possible." He told Wells that he believed the typescript synopsis for *The Ambassadors* had been destroyed after submission to *Harper's* magazine. In

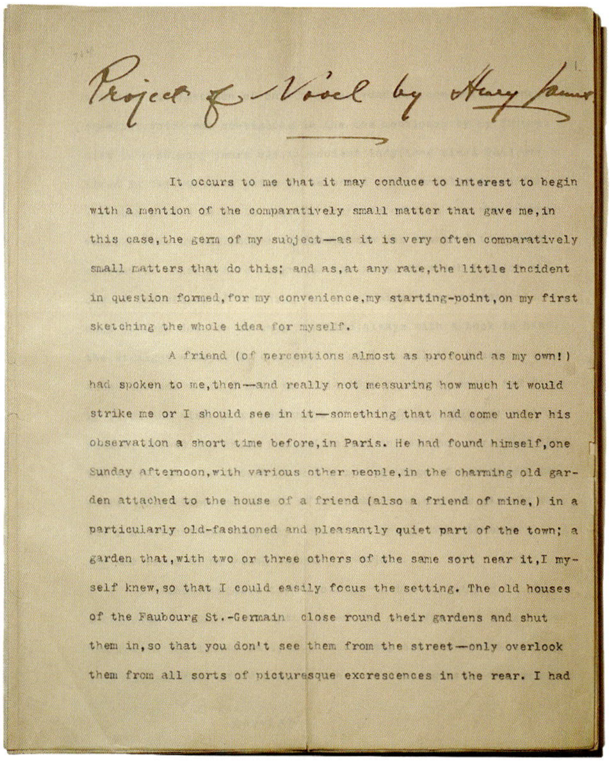

Project of Novel by Henry James

1.

It occurs to me that it may conduce to interest to begin with a mention of the comparatively small matter that gave me,in this case,the germ of my subject—as it is very often comparatively small matters that do this; and as,at any rate,the little incident in question formed,for my convenience,my starting-point,on my first sketching the whole idea for myself.

A friend (of perceptions almost as profound as my own!) had spoken to me,then—and really not measuring how much it would strike me or I should see in it—something that had come under his observation a short time before,in Paris. He had found himself,one Sunday afternoon,with various other people,in the charming old garden attached to the house of a friend (also a friend of mine,) in a particularly old-fashioned and pleasantly quiet part of the town; a garden that,with two or three others of the same sort near it,I myself knew,so that I could easily focus the setting. The old houses of the Faubourg St.-Germain close round their gardens and shut them in,so that you don't see them from the street—only overlook them from all sorts of picturesque excrescences in the rear. I had

FIG. 18. Henry James, page 1 of "Project of a Novel," 1 September 1900, The Morgan Library & Museum, New York.

this mistaken belief, he also informed Wells that "those wondrous and copious preliminary statements (of my fictions that are to be) don't really exist in any form in which they can be imparted."

Wells knew that Joseph Conrad had seen the scenario for *The Wings of the Dove* and had asked if James might share that typescript with him. But, in the same letter, James reported: "*that* synopsis too has been destroyed; it was returned from the U.S., but I had then no occasion to preserve it." This tells us, of course, that James was in the habit of occasionally destroying his papers well before the great conflagrations of 1909 and 1915.

James's letter to Wells is particularly useful in clarifying our understanding of the relation of the scenario to the finished work as well as the evolution of James's late style. He characterized his synopsis of *The Ambassadors* as a "voluminous effusion" that constituted only "a preliminary *private* outpouring."[57] The scenario was, for James, something "so extremely familiar, confidential, and intimate—in the form of an interminable garrulous letter addressed to my own fond fancy—that, though I always for easy reference, have it carefully typed, it isn't a thing I would willingly expose to any eye but my own. And even *then*, sometimes, I shrink!" James expressed some bitterness that his novel had not yet been published—he declared "I shall not again draw up detailed & explicit plans for unconvinced & ungracious editors"—and ended his letter to Wells with an appeal to "pardon my too many words."[58]

Contrary to James's belief, the ninety-page typescript scenario for *The Ambassadors* was not destroyed. It first surfaced in 1925 and, while the precise logistics of its preservation remain unclear, it has been part of the Morgan's collection since 1974, when Mr. and Mrs. A. Hyatt Mayor donated it. Prior to that, provenance records indicate that the earliest traced owner was Joseph B. Ames of Morristown, New Jersey. Along with James's typescript, there is a letter from Percy Lubbock to Ames, written on 11 February 1925 (MA 3140.7), in which the editor states: "I am very glad to learn that you have found & rescued it. Will you think it a great nuisance if I ask whether I might some time see a copy of it? It would of course interest me immensely; for nothing else of quite the same kind has survived & it must throw light upon his methods of work etc." Ames did not hold on to James's typescript for long: in 1929 Bernard Bandler purchased it at auction in New York for $200. Bandler subsequently gave the typescript to Mr. and Mrs. A. Hyatt Mayor in 1932 (Fig. 19).[59]

It would not be an overstatement to say that the typescript scenario of *The Ambassadors* is, indeed, "a mine

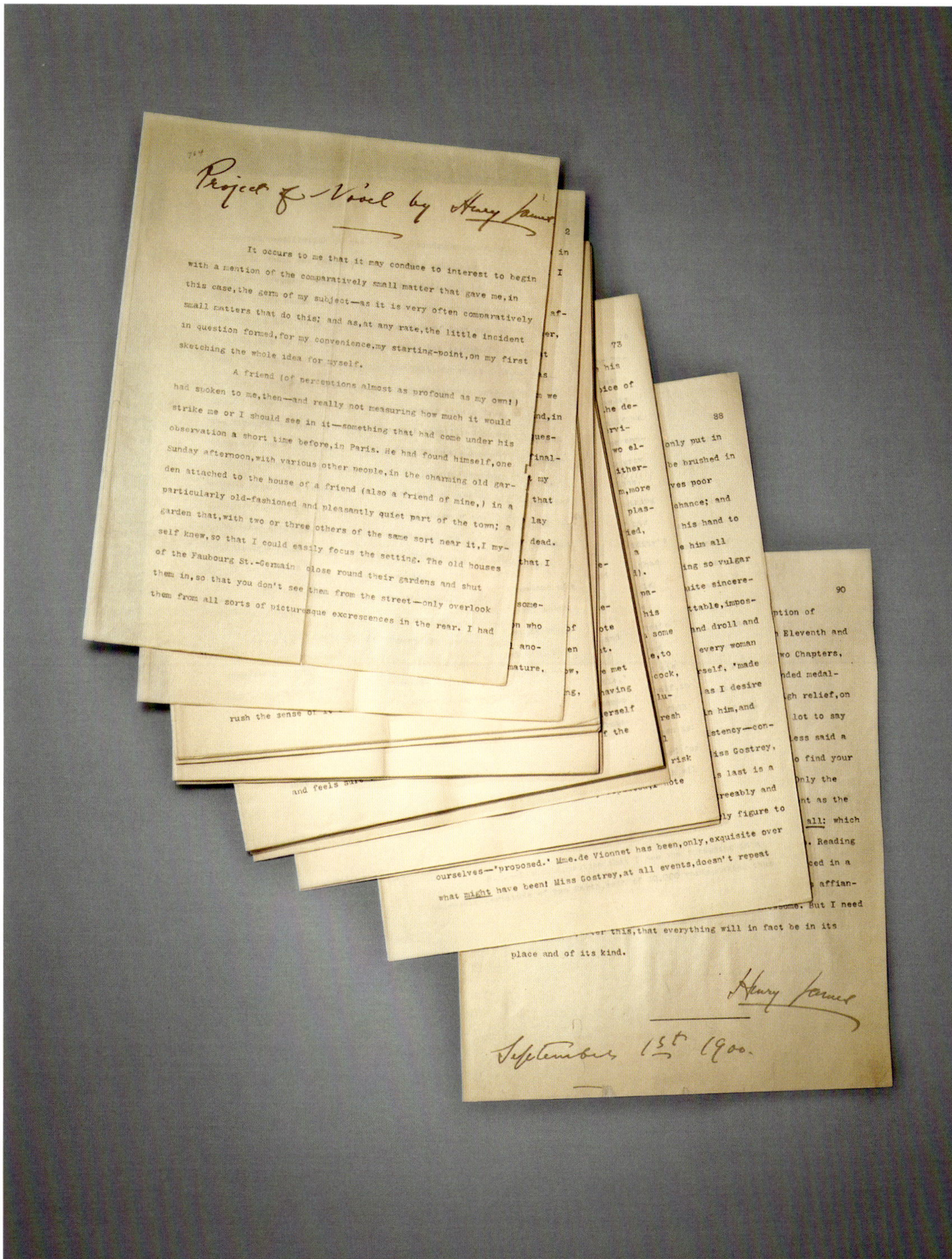

FIG. 19. Henry James, pages of "Project of a Novel," 1 September 1900, The Morgan Library & Museum, New York.

of gold, a precious independent work." It is, in fact, the only surviving scenario of a novel by James. As F. O. Matthiessen and Kenneth B. Murdock (the editors who first published it in 1947) explained, this synopsis "lets us have, for the work he regarded as his best, four successive visions of it: his first record of its 'germ' [in his notebooks], this detailed synopsis, the novel itself, and the preface that he composed six or seven years after the book's completion." The synopsis offers readers a unique insight into the published work because it "contains James's amplest account of how a 'dropped seed' germinated . . . the synopsis itself is the most substantial example of the thoroughness with which he worked out his *donnée*."[60]

The chance survival of this typescript—James probably would have destroyed it along with the synopsis of *The Wings of the Dove*, had it been returned to him from the publisher—also sheds light on the first serial publication of the novel. Alongside James's synopsis, there are other papers that constitute a miniature archive, including a typed letter from William D. Fitts of Harper & Brothers, London (MA 3140.2); Henry Mills Alden's reader's report of James's synopsis (MA 3140.3); a letter from James B. Pinker (Henry James's agent) arranging the terms for publishing *The Ambassadors* (MA 3140.4);[61] a manuscript note, presumably from someone at *Harper's*, discussing publication terms (MA 3140.5); a typed copy of a letter from James to Harper & Brothers (MA 3140.6); and the 1925 letter from Percy Lubbock to Joseph Ames discussing James's outline for *The Ambassadors* (MA 3140.7) mentioned above.

These letters provide unparalleled insight into the background and earliest reception of *The Ambassadors*. Writing on 19 September 1900, Fitts informed George B. M. Harvey—who had, only a few months before, been appointed president of *Harper's*—that:

> *Mr. James has begun work upon his story, a scenario of which I am sending you. After you have read it, please hand it to Mr. Alden. Mr James is now "pegging away" at the story and can let you have it by the end of the year. I don't know when I have been so pleased and satisfied with a synopsis as with this one of James's. It is exactly what I wanted him to do. The American life in it, transplanted to Paris, where James is absolutely at home, will I am sure appeal to a large audience in the United States.*
>
> *Mr. James is keen upon the work and I feel sure from his letters and talks with me, that you will have one of the best novels written by him, and it looks to me as if it ought to be become one of the books of the year. At all events, after some months of thought and consultation this is the point at which James and I have arrived.*
>
> *I am sure Mr. James would be glad to receive a letter of appreciation from you about the story. It would be helpful if you came into sympathetic relations with authors over here. As yet they only know of you by name and as a successful financier, but I should like to have them know you from the literary side.*[62]

Harvey duly passed along the typescript to Alden, the reader for *Harper's*. So much for "sympathetic relations"—the reader's report, described by Matthiessen and Murdock as "a masterpiece of miscomprehension," attests to James's difficulties in the popular literary marketplace at the beginning of the new century. Alden's excoriating assessment (MA 3140.3; Fig. 20) was that "The scenario is interesting, but it does not promise a popular novel. The tissues of it are too subtly fine for general appreciation. It is subjective, fold within fold of a complex mental web, in which the reader is lost if his much-wearied attention falters. . . . I do not advise acceptance. We ought to do better." As one of the first readers of the planned novel, Alden registered James's disregard for the general reader's expectations and the well-established conventions of contemporary commercial fiction. Despite Alden's unsympathetic report, the novel was serialized in

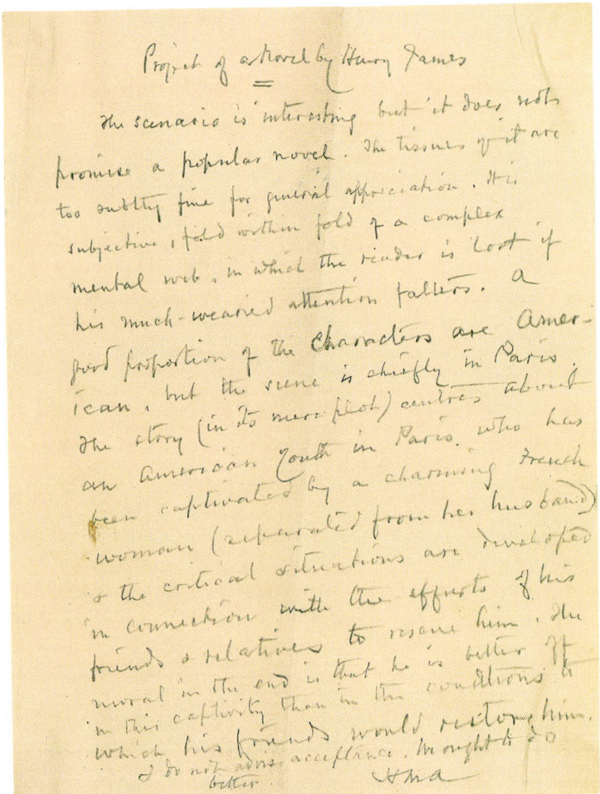
Project of a Novel by Henry James

The scenario is interesting but it does not promise a popular novel. The tissues of it are too subtly fine for general appreciation. It is subjective, fold within fold of a complex mental web, in which the reader is lost & his much-wearied attention falters. A good proportion of the characters are American, but the scene is chiefly in Paris. The story (in its mere plot) centres about an American youth in Paris, who has been captivated by a charming French woman (separated from her husband) & the critical situations are developed in connection with the efforts of his friends & relatives to rescue him. The moral in the end is that he is better off in this captivity than in the conditions to which his friends would restore him. I do not advise acceptance. He ought to do better.

HMA

FIG. 20. Henry Mills Alden (1836–1919), autograph reader's report of the scenario for *The Ambassadors* ("Project of a Novel"), 1 September 1900, The Morgan Library & Museum, New York.

the *North American Review* between January and December 1903. James thought it the most perfectly constructed of his novels—hailing it, in his preface, as "frankly, quite the best 'all round,' of my productions"—and it is now widely regarded by critics as his towering masterpiece.[63]

"Caro dottore mio"

The Morgan's most extensive collection of letters by Henry James were written to William W. Baldwin (MA 8732; former accession number MA 3564).[64] Dr. Baldwin (1850–1910) was an internationally famous American physician specializing in cardiology. He set up a practice in Florence in the 1880s and was physician to Queen Victoria, her daughter-in-law, the Princess of Teck (who later became Queen Mary), and the Duchess of York and her family. Baldwin also attended to the medical needs of the expatriate American community in Italy and many Americans who passed through the country. Among his famous American patients were Mark Twain and his wife, Olivia; Edith Wharton; William Dean Howells; Constance Fenimore Woolson; the artist Cecilia Beaux; Henry, William, and Alice James; and Pierpont Morgan.[65]

In a letter to Grace Norton, written from Palazzo Barbaro on 30 June 1890, James described Baldwin as "a charming and glowing little man, who, coming here eight or ten years ago, has made himself a first place."[66] Baldwin was regarded as a brilliant diagnostician and correctly diagnosed Alice James's cancer in 1891. Writing to William James on 31 July 1891, James described Dr. Baldwin as "very 'live'—clever, intelligent and ingenious and remarkable in his way; and, as a good friend of mine, has taken an added interest in her [Alice James], besides having evidently been most careful and attentive. He appears to have been almost the only doctor that she has ever *liked* to see." [67] Leon Edel believed that Baldwin was the model for the character Sir Luke Strett in *The Wings of the Dove* (1902).[68]

James occasionally used the salutation *"Caro dottore mio"* when writing to Dr. Baldwin. His letters, written mostly from England and Italy, span the years 1887 to 1907 and comprise 402 pages. The sixty-nine autograph letters, three typed letters, and two telegrams James sent from a wide range of locations attest to the peripatetic life he led in those years. Letters are addressed from London, Lamb House, Rye, Venice, Siena, Rome, Naples, Vallombrosa, Innsbruck, and several other locations in Great Britain and Europe. James initially sought Baldwin's help with a

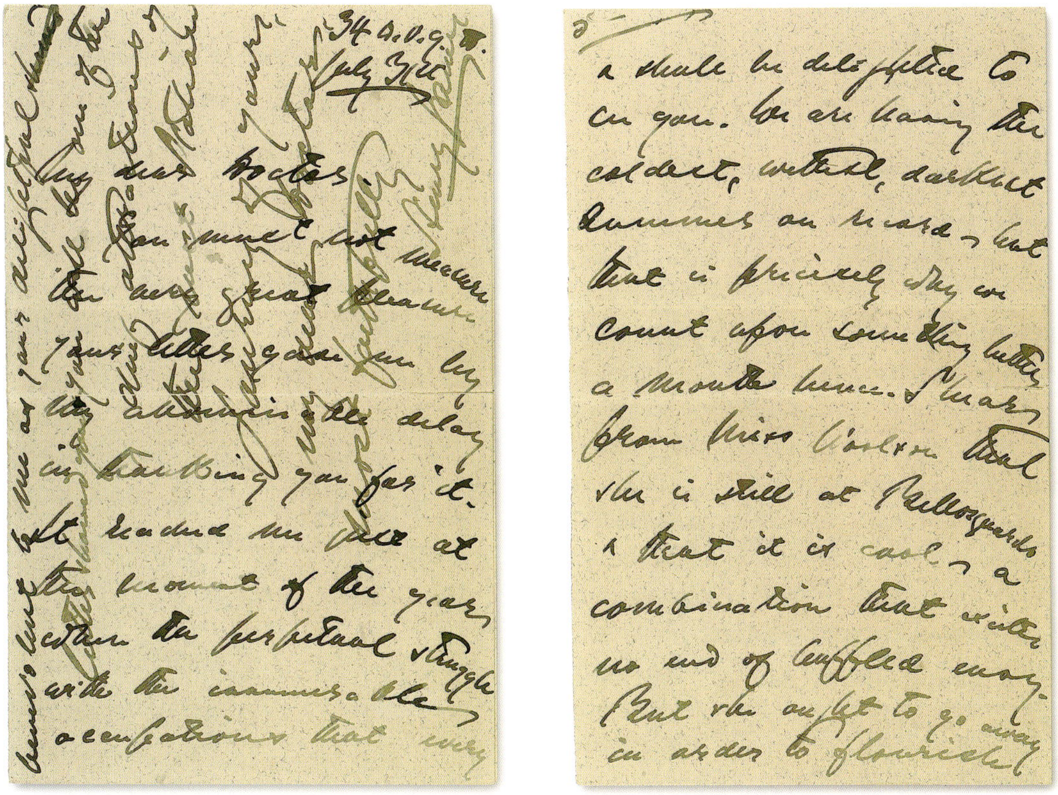

FIG. 21. Henry James, autograph letter, signed, to Dr. William W. Baldwin, 31 July [1888], The Morgan Library & Museum, New York.

urinary problem in March 1887, and his early letters contain a considerable amount of personal detail about James's fluctuating health and dietary habits. Many of his later letters read like travelogues, while others relate the current state of his health and his concerns about his general well-being, his work—in particular the production of his play *The American*—and other literary enterprises. Numerous letters concern the illness and eventual death of Alice James and the declining health and suicide of Constance Fenimore Woolson (1840–1894). James also wrote about the health of Paul Bourget and Wolcott Balestier, news of their mutual friends, current affairs in Italy and the United States, and the Dreyfus case. The onerousness of Dr. Baldwin's wealthy clients is also a recurrent theme of these letters. Only five of James's letters to Baldwin were published in Edel's *Henry James Letters,* and there is sparse quotation from others in Edel's biography.

Several highlights from James's correspondence with Baldwin may serve to convey the interest and importance of this extensive archive; a complete checklist of letters is provided in an appendix. On 31 July 1888 (MA 8732.6; Fig. 21), he wrote to Baldwin about his concerns for the health of their mutual friend, Constance Fenimore Woolson: "I hear from Miss Woolson that she is still at Bellosguardo. . . . But she ought to go away in order to flourish when she comes back. I take it for granted she is overworking—but her power to keep that up has long mystified me. Anything beyond three hours a day (with continuity) in the sort of work she does is a nail in her coffin. But she appears to desire that her coffin shall have

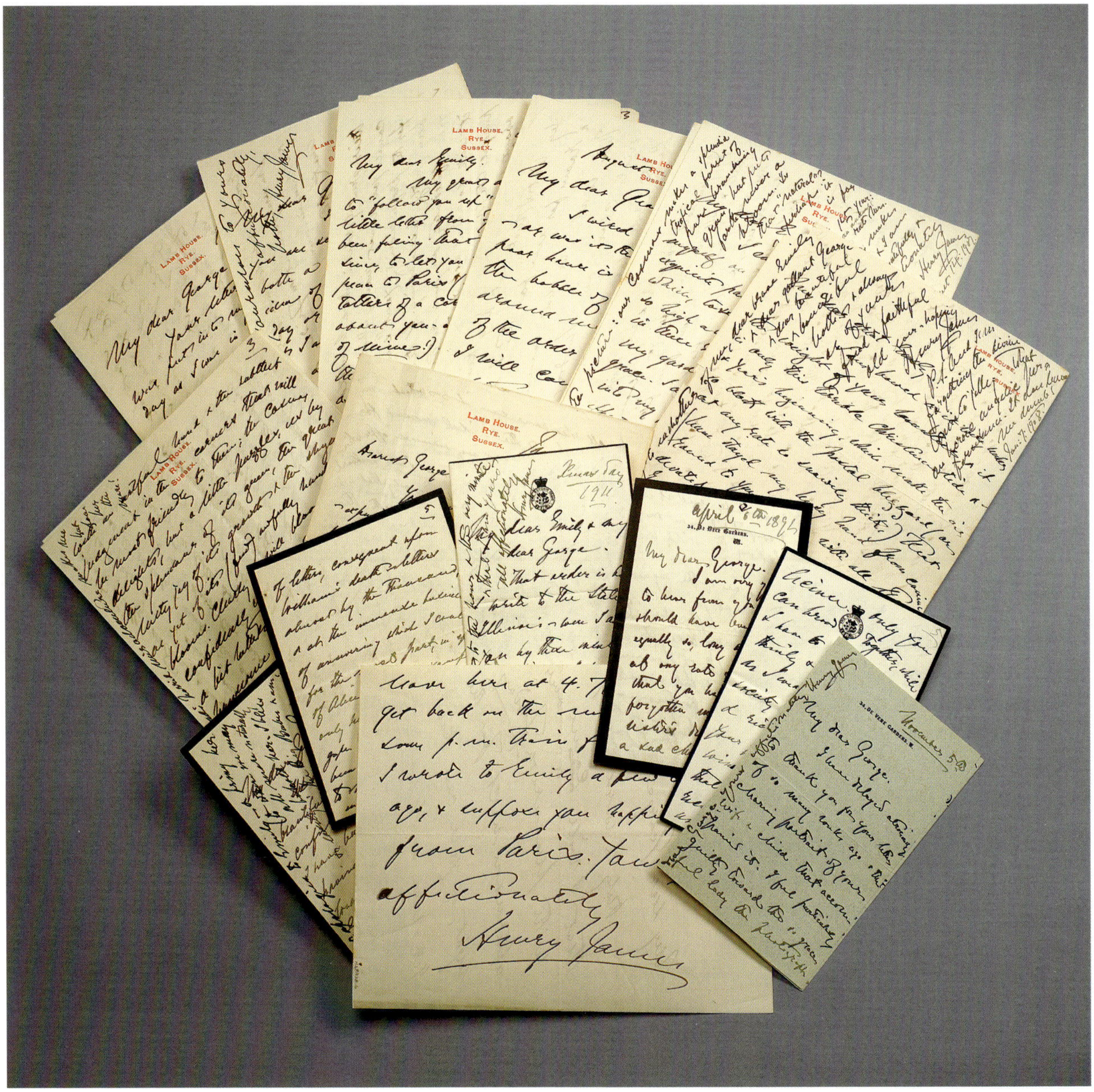

FIG. 25. Henry James, group of autograph letters, signed, to George Higginson, 1892–1911, The Morgan Library & Museum, New York.

the existence of these letters from James to his cousin. But the correspondence suggests a larger place for Higginson in James's life. Incidentally, the March 1905 letter James sent to Mrs. Sullivan, aunt of J. P. Morgan, Jr., was begun at the Winnetka, Illinois, home of Higginson, to whom James referred as "a most blessed cousin of mine."

James's letters to his cousin concern the loss of his sister Alice in 1892 and that of his brother William in 1910. Some letters include his thoughts on the life that George and his wife, Emily, were leading in America and offer travel advice, including detailed recommendations, on the Higginsons' travels in Europe. The letters provide an insight into James's emotions in the midst of several major events of his life and reveal what we might call the avuncular side of his personality.

Using customary black-bordered mourning stationery, on 6 April 1892, James wrote to Higginson that "My sister's death makes a sad change in my life—I saw her with such frequency & such interest; but it represents the cessation of a lifetime of suffering." James congratulated his cousin on his marriage and on "liking the wild west, as to which I fear my ideas are of the vaguest and most prejudiced; if you are happy there I shall try to see it in the light of that romance." James hoped that after Higginson had made his fortune he would come "to London again, that is if you will still be prepared to recognize your indigent, but, my dear George, very faithful relative."

Over two years later, on 5 November 1894, he apologized for his delay in thanking Higginson for a photograph of his wife and child, saying "There are times when, from the mere force of hostile circumstances, my correspondence goes utterly to pieces & I have to be patient & to ask for patience, while I dress its wounds & repair its gaps & set it on its feet again." Written after reading Higginson's description of the Chicago World's Fair, James commented: "Your roaring Chicago seems very far away from me, & what I hear of its wonders make it seem further still—the exhibition must have been, for you residents, a rather fierce ordeal. . . . To me such things are things of dread & such places of despair. Colossal size & colossal numbers or colossal crowds make me long to fly to the desert. London is too big & one's constant battles with its dimensions of all kinds, leaves one, I suppose, prejudiced in favour of something shy & shrunken."

James visited Chicago in 1905 and found it very much as he anticipated. His stay with the Higginsons proved to be a comfortable respite from the demands of his lecture tour. The visit seems to have cemented his relationship with his cousin, for the following summer, on 7 June 1906, he told Higginson that he was delighted to learn that he was in Europe and would come to visit. Sharing information on "quiet watering-places" in England, James advised that "The Seaside watering-place is here, nowadays, mostly, an inferior—a third-rate resort (save the case of the few winter places, like Brighton, Torquay, &c, which are impossible in summer.) Hastings & St. Leonard's, near me here (12 miles away) are for instance, mere shadeless deserts of bricks & mortar without a redeeming feature & given over to mobs of intoxicated cheap trippers."[75]

At James's recommendation, Higginson brought his family to Folkestone, and the family visited James at Lamb House in Rye. From there, they went on to Paris. On 3 August 1906, James told Higginson and his wife how much pleasure their summer visit had given him and expressed his hope that "Paris will have been really convenient, & completely rewarding, & not too hot or too complicated or too monstrous. The Louvre is

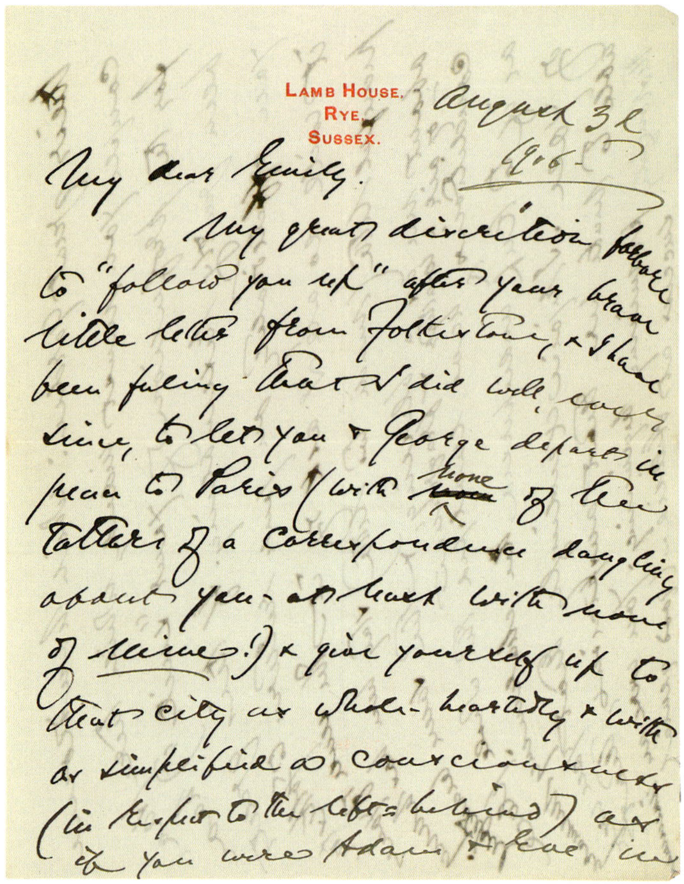

LAMB HOUSE,
RYE,
SUSSEX.

August 3d
1906.

My dear Emily.

My great discretion forbade to "follow you up" after your brave little letter from Folkestone, & I have been feeling that I did well, ever since, to let you & George depart in peace to Paris (with none of the tatters of a correspondence dangling about you—at least with none of mine!) & give yourself up to that city as whole-heartedly & with as simplified a consciousness (in respect to the left-behind) as if you were Adam & Eve in

FIG. 26. Henry James, autograph letter, signed, to Emily Higginson, 3 August 1906, The Morgan Library & Museum, New York.

monstrous—but a monster you will probably have spent most of your time stroking the ears & pulling the tail of! I envy you the freshness of that impression. I had it 1st too long ago" (Fig. 26). James paid a three-day visit to the Higginsons when they returned from Paris to Folkestone at the beginning of August.

This visit seems to have gone very well—aside from a little forgetfulness on James's part. On 13 August 1906, he wrote to ask Higginson to "rescue" his razor and strop, which he had left "hanging in my room on the hook for the loop of one of the curtains," and to mail it to him, adding that he recognized this request as an "odious little care." He suggested that Higginson could "keep it & use it & find it good yourself—all with the blessing of its poor perpetually inadvertent & oblivious ex-proprietor." He assured his cousin that: "My memory of you both & the babes & the walks & the talks & the drives & the dinners remains lustrous & tender, without a flaw."

James next wrote to his cousin on 11 January 1907, thanking him for a Christmas gift in fulsome terms: "I deeply rejoiced to get it, & there was a rare thrill in being put in such strangely immediate relation with far & fabulous Winnetka—yet as out of my present picture as if I had been there once but in a balloon or a hascheesh vision!" Reflecting on his relatives' visit the previous summer and the passage of time, he told Higginson: "At my age, as you'll see one of these years, the weeks & the months pass like the telegraph-posts at a car-window."

James's letter to Emily Higginson of 14 August 1907 expressed his deep fondness for his cousin's wife and invited her to return the next summer. Thinking of the contrast between his life at Rye and their life at Winnetka, he wrote wistfully:

> *What a life you must lead & how I hope it thoroughly agrees with you & that George, dearest & best of men, rejoices & thrives. . . . I think of your vast barns & granaries resounding with the neigh & the other mellow music of innumerable beasts, I think of your plantations already nodding in the lakeside breeze, on the vastest scale, I think of your wide hospitable house all redolent of tomato-jelly, & above all, my dear Emily, I focus your glorious garden where no plant is less than ten feet high or has a name in less than ten syllables!*

Emily and George Higginson evidently continued to correspond with and send gifts to cousin Henry. On 7 January 1908, James wrote to thank Emily for her "divine tomato jelly." There is a New Year's letter for 1909, and on 2 January 1910, James wrote to thank them for a cable message sent at Christmas. He assured them that "your sign of remembrance has touched me—very deeply, I assure you." He told them that he hadn't "had a very famous year—but rather a disabled & disqualified or depressed one; but the ills in question I seem really to have been able to handle intelligently enough mainly to shuffle them off & to enjoy now a clearer prospect. It has been an infamous year climatically & pluvially; it has rained—in a single sustained deluge—for the hapless twelvemonth on end, & we are all soaked & sodden, mouldy & miserable, in consequence." Remarking on the circumscribed nature of his life he told them: "I practically never travel now, but just change, as you see, from the blue bed to the brown."[76]

His next letter, written on 26 October 1910 from Cambridge, Massachusetts, is even darker in tone. James told his cousins that he had been "perpetually & miserably ill—with the obstinate remains of my quite dreadful & horrible illness of last year (I mean of this past one, from Christmas back to the present autumn.)" He had become unwell even before he accompanied his brother William back to the United States. A week after their arrival came William's "dreadful accelerated death, the shock & pain & strain of which made me lose all the ground I had managed to gain. I was thrown back again, dismally, into my worst condition, with which I have still constantly to struggle. At the same time we were all overwhelmed by an avalanche of letters, consequent upon William's death—letters almost by the thousand, & at the immense business of answering which I could for the most part, in spite of Alice's heroic example, only helplessly & shrinkingly gape." He invited his cousins to spend Thanksgiving with the James family in Boston but declined an invitation to visit them in Winnetka and

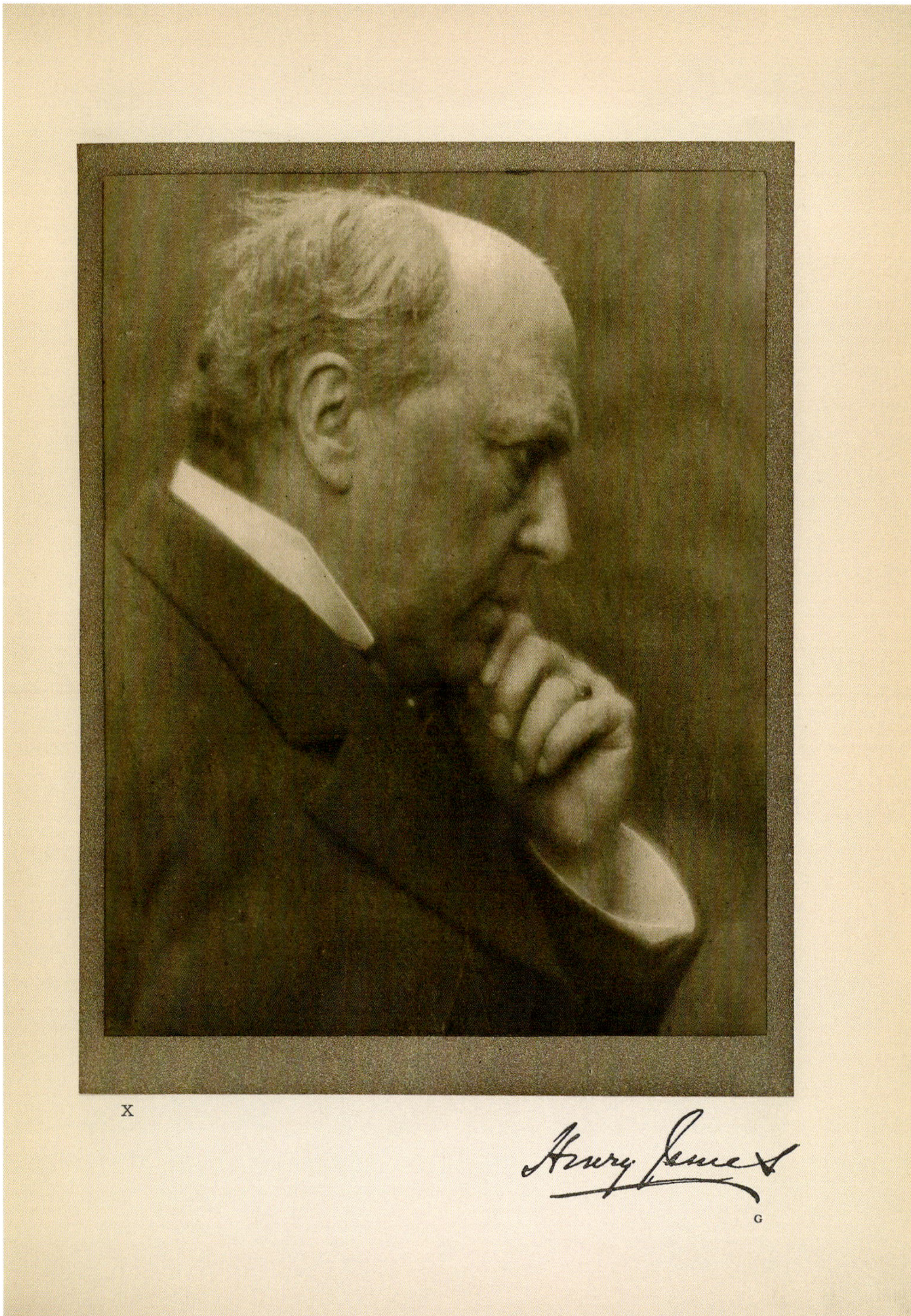

FIG. 27. Alvin Langdon Coburn (1882–1966), photogravure portrait of Henry James in *Men of Mark*, 1913.

lamented that he was unable to travel much farther than Boston or New York.

In the final letter in the group, written on Christmas Day 1911 from the Reform Club, James described the scene in the city. As he sat "'doing letters,' as we say, this still soft Xmas morning . . . London presents its usual (at this moment) vast vacancy & quietude; the whole population (some say 4 million) flies to the country & abroad & the result for those who artfully stay still, is delightful in respect to peace & ease." He told them that his health had much improved since they last saw him because "I hibernate no more, & shall never again hibernate, at Rye—I treated myself for years to too much of that—which meant an excess of solitude & confinement. Here I can circulate as well as brood."

Circulate and *brood*. These antithetical activities were central to James's life and art. His letters record just how extensively he circulated among his fellow expatriates in Europe, at home in his adopted England and, occasionally, abroad in the United States, from which he had emigrated in his early thirties. Few authors were as gregarious and well traveled as James; he appears to have seldom refused an invitation to a social gathering. But solitude and confinement were essential for him to brood, and out of this incubation his letters and his fiction hatched. James's correspondence, through which he maintained contact and nurtured friendships, speaks richly of his equal need for epistolary circulation—for relationships across time and distance—and of his need for the many varieties of intimacy a letter affords the writer, even while it protects the writer's privacy. Alvin Langdon Coburn's (1882–1966) 1906 photogravure portrait of the author at his home in Rye (Fig. 27) seems to capture him in the very act of brooding, for James had, as William Hazlitt put it in a more poetic context, "a mind for ever brooding over itself."[77]

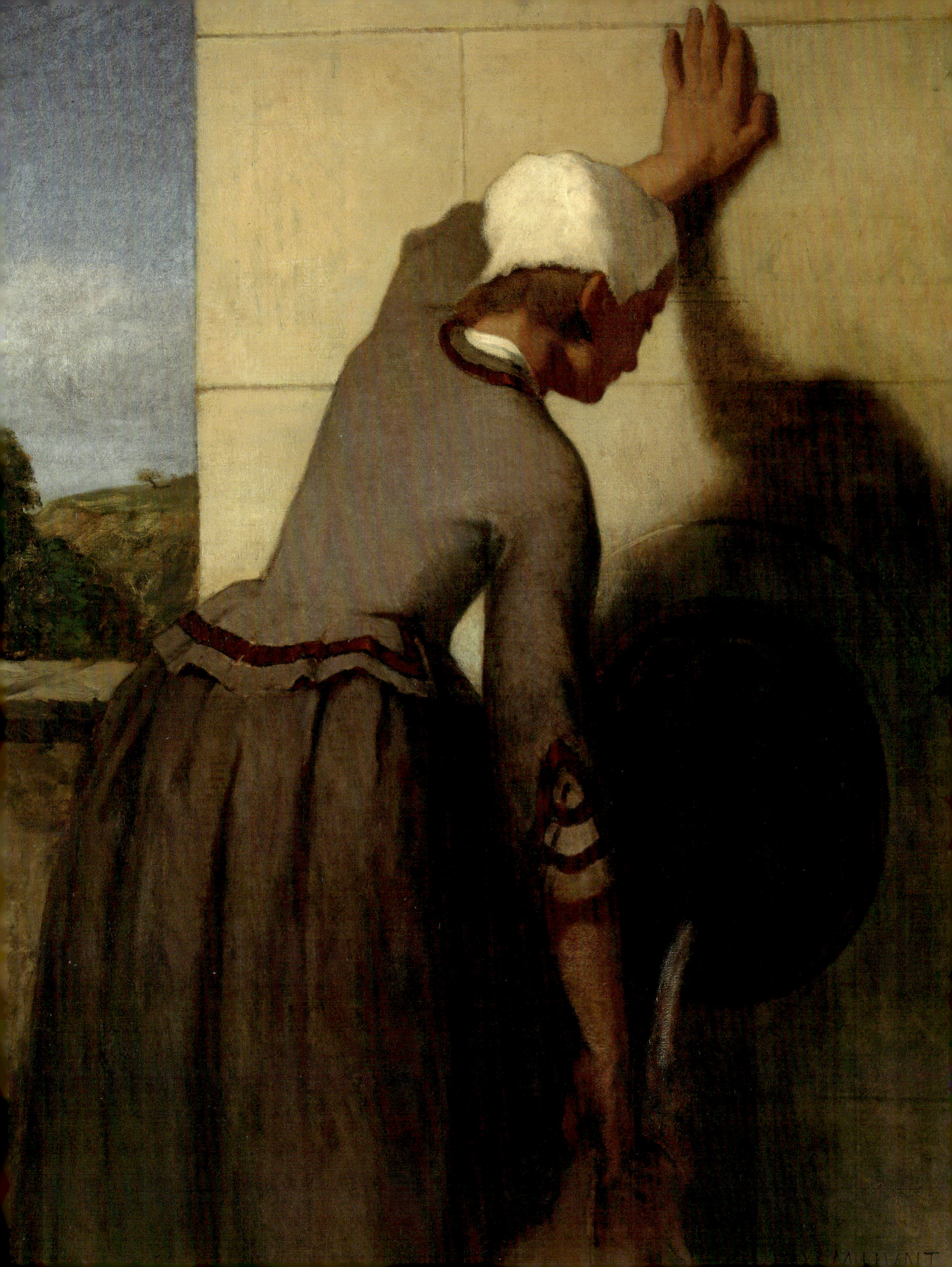

Notes

HENRY JAMES: SHADOW AND SUBSTANCE

COLM TÓIBÍN

1. Gunter and Jobe 2004, p. 15.
2. Ibid., p. 21.
3. Ibid., p. 49.
4. Ibid., p. 53.
5. Ibid., p. 58.
6. Ibid., p. 59.
7. Ibid., p. 61.
8. Ibid., p. 77.
9. Ibid., p. 72.
10. Ibid., p. 73.
11. Ibid., p. 78.
12. James 1986, p. 112.
13. Ibid., p. 123.
14. Ibid., p. 140.
15. Ibid., p. 119.
16. Quoted in Edel 1953, p. 300.
17. Howard 1993, p. 306.
18. Edel 1974–84, vol. 1, p. 160.
19. Ibid., p. 166.
20. Ibid., p. 180.
21. Edel 1962, p. 85.
22. Ibid., p. 91.
23. Ibid., p. 91.
24. Ibid., p. 92.
25. Quoted in Edel 1953, p. 62.
26. Horne 2016, p. 311.
27. Edel 1953, p. 161.
28. Horne 2016, p. 31.
29. Quoted in Collister 2007, p. 230. James was writing to Mary Cadwalader Jones on 26 December 1902; Harvard University, Houghton Library, James Papers.
30. Washington and elsewhere 1987–88, p. 17.
31. Edel 1974–84, vol. 4, p. 566.
32. Cortissoz 1911, p. 13.
33. Sweeney 1956, p. 87.
34. Ibid., p. 51.
35. Ibid., p. 52.
36. Ibid., p. 53.
37. Ibid., p. 39.
38. Ibid., pp. 114–15.
39. Ibid., p. 227.
40. Ibid., p. 25.
41. Ibid., p. 28.
42. Quoted in Rioux 2016, p. 203.
43. James 2011, p. 278.
44. James 1986, p. 333.
45. Edel 1974–84, vol. 1, p. 324.
46. Quoted in Edel 1962, p. 164.
47. Ibid., p. 296.
48. Quoted in Ott 2016, p. 108.
49. Horne 2016, p. 564.
50. Ibid., p. 565.
51. Quoted in Edel 1953, p. 315.
52. Edel 1962, p. 94.
53. Ibid., p. 262.
54. Florence 2012, pp. 28–29.
55. Quoted in Ott 2016, pp. 89–90.
56. Quoted in ibid., p. 24.
57. Quoted in ibid., p. 27.
58. Quoted in ibid., p. 48.
59. Edel 1974–84, vol. 1, p. 245.
60. Quoted in Ott 2016, pp. 48–49.
61. Quoted in ibid., p. 52.
62. Quoted in ibid., p. 55.
63. Howells 2004, pp. 46–47.
64. Ibid., pp. 84–85.
65. Quoted in Kaplan 1992, p. 222.
66. Edel 1974–84, vol. 2, p. 264.

67. Ibid., p. 167.
68. Sweeney 1956, p. 165.
69. Anderson and Koval 1994, p. 215.
70. Quoted in Honour and Fleming 1991, p. 37.
71. Ibid., p. 37.
72. Ibid., p. 40.
73. Ibid., p. 40.
74. Quoted in Ott 2016, p. 34.
75. Honour and Fleming 1991, p. 44.
76. Bacher 1909, pp. 101–2.
77. Honour and Fleming 1991, p. 48.
78. Bacher 1909, p. 44.
79. Edel 1974–84, vol. 3, p. 43.
80. Edel 1974–84, vol. 4, p. 41.
81. Quoted in Boyd 2010.
82. Edel 1962, p. 403.
83. Edel 1974–84, vol. 2, p. 277.
84. Ibid., p. 280.
85. Quoted in Edel 1962, p. 404.
86. Edel 1974–84, vol. 2, p. 349.
87. James 2011, p. 237.
88. Ibid., p. 238.
89. Quoted in Ott 2016, p. 123.
90. Ibid., p. 125.
91. Edel 1974–84, vol. 3, pp. 111–13.
92. Ibid., p. 113.
93. Ibid., p. 117.
94. Ibid., pp. 119–20.
95. Gordon 1999, p. 204.
96. New York 1996, p. 26.
97. Quoted in Rioux 2016, p. 133.
98. Ibid., p. 135.
99. Ibid., p. 188.
100. Quoted in ibid., p. 191.
101. Edel 1974–84, vol. 3, p. 138.
102. Rioux 2016, p. 192.
103. Edel 1974–84, vol. 3, p. 232.
104. Ibid., pp. 230–31.
105. Ibid., p. 233.
106. Quoted in Rioux 2016, p. 226.
107. Quoted in Edel 1962a, p. 249.
108. Edel 1974–84, vol. 3, p. 246.
109. Ibid., p. 249.
110. Quoted in Edel 1962a, p. 249.
111. Quoted in Rioux 2016, p. 228.
112. Florence 2012, p. 47.
113. Quoted in Ott 2016, p. 171.
114. Edel 1974–84, vol. 3, p. 418.
115. Ibid., p. 494.
116. Matthiessen and Murdock 1947, p. 125.
117. Ibid., p. 130.
118. Ibid., p. 131.
119. Ibid., p. 232.
120. James 1934, p. 330.
121. Quoted in London and elsewhere 1998, p. 171.
122. Ibid., p. 171.
123. Quoted in Williamstown 1997, p. 23.
124. Edel 1974–84, vol. 3, p. 456.
125. Edel 1974–84, vol. 3, p. 42.
126. James 1999, p. 720.
127. Ibid., p. 739.
128. Sweeney 1956, p. 217.
129. Elaine Kilmurray in London and New York 2015, p. 82.
130. Ibid., p. 82.
131. James 2008, p. 339.
132. Edel 1974–84, vol. 3, p. 390.
133. Quoted in London and elsewhere 1998, p. 152.
134. James 2008, p. 336.
135. Edel 1974–84, vol. 4, p. 605.
136. Quoted in Edel 1972, p. 488.
137. Quoted in London and elsewhere 1998, p. 171.
138. Private collection.
139. London and elsewhere 1998, p. 171.
140. Seattle 2000–2001, pp. 106 and 134.
141. Ibid., p. 179.
142. Anesko 2012, p. 56.
143. Ibid., p. 55.
144. Ibid., p. 93.
145. Ibid., pp. 158–59.
146. Ibid., p. 160.

147. Ibid., p. 183.
148. Ibid., p. 183.
149. Quoted in Gunter 2009, p. 299.

"I LIKE AMBIGUITIES AND DETEST GREAT GLARES" HENRY JAMES AND AMERICAN PAINTINGS

MARC SIMPSON

1. Tintner 1986, p. 2.
2. Winner 1970, p. 69. Robert L. Gale wrote, "The largest single category of similes and metaphors from James's fiction is that of art"; quoted in Vanderlaan 2008, p. 12n2.
3. Notable in the bibliography on the topic are the works by Tintner and Winner cited above. Significant contributions also include, among many others: Edwin T. Bowden, *The Themes of Henry James: A System of Observation Through the Visual Arts* (New Haven: Yale University Press, 1956); Marianna Torgovnick, *The Visual Arts, Pictorialism, and the Novel: James, Lawrence, and Woolf* (Princeton: Princeton University Press, 1985); Paul Fisher, *Artful Itineraries: European Art and American Careers in High Culture, 1865–1920* (New York: Garland Publishing, 2000); Kendall Johnson, *Henry James and the Visual* (Cambridge: Cambridge University Press, 2007); and Peter Collister, *Writing the Self: Henry James and America* (London: Pickering & Chatto, 2007). For biographical context throughout, I have leaned heavily on (and borrowed freely from) Leon Edel's five-volume biography of James and his four-volume compilation of letters (I cite these more fully in subsequent notes); I have also consulted the University of Nebraska's publication of *The Complete Letters of Henry James,* edited by Pierre A. Walker and Greg W. Zacharias, which to date covers material from 1855 to 1880, but have, for consistency's sake and its more ready accessibility, cited Edel when possible.
4. James 2011a, p. 280.
5. Leon Edel notes, however, and almost all other commentators agree on this point, that James's art criticism is of a kind "that belongs not to the specialist, but that of the genius who uses pictures to feed his own art; a visual sense that, in the end, came to regard pictures as life itself" (Edel 1974, p. 12).

Painting rather than sculpture seems to animate James's enthusiasm, and it is with painters that I will deal in this essay. In addition to the sculptors in his fiction, he wrote much about the American sculptor William Wetmore Story (1819–1895), with whose work he had little sympathy. James much regretted late in life having agreed, as a friend of the Story family, to write *William Wetmore Story and His Friends: From Letters, Diaries, and Recollections* (1903). In one of the kinder of his private comments on the project, he wrote to Millicent, Duchess of Sutherland, "Story was the dearest of men, but he wasn't massive, his artistic and literary baggage were of the slightest and the materials for a biography *nil*" (23 December 1903; in Edel 1974–84, vol. 4, p. 302). Through Story, James met Harriet Hosmer (1830–1908), who "looks like a remarkably ugly little grey-haired boy, adorned with a diamond necklace, but she seems both 'vivacious' and discreet and is better, I imagine, than her statues" (James to Alice James, 10 February 1873, in Edel 1974–84, vol. 1, p. 339). Other of his letters from Rome in 1873 document his socializing with the "lethargic" Luther Terry (1813–1900), the "irrepressible" Eugene Benson (1839–1908), and the "atrocious [J. Rollin] Tilton, the transcendental painter" (1828–1888); he did not, however, publish on their art (in Edel 1974–84, vol. 1, pp. 392 and 372). In later life he also knew, owned work by, and corresponded at length with (and about) the American sculptor Hendrik Andersen (1872–1940), but he did not write about him for publication, either.
6. Peter Collister has edited and annotated James's memoirs insightfully: *A Small Boy and Others* (1913; Charlottesville: University of Virginia, 2011) and *Notes of a Son and Brother* and *The Middle Years* (1914 and 1917; Charlottesville: University of Virginia, 2011).
7. James 2011a, p. 50.
8. Ibid., p. 210.
9. Ibid., pp. 52–54 and 210.
10. Ibid., p. 207.
11. Ibid., p. 208. Collister identifies the Stuyvesant Institute—a museum, lecture hall, and library at 659 Broadway—not only as the site where the Leutze was on view in the winter of 1851–52 but also as where Henry James, Sr., gave many of his public lectures and where New York's Swedenborgian Society met.
12. Ibid., p. 208.
13. Ibid., pp. 210 and 212.
14. Ibid., p. 210. He declared, in fact, that his lifelong fascination with Tuscany began not with his time in and around Florence but with this picture.
15. Ibid., p. 210.
16. Henry James, *The American Scene* (1907), in Howard 1993a, pp. 809–10. The text combined ten articles published between April 1905 and November 1906 with four previously unpublished essays.

17. Ibid., pp. 561; 405–6 and 513; 433–34; 665 and 498; 497–99 and 561; 393. James described the Pope home, Hill-Stead, which he apparently visited twice—once probably in October 1904 with Edith Wharton and then again, according to Hill-Stead records, on 20 May 1911—as: "a house apparently conceived—and with great felicity—on the lines of a magnified Mount Vernon, and in which an array of modern 'impressionistic' pictures, mainly French, wondrous examples of Manet, of Degas, of Claude Monet, of Whistler, of other rare recent hands, treated us to the momentary effect of a large, slippery sweet inserted, without a warning, between the compressed lips of half-conscious inanition. One hadn't quite known one was starved, but the morsel went down by the mere authority of the thing consummately *prepared*. . . . [N]o proof of the sovereign power of art could have been, for the moment, sharper. It happened to be that particular art—it might as well, no doubt, have been another; it made everything else shrivel and fade: it was like the sudden trill of a nightingale, lord of the hushed evening" (pp. 393–94). For the 1911 visit, see http://www.hillstead.org/about-us/historical-timeline/. In his otherwise enlightening discussion of James and Impressionism, Fisher misidentifies Hill-Stead as the "Clarke [*sic*] Institute in Williamstown," which was not founded until fifty years later (Fisher 2000, p. 98). Pope owned five paintings by Whistler, as well as many works of art on paper. The paintings were an urban landscape (*The Last of Old Westminster* [1862; Museum of Fine Arts, Boston]), three seascapes (*Blue and Silver: Blue Wave, Biarritz* [1862], *Dark Blue and Silver* [1893; both still at the Hill-Stead Museum, Farmington, Connecticut], and *The Selsey Shore* [ca. 1878; New Britain Museum of American Art, Connecticut]), and a portrait head (*Crimson Note—Carmen* [ca. 1895; Hill-Stead Museum]).

18. Not, however, that the references are casual. In his "American Journal II" James plotted how to move his prose from the "splendid portrait" of Henry Higginson to the murals in the Boston Public Library. "I swim a little, in fancy, in imagination, in association, in the Sargent connection," he writes (Edel and Powers 1987, p. 236).

19. The basic text for James's art criticism is *The Painter's Eye: Notes and Essays on the Pictorial Arts by Henry James*, edited by John L. Sweeney (Cambridge, Massachusetts: Harvard University Press, 1956), with Sweeney's truly seminal introductory essay on the form. A more recent compilation is *Henry James: Essays on Art and Drama*, edited by Peter Rawlings (Aldershot: Scolar Press, 1996). Many of James's art reviews were unsigned, and there is disagreement in published sources over whether a review may or may not be by him; those in the *Atlantic Monthly* by his friend Thomas Sergeant Perry from 1876 and 1877, in particular, are sometimes given to James. I have relied largely on Sweeney and Rawlings to define the corpus. Cambridge University Press is about to issue Collister's *The Complete Writings of Henry James on Art and Drama*, 2 volumes, which will appear too late for use in this essay but which promises to be a superb resource; from the available table of contents, we seem to be in accord concerning the sixty items that can be ascribed to James.

20. [Henry James], "Hamerton's Contemporary French Painting," *North American Review* 106 (April 1868), p. 718. See, for an example of the subject's return, the opening of "On Some Pictures Lately Exhibited," *The Galaxy* 20, no. 1 (July 1875), p. 89.

21. [Henry James], "Hamerton's Contemporary French Painting," *North American Review* 106 (April 1868), p. 717. He continued: "It is no more than just, that, before sitting down to discourse upon works of art, a writer should be required to prove his familiarity with the essential conditions of the production of such works, and that, before criticising the way in which objects are painted, he should give evidence of his knowledge of the difference between the manner in which they strike the senses of persons of whom it is impossible to conceive as being tempted to reproduce them and the manner in which they strike the senses of persons in whom to see them and to wish to reproduce them are almost one and the same act. With an accomplished sense of this profound difference, and with that proportion of insight into the workings of the painter's genius and temperament which would naturally accompany it, it is not unreasonable to believe that a critic in whom the faculty of literary expression is sufficiently developed may do very good service to the cause of art,—service similar to that which is constantly performed for the cause of letters. . . . It is certain that painters need to be interpreted and expounded, and that as a general thing they are themselves incompetent to the task" (pp. 717–19).

22. [Henry James], "Hamerton's Contemporary French Painting," *North American Review* 106 (April 1868), p. 717.

23. James to Charles Eliot Norton, 4 February 1872, in Edel 1974–84, vol. 1, pp. 272–73. He continued, self-mockingly, "It's pitiful work and I shall of course soon collapse for want of material."

24. James to William James, 30 May 1869, in Skrupskelis and Berkeley 1992–2004, vol. 1, p. 76.

25. For details of the trip, see Edel 1953 (1978), pp. 281–322.
26. In late January, he wrote to his friend Lizzie Boott announcing his activities: "Do you read the new musical *critiques* in the *Atlantic*? They are (if you don't know it) by your friend Apthorp junior. . . . I hardly dare in the same breath, to mention that the little art-notices, if you look at 'em, are by your humble servant. The thing is hard to do, for want of matter and occasion. If I only had Beato Angelico to start me up! But he, poor man, has been done to death!" (James to Elizabeth Boott, 24 January 1872, in Edel 1974–84, vol. 1, p. 269). The pride is apparent, as is the complaint of the materials he has to work with.
27. Charles Eliot Norton, too, penned a largely negative review in the *Harvard Advocate* 18, no. 2 (16 October 1874), p. 23.
28. [Henry James], "Art," *Atlantic Monthly* 35, no. 207 (January 1875), p. 119. The review closed with one of the most overtly condemnatory paragraphs James ever published on an art object, dedicated to an "apotheosis of cleverness of the vulgar order," "a most extraordinary piece of artistic depravity" from the brush of the Hispano-Roman Rogelio de Egusquiza (1845–1915) at Williams and Everett's gallery, a work now at the Museo de Arte de Ponce (*Woman in Blue Dress*, 1873).
29. [Henry James], "Art," *Atlantic Monthly* 34, no. 205 (November 1874), p. 636.
30. [Henry James], "Notes," *The Nation* 532 (9 September 1875), pp. 165–66.
31. Ibid., p. 166. James continued, granting that we "finally perceive, however, that it can be a little more graceful and a little more suggestive. Even in so happy a performance as the portrait of Mrs. Skinner, Copley remains a trifle hard and rigid; here and there his surfaces are more like carving than painting."
32. The twenty columns (and associated correspondence with editor Whitelaw Reid and James's friend John Hay, who had translated columns from the French of the previous correspondent, Arsène Houssaye, and was responsible for recommending James to Reid) have been gathered together and published in Edel and Lind 1957.
33. John L. Sweeney, "Introduction," in Sweeney 1956a, p. 31. A fine analysis of the whole book is in Bogardus 1978, pp. 77–94.
34. James to Charles Eliot Norton, 4 July 1892, in Edel 1974–84, vol. 3, p. 389.
35. [Henry James], "French Pictures in Boston," *Atlantic Monthly* 29, no. 171 (January 1872), p. 117. This echoes some of what William James, visiting La Farge's studio in 1869 and seeing a number of pictures, had written to his brother Henry of them: "you've no idea of the pure splendor of some of those things." Of this canvas, he was most enthusiastic: "his big landscape of the gorge. A most honest, solid bit of study fm. nature, with less of his subjectivity than anything else of his I know. Full of light & splendor, and it kept 'growing' on me all the time I was there. There is an immense amount of labor in it, and it must have taught him a great deal, which will be some consolation if it brings nothing to his pocket. It wants some man or animal in the foreground. . . . If I hd. money I wd. immediately buy his big landscape" (William to Henry James, 2 October 1869, in Skrupskelis and Berkeley 1992–2004, vol. 1, p. 101).
36. Decamps's *Christ and the Centurion* was at the gallery. At least some of the works were evidently from the Hollis Hunnewell Collection.
37. For a general overview of John La Farge (1835–1910) and his achievement as a painter, muralist, watercolorist, stained glass designer, and aesthetician, see Washington and elsewhere 1987–88.
38. James 2011b, p. 67.
39. Cortissoz 1911, p. 117.
40. James to Elizabeth Boott, 27 January 1875, in Edel 1974–84, vol. 1, p. 472.
41. James to Sir John Clark, 13 December 1891, in Edel 1974–84, vol. 3, p. 367. Although in 1870 James, in England and wishing for a companion, contemplated La Farge with the qualification, "I feel as if I could endure his peculiarities much better now than formerly" (James to William James, 8 March 1870, in Skrupskelis and Berkeley 1992–2004, vol. 1, p. 150). In 1895, he wrote of hoping to leave London before La Farge was due to arrive—so things are, as always with human beings, more complex than they might seem (James to William James, 3 July 1895, in Skrupskelis and Berkeley 1992–2004, vol. 2, p. 366).
42. James to Margaret La Farge, 15 November 1910, in Edel 1974–84, vol. 4, p. 566.
43. James 2011b, p. 83.
44. My thanks to James L. Yarnall for clarifying which one of La Farge's two large Paradise landscapes was on display in the Memorial Exhibition (e-mail to author, 5 April 2016). For a clear and detailed account of La Farge's work in and around this site, see Newport 1995. James, writing in 1869, noted that he had already seen both of the big landscapes (James to William James, 30 October 1869, in Skrupskelis and Berkeley 1992–2004, vol. 1, p. 117).
45. Of this picture, William James had written, back in 1869, again

stressing the radiance of the light: "a vast green landscape of the fields near Paradise, originally meant as background to a white figure but with the latter painted out. Also as big as all out doors and flooded with light even in its botchy state. He ought to repaint a figure in it no matter how 'quaint' it will look to the vulgar" (William to Henry James, 2 October 1869, in Skrupskelis and Berkeley 1992–2004, vol. 1, p. 101).

46. James 2011b, pp. 82, 83, and 85–86.

47. James to Thomas Sergeant Perry, 18 July 1860, in Edel 1974–84, vol. 1, p. 22.

48. James 2011b, p. 64.

49. Ibid., p. 65. He later wrote to Lizzie Boott, jokingly (29 July 1874), "If I were a paintist," but the sensibility did not stay with him (Walker and Zacharias 2009, vol. 2, p. 190).

50. [Henry James], "Art," *Atlantic Monthly* 29, no. 172 (February 1872), p. 246.

51. James 2011b, p. 65.

52. [Henry James], "The London Exhibitions—The Grosvenor Gallery," *The Nation* 26 (23 May 1878), p. 338.

53. Ibid., p. 338.

54. Henry James, Jr., "The Picture Season in London," *The Galaxy* 24, no. 2 (August 1877), p. 156.

55. For the fullest account, see Merrill 1992.

56. [Henry James], "The Grosvenor Gallery and Royal Academy," *The Nation* 24 (31 May 1877), p. 320. James mistook the identity of the latter portrait; *Arrangement in Black and Brown: The Fur Jacket* (1876; Worcester Art Museum) portrays Maud Franklin, not the actress Ellen Terry (Merrill 1992, p. 40). Curiously, James did not write of the third portrait in the exhibition, the *Arrangement in Grey and Black, No. 2: Portrait of Thomas Carlyle* (1872–73; Kelvingrove Art Gallery and Museum, Glasgow), which, although *hors catalogue*, was given a prominent place in the gallery's vestibule; this would seem to have been a picture—given his enthusiasm for the portrait of the artist's mother, which it resembles—that James might have liked (for the picture's inclusion, see Merrill 1992, p. 35).

57. Henry James, "London. June 1, 1897," *Harper's Weekly* 41, no. 2114 (26 June 1897), p. 640.

58. Ibid., p. 640.

59. Ibid., p. 640.

60. Spassky et al. 1985, pp. 378–85.

61. James to his father, 19 April 1878, in Edel 1974–84, vol. 2, p. 167. The two men evidently met through their mutual friend Mrs. Rogerson: "I dined the other day with Mrs. Kemble. . . . Scatter all through this an occasional dinner with my friend Mrs. Rogerson (whose entertainments, though numerous, are always informal and easy—Whistler, the painter, has always been there of late) and you will have as complete a record as you need desire of my social existence" (James to his father, 25 March 1878, in Edel 1974–84, vol. 2, p. 161).

62. [Henry James], "Notes," *The Nation* no. 703 (19 December 1878), p. 385.

63. Ibid., p. 385.

64. [Henry James], "London Pictures and London Plays," *Atlantic Monthly* 50, no. 298 (August 1882), pp. 256–57.

65. Letter to Elizabeth Boott, 2 June 1884, in Edel 1974–84, vol. 3, p. 43.

66. Edel 1962a (1978), p. 152.

67. James to Whistler, 18 February 1889, in MacDonald et al. 2003–; GUL J24, GUW 02403.

68. Letter to Isabella Stewart Gardner, 1 May 1893, in Horne 1999, p. 265.

69. Whistler to James, 22 February 1897, in MacDonald et al. 2003–; GUL J26, GUW 02405.

70. James to Whistler, 25 February 1897 in MacDonald et al. 2003; GUL J25, GUW 02404. For a recent essay on the relations between James and Whistler, see Boyd 2010.

71. Henry James, "London. June 1, 1897," *Harper's Weekly* 41, no. 2114 (26 June 1897), p. 640.

72. James 2011b, p. 97.

73. Ibid., p. 97.

74. A token of the current disregard among art historians is visible in, to cite but one example, Sarah Burns and John Davis's splendid compilation *American Art to 1900: A Documentary History* (Berkeley: University of California Press, 2009). Whistler, Sargent, La Farge, Duveneck, and Abbey all have multiple entries; in its 1,000-plus pages, Boughton is not mentioned.

75. de Leeuw 1995.

76. Merrill 1992, p. 57.

77. Henry James, "Our Artists in Europe," *Harper's New Monthly Magazine* 79, no. 469 (June 1889), p. 60.

78. For a recent consideration of this work, see Glesmann 2002.

79. [Henry James], "Art," *Atlantic Monthly* 35, no. 207 (January 1875), p. 118.

80. Henry James, "Our Artists in Europe," *Harper's New Monthly Magazine* 79, no. 469 (June 1889), p. 62.
81. Henry James, Jr., "On Some Pictures Lately Exhibited," *The Galaxy* 20, no. 1 (July 1875), p. 96.
82. Ibid., p. 97.
83. Letter to William James, 28 February 1877, in Edel 1974–84, vol. 2, p. 102.
84. [Henry James], "The Grosvenor Gallery and the Royal Academy," *The Nation* 24 (31 May 1877), p. 321. *Snow in Spring* was recently at auction: Heritage Auctions, 19 June 2015, lot 69024.
85. "An Occasional Correspondent" [Henry James], "The London Exhibitions—The Grosvenor Gallery," *The Nation* 26 (23 May 1878), p. 339.
86. James to Elizabeth Boott, 11 December 1883, in Edel 1974–84, vol. 3, p. 18.
87. Henry James, "London. May, 1897," *Harper's Weekly* 41 (5 June 1897), p. 563.
88. James fully approved of these intimate environments for art viewing. He wrote in 1872: "The excellent custom of exhibitions of an artist's collected works seems to be coming into favor. It is a fashion by which a sincere and honest painter, of however modest merit, can hardly fail to profit. There is sure to be something interesting in any full presentation of a talent. Certain frank weaknesses legitimate themselves and are accepted as the inevitable condition of its exercise, and scattered merit joins forces to demand proper credit" ("Art," *Atlantic Monthly* 29, no. 173 [March 1872], p. 372).
89. Conrads 2000, pp. 97 and 104n43.
90. Henry James, Jr., "On Some Pictures Lately Exhibited," *The Galaxy* 20, no. 1 (July 1875), p. 89.
91. Ibid., p. 89.
92. Ibid., p. 90.
93. Ibid., p. 90.
94. There were, in fact, four: *Course of True Love, Milking Time, Uncle Ned at Home* (1875; private collection), and *Landscape*—perhaps *Hatstacks and Children* (1875; Smithsonian Institution, Cooper-Hewitt Museum); Conrads 2001, pp. 78–84.
95. Any close study of one of Homer's major pictures reveals the falsity of this assertion; Homer composes, selects, adjusts, and combines as avidly as any of his colleagues. As one case study of this, relevant to one of the NAD 1875 pictures, see Simpson 2000.
96. Henry James, Jr., "On Some Pictures Lately Exhibited," *The Galaxy* 20, no. 1 (July 1875), pp. 93–94.
97. Ibid., p. 94.
98. Ibid., p. 91.
99. Ibid., p. 96. Several years later, in his review of the 1878 Royal Academy summer exhibition, James had a chance to comment again on a panoramic painting by Bierstadt, *The Rocky Mountains, Longs Peak* (on view as *Estes Park, Colorado, U.S.*; 1877; Denver Public Library). His commentary was restrained: "American art (and American nature, I may add), are represented in a large view of Colorado scenery by Mr. Albert Bierstadt. The picture is unfavorably hung" ([Henry James], "The London Exhibitions—The Royal Academy, 1878," *The Nation* 26 [6 June 1878], p. 372). Note that he did not protest the justice of the hanging committee's decision.
100. Henry James, Jr., "On Some Pictures Lately Exhibited," *The Galaxy* 20, no. 1 (July 1875), p. 95.
101. Ibid., pp. 95–96.
102. Ibid., pp. 92–93. Patricia Hills, principal scholar of Johnson, believes that he dated the pcture only in 1876 (email to author, 23 December 2016).
103. Ibid., pp. 94 (Loop, Chase, and Neal) and 96 (Church).
104. Ibid., p. 96.
105. Ibid., p. 94.
106. For an extended consideration of the Velázquez phenomenon at midcentury, see New York 2002.
107. Elizabeth Boott and her father, Francis, "immediately" acquired this picture (Osborne 1992, p. 191).
108. Henry James, Jr., "On Some Pictures Lately Exhibited," *The Galaxy* 20, no. 1 (July 1875), p. 95.
109. [Henry James], "Note," *The Nation* 20 (3 June 1875), pp. 376–77.
110. Ibid., pp. 376–77.
111. [Henry James], "Notes," *The Nation* 21 (9 September 1875), pp. 165–66.
112. Ibid., pp. 165–66. Currently unlocated, but I wonder if it may not be the portrait of Frank Currier in the collection of the Art Institute of Chicago (acc. no. 1917.263). The portrait is given a date of ca. 1877, but the connoisseurship of Duveneck's early work could readily allow an earlier dating. Currier, of course, is not Italian, but not knowing the source of that supposition on James's part casts some doubt concerning its validity.

113. [Henry James], "Notes," *The Nation* 21 (9 September 1875), pp. 165–66.
114. Ibid., pp. 165–66.
115. Duveneck kept the portrait until 1894, then sent it to James. James wrote to his brother William after Francis Boott had stressed that the picture was a loan and not a gift and should eventually be returned to Duveneck's son: "I will immediately add a codicil to my will directing that Father's portrait be given to the boy, & stating that it's his property & never was mine. But if Boott had ever, in his life, a chance to do a graceful thing to the man & author he has lifelongly professed to 'admire' and who has always been infinitely responsive to his exactions & indulgent to his idiosyncracies, it was to make *mine*, by gift, this memorial of my own father, which can have no meaning whatever for that indifferent child—who will have quantities of *his* father's unsold pictures. When Boott was last here he shocked me by the merely grudging, jealous, ungracious way in which he treated my having the thing at all. I had originally *asked* him, candidly, for it—and he declined; whereupon Duveneck himself generously packed it off to me—from Florence, at the time of the break-up of the villa after Lizzie's death. I have a mind (if I can presently afford it,) to write and offer to *buy* it of him—of Boott; & if he refuses, then to send it regretfully back to him—immensely as I prize it" (James to William James, 22 December 1894, in Skrupskelis and Berkeley 1992–2004, vol. 2, p. 333). The work, evidently, remained in the James family.
116. For graceful and informative discussions of Duveneck and the Bootts, see Osborne 1992, pp. 188–99; and Carol M. Osborne, "Frank Duveneck & Elizabeth Boott: An American Romance," in New York 1996. By marriages, the Bootts were related to the Greenough and Curtis families, each with artist members with whom James was acquainted, but of whom he did not, apparently, write.
117. Osborne 1992, p. 188.
118. For an illustration of one of the works that James tried to place on the London market, *Oranges on a Branch, Castel Fusano* (1877; private collection), see Osborne 1992, p. 193. Earlier James had written to his brother William: "Her painting has developed into a resource that most girls would feel very thankful to possess. . . . Her work will always lack the last delicacy, but if she would only paint a little less *helplessly*, she would still go far—as women go. I should think she might make very successful little drawings for books" (Henry to William James, 9 April 1873). In 1880 he wrote of Lizzie's art, again to William: "She is trying to form herself upon Duveneck, & produces dozens of canvases & panels, many of which show a zealous effort. But the quality of her powers has not radically altered" (9 May 1880; both in Skrupskelis and Berkeley 1992–2004, vol. 1, pp. 201 and 324). James recounts his efforts on her behalf in letters to her of 11 and 26 February, 17 March, 14 April, 4 and 26 May, 28 June, and 21 July 1879 (in Walker and Zacharias 2014–15, vol. 1, pp. 107, 118, 131, 156, 164, 185–86, 223, and 242).
119. James to Charles Eliot Norton, 31 March 1880, in Edel 1974–84, vol. 2, p. 280. He began the reference by likening Duveneck to the violent Hannibal Challop, a character from Charles Dickens's *Martin Chuzzlewit*.
120. James to Catherine Walsh, 3 May 1880, in Walker and Zacharias 2014–15, vol. 2, p. 178. He had begun the passage by writing that Lizzie seemed both "pupil & adoptive mother—or at least adoptive sister" to Duveneck. He continued, in vain, as it turned out, "I hope she won't ever become his adoptive any-thing-else. . . . But of this there is probably no danger."
121. James to Henrietta Reubell, 11 March 1886, in Edel 1974–84, vol. 3, p. 117. This just a few weeks after writing to Boott in an understandably different vein: "I value greatly the prospect of renewing my relations with the gifted Frank, whom I always liked and esteemed and whom I congratulate still more than I congratulate you. Give him, please, my friendliest regards, and tell him my interest in him, always great, will be redoubled" (James to Lizzie Boott, 22 February 1886, in Edel 1974–84, vol. 3, p. 111).
122. Alice James, Henry's sister, wrote to her brother William of how Lizzie's "having so violently discontinued herself was a great shock" (4 November 1888, quoted in Strouse 1982, p. 298). The condolence letter that James wrote to Francis Boott does allow of this interpretation, but is ambiguous (3 April 1888, in Edel 1974–84, vol. 3, p. 232).
123. This was an expansion of the conversational limit. Writing to his brother William in late 1886, James characterized Duveneck as "a good frank fellow, without any small or nasty qualities—but it is impossible to converse with him for more than 2 minutes. . . . He is only 1/2 civilized—though he is very 'civil'" (James to William James, 23 December 1886, in Skrupskelis and Berkeley 1992–2004, vol. 2, p. 56).
124. James to Henrietta Reubell, 1 April 1888, in Edel 1974–84, vol. 3, pp. 230–31.
125. For extended studies of the work, see Mills 2014, pp. 25–32 and 115–25; and Dinnerstein 1992.
126. James to Francis Boott, 14 July 1893, in Edel 1974–84, vol. 3, pp. 417–18.

127. James to William James, 22 December 1894, in Skrupskelis and Berkeley 1992–2004, vol. 2, pp. 333–34.
128. James to Francis Boott, 15 December 1894, in Edel 1974–84, vol. 3, p. 493.
129. James to Margaret Mary James, 1 December 1915, in Edel 1974–84, vol. 4, p. 783.
130. James to Grace Norton, 23 February 1884, in Edel 1974–84, vol. 3, p. 32. For a rich and detailed consideration of James and Sargent as artistic confreres, see Miyabe 2007.
131. James had written of Sargent earlier, but in a fashion that is unclear concerning his own opinion of the man or his art: "I met Mrs. Boit several times since at the Sturgis's and she gave me a famous account of Sargent, whom she constantly sees. She says he is *de plus en plus fort*—but I don't know that she is a judge" (James to Lizzie Boott, 14 October 1883, in Edel 1974–84, vol. 3, p. 9). Earlier still, James's brother William, in Venice, wrote of various Americans in the city, including, in a less equivocal fashion, "Sargent the painter, a charming young fellow" (William to Henry James, 16 October 1882, in Skrupskelis and Berkeley 1992–2004, vol. 1, p. 336).
132. [Henry James], "London Pictures and London Plays," *Atlantic Monthly* 50, no. 298 (August 1882), p. 259. James knew Story, son of the sculptor, from his time in Rome. He wrote in 1880 that the younger Story "paints apparently with a good deal of industry & a promise of success. He is such a charming, handsome, taking fellow that one feels all sorts of kindness for him; but he strikes me rather as a member of the ornamental than of the useful class" (James to Sarah Butler Wistar, 16 April 1880, in Walker and Zacharias 2014–15, vol. 2, p. 160).
133. See Edel 1962a (1978), pp. 108–11.
134. James to Grace Norton, 6 May 1884, in Bowden 1956, p. 5.
135. For a detailed account, see Simpson 1993.
136. James to Elizabeth Boott, 2 June 1884, in Edel 1974–84, vol. 3, p. 42.
137. Leon Edel, " Introduction," in Edel 1974–84, vol. 3, p. xix.
138. James to Elizabeth Boott, 2 June 1884, in Edel 1974–84, vol. 3, pp. 42–43.
139. James to Grace Norton, 6 May 1884, in Bowden 1956, p. 5.
140. James to Henrietta Reubell, 18 November 1885, Harvard University, Houghton Library, bMS Am 1094 (1061). Sargent painted Stevenson three times: in 1884 (a portrait said to be destroyed, but a record of which, I believe, is in the drawing currently at Yale University's Beinecke Library [accession number 1952.36.3]; this, rather than being a drawing by Sargent, as currently catalogued, seems instead to be an amateur's copy of Sargent's lost painting); the 1885 double portrait James comments on in this letter; and a depiction of Stevenson seated in a wicker chair (1887; Taft Museum, Cincinnati). It is surely no coincidence that James, seeing at least two of Sargent's portraits during his visits to Bournemouth, starts his literary portrait of Stevenson with page after page decrying the sad fact that one no longer relies on portraiture, since Stevenson is such an apt subject for a portraitist; see "Robert Louis Stevenson," *Century Magazine* 35, no. 6 (April 1888), pp. 869–70; later reprinted in *Partial Portraits* (1888).
141. James to Henrietta Reubell, 19 May 1886, Harvard University, Houghton Library, bMS Am 1094 (1066).
142. Henry James, "John S. Sargent," *Harper's New Monthly Magazine* 75, no. 449 (October 1887), pp. 683–91.
143. James considers that "we shall be well advised to claim him, and the reason of this is simply that we have an excellent opportunity. Born in Europe, he has spent his life in Europe, but none the less the burden of proof would rest with those who should undertake to show that he is a European" (ibid., p. 683).
144. Ibid., p. 684.
145. James had visited the second Impressionist exhibition of 1876, held at the Galerie Durand-Ruel, and he dismissed "the young contributors of whom I speak" (without mentioning anyone by name) as "absolute foes to arrangement, embellishment, selection. . . . The beautiful, to them, is what the supernatural is to the Positivists—a metaphysical notion. . . . None of its members show signs of possessing first-rate talent" (Henry James, Jr., "Parisian Festivity," *New-York Tribune,* 13 May 1876).
146. Henry James, "John S. Sargent," *Harper's New Monthly Magazine* 75, no. 449 (October 1887), p. 684.
147. Ibid., pp. 686 and 688. I am grateful to an anonymous reader for Penn State University Press who emphasized to me the ubiquity of the phrase "air of reality" and the high approbation accorded to the writer who attains it in James's essay "The Art of Fiction" (1884).
148. Henry James, "John S. Sargent," *Harper's New Monthly Magazine* 75, no. 449 (October 1887), p. 688.
149. James had sent the article to New York on 1 December 1886, writing: "I send you herewith (that is, by this post, but in a different cover,) my article on Sargent, promised so long since. I hope it is about the sort of thing that suits you. I send also in two different parcels all the

photographs (7 or 8, I forget which) I have been able to obtain of Sargent's pictures. I have a hope that you will use (assuming that about *three* are what you would wish) the large picture of the 4 children, which seems to me so fine; the portrait of the young lady holding out her flower, & the little oriental figure" (James to Henry Alden, 1 December 1886, Boston Athenaeum, Sargent Papers, box 1, folder 18).

150. James to James R. Osgood, 5 August 1887, Yale University, Beinecke Rare Book and Manuscript Library (Za 13-17).

151. "I hoped it would appear immediately after the great success he [Sargent] had at the Academy this year—the Academy buying his picture out of the Chantrey fund &c—& lately I heard from him that he had been asked for material by the *Art Journal* (Fine Art Society) who propose to publish an article about him. He gave the materials & never thought till afterwards that this might interfere with or anticipate the paper I had prepared about him for *Harper*. He wrote to the *Art Journal* telling them of this & requesting them to hang back: but I am afraid the circumstance will have just the opposite effect. It would distress me very much if my article should be forestalled. Moreover it is already antiquated—if it appears some months after the Academy episode of this year (the most important that has ever happened to him) & contains no mention of it" (James to James R. Osgood, 5 August 1887, Yale University, Beinecke Rare Book and Manuscript Library [Za 13-17]). Stevenson's extremely good and acute article, "J. S. Sargent," with a focus decidedly distinct from James's, appeared in the March 1888 issue of the *Art Journal*.

152. Sargent wrote, when offering the painting: "I suppose it is the best thing I have done" (Sargent to Edward Robinson, 8 January 1916, The Metropolitan Museum Archives).

153. Henry James, "John S. Sargent," *Harper's New Monthly Magazine* 75, no. 449 (October 1887), p. 690.

154. Ibid., p. 691.

155. Ibid., p. 684.

156. Ibid., p. 690.

157. Ibid., p. 691.

158. Ibid., p. 691.

159. There were four illustrations in the article, wood engravings after a photograph of the artist (a profile view that looks distinctly like a police mug shot) and after three paintings: *The Daughters of Edward Darley Boit* (Fig. 16), *Lady with the Rose (Charlotte Louise Burckhardt;* Fig. 15), and *Carolus-Duran* (1879; Sterling and Francine Clark Art Institute, Williamstown, Massachusetts). Rather than the latter, James had hoped *Fumée d'ambre gris* (Fig. 14) would be used (as noted above—James to Henry Alden, 1 December 1886, Boston Athenaeum, Sargent Papers, box 1, folder 18), but the editors chose otherwise.

160. Henry James, "John S. Sargent," *Harper's New Monthly Magazine* 75, no. 449 (October 1887), pp. 684–85.

161. Ibid., p. 686.

162. Ibid., p. 688.

163. Ibid., p. 686.

164. Ibid., p. 691.

165. Henry James, *The Tragic Muse* (1890), in James 1989, p. 973.

166. Ibid., p. 992.

167. H. B., "The London Letter," *The Critic* 5 (22 May 1886), pp. 258–59; quoted in Fairbrother 1981, p. 89.

168. For a graphic presentation of his exhibition practice, see Appendix in Williamstown 1997, pp. 172–85.

169. Henry James, *The Tragic Muse* (1890), in James 1989, p. 1222. Even genre painters in this circle felt this way. Frank Millet, for example, wrote: "We should include in our reply to the question, 'What shall our artists paint?' first of all portraits, because portraiture demands the highest quality of mind joined with a complete mastery of execution" (F. D. Millet, "The Watts Exhibition," *Harper's Magazine* 71, no. 421 [June 1885], p. 99).

170. Until the cataclysm of the Great War, that is, and his immensely moving portrayal of its victims in *Gassed* (1918–19; Imperial War Museum, London).

171. James to Theodore Child, 23 March 1888, in Edel 1974–84, vol. 3, p. 228.

172. James to Henrietta Reubell, 1 April 1888, in Edel 1974–84, vol. 3, pp. 230–31.

173. Over the years, James tempered his disappointment, writing of Sargent to Lily Millet in 1902: "What a prodigious show of genius & power *he* makes this year!—What a palpable proof for us that we *have* been living all this time with a Great Big Man, in the fine old sense of the term. His show was the one consoling beautiful fact in the huge hideous mist of the London that has so strangely & exactingly collapsed" (James to Lily Millet, 27 June 1902, Archives of American Art).

174. James to Henrietta Reubell, 24 May 1888, Harvard University, Houghton Library, bMS Am 1094 (1078).

175. Henry James, "London. January 1, 1897," *Harper's Weekly* 41 (23 January 1897), p. 78.
176. Henry James, "London. June 1, 1897," *Harper's Weekly* 41 (26 June 1897), p. 640.
177. Henry James, "London. February 1, 1897," *Harper's Weekly* 41 (20 February 1897), p. 183.
178. Henry James, "London. May 5, 1897," *Harper's Weekly* 41 (5 June 1897), p. 563.
179. James to William James, 24 June 1893, in Skrupskelis and Berkeley 1992–2004, vol. 2, p. 270.
180. Henry James, "London. May 5, 1897," *Harper's Weekly* 41 (5 June 1897), p. 563.
181. William Rothenstein, *English Portraits: A Series of Lithographed Drawings* (London: Grant Richards, 1898). The drawing of Sargent is number 8 of 24; the final drawing in the book is of Henry James.
182. James to William Rothenstein, 13 July 1897, in Edel 1974–84, vol. 4, pp. 50–51.
183. James to Thomas Bailey Aldrich, 3 March 1888, in Edel 1974–84, vol. 3, p. 223.
184. Henry James, "London. May 5, 1897," *Harper's Weekly* 41 (5 June 1897), p. 563.
185. Illustration was "always," as he was to write in the "Preface" to the New York Edition of *The Golden Bowl*, "to my sense a lawless incident." For a recent discussion of the subject, see Tucker 2010. Of all his earlier illustrators, he seems to have been closest to Joseph Pennell (1857–1926). A note concerning the illustrations for the essay "London," to appear in *Century Magazine*, conveys the general tone: "As for the illustrations I have really nothing to suggest save that you follow your own fancy. If you too are fond of London let that fondness be your guide and you will fall in sufficiently with my text. The article from being so general is difficult to illustrate—and the thing, I should say, should be freely and fancifully done; *not* with neat, definite, photographic 'views.' Into that, however, you are not in danger of falling. . . . But do your own London, and it will be sufficiently mine" (James to Joseph Pennell, 6 January 1888, in Edel 1974–84, vol. 3, p. 218).
186. Gernsheim 1966, pp. 54 and 58. For a detailed consideration of the relations of the two men, see Bogardus 1984.
187. Boughton, student and colleague of Gertrude Käsebier and a successful New York City portraitist, whose Photo-Secessionist figural work was admired by Alfred Stieglitz, later wrote that James "was, I may truthfully say, the only sitter who ever terrified me. I was to do him for publication, and though the time was set for early afternoon, he did not come until nearly four o'clock. It was April, and a warm day, ending in a thunder shower, the sky getting blacker by the minute and the light going. Finally he came; dignified and impressive, with manners almost courtly, and wearing a top hat several sizes too big" ("Henry James," *Photographing the Famous* [Avondale Press, 1928; quoted in Haralson and Johnson 2009, p. 256]).
188. James to Gaillard T. Lapsley, 22 June 1902; in Lubbock 1920, vol. 1, p. 392. James had earlier written to his brother William of Bay, of whom they were both terribly fond, as his portraits were being painted: "Bay is a pure *painter*, a real one, a good one; without imagination, a grain, but with a large capacity, which will increase; & if *she* doesn't marry I think her future is safe. If she does, it will go—I mean as a painter" (James to William James, 18 July 1900; in Skrupskelis and Berkeley 1992–2004, vol. 3, p. 124). Of course, she did, in 1911, marry William Blanchard Rand and within three years had three sons.
189. James L. Yarnall reports that when the work was auctioned at Ortgies & Co., New York, in 1884, it had both a date and a signature, although neither is apparent now (Yarnall 2012, p. 87n60).
190. James 2011b, p. 326.
191. Henry Adams, "The Mind of John La Farge," in Washington and elsewhere 1987–88, p. 17.
192. In 1884 James learned from his brother William that the painting was at auction. He responded: "I regret that 'the family' should n't possess it—but it can't be helped. If I had been at home I might have been able to buy it myself; but after this delay I fear it is too late" (James to William James, 22 March 1884, Skrupskelis and Berkeley 1992–2004, vol. 1, p. 376).
193. Yarnall 2012, p. 60.
194. James to Lily Millet, 12 November 1886, Archives of American Art.
195. Abbey to Austin Dobson, 8 November 1885, University of London, Austin Dobson Collection, MS 810.I.9.
196. Lucia Millet to her family, 6 September 1886, Archives of American Art. She continued: "They are all making fun of me and say I have made a 'mash' but I always think he is after a new character and may possibly make me ridiculous in one of his novels later on."
197. Edmund Gosse quoted in Lubbock 1920, vol. 1, pp. 88–89.
198. Charteris 1927, p. 79.
199. Henry James to William James, 10 September 1886, Harvard

University, Houghton Library bMS Am1094 (2030). A close version, with regularized punctuation and expanded abbreviations appears in Edel 1974–84, vol. 3, p. 132. He writes *(here)* to distinguish James's sister in London from his sister-in-law, William's wife, also named Alice.

200. "Portrait of Henry James," *The Yellow Book* 2 (July 1894), pp. 191–94 (the illustration is on 193). It was accompanied solely by the text: "Portrait of Henry James: By John S. Sargent A.R.A." Apparently both artist and sitter approved its use—to judge from a later request from the periodical concerning Gosse's portrait, which Sargent declined. Sargent did not approve of the journal. He wrote to Gosse: "I have just replied in the negative to a note from Mr. Aubrey Beardsley asking my permission to reproduce your portrait in the 'Yellow Book.' From an artistic point of view I dislike that book too much to be willing to seem an habitual contributor. My only regret is that it should be *à propos* of your portrait, especially if you were ever willing that it should be reproduced, which I should consider a great compliment" (Sargent to Gosse, 1894; quoted in Charteris 1927, p. 142).

201. Edel and Powers 1987, p. 353.

202. James to Edmund Gosse, 30 January 1912, in Edel 1974–84, vol. 4, pp. 600–601.

203. "Sit Sargent 11. Bill and Alice present, and then Mrs. Hunter, who took us 3 to lunch with her" (Edel and Powers 1987, p. 353).

204. James to Edith Wharton, 5 February 1912, in Powers 1990, p. 212.

205. James to Edmund Gosse, 5 February 1912, in Edel 1974–84, vol. 4, p. 601.

206. Hunter was a close friend of both men; James had just reported to Wharton that Hunter was depressed over the legal status of her suffragette sister, composer Ethyl Smyth, who had been sentenced to two months' hard labor in Holloway Prison for window-breaking activities.

207. James to Edith Wharton, 13 March 1912; in Edel 1974–84, vol. 4, pp. 603–4. The pocket diary for 1912 reports that the third sitting was on the 13th (Edel and Powers 1987, p. 355).

208. James to Edith Wharton, 16 March 1912, in Edel 1974–84, vol. 4, p. 605.

209. James to Alice James, 23 March 1912, in Gunter 1999, p. 87.

210. Sargent to Wharton, 28 March 1912, in Ormond and Kilmurray 2003, p. 229. He could not have thought too ill of it, however, for in March 1916, just after James's death, Sargent donated it to the Royal Collections.

211. Edel 1972 (1978), pp. 483–84. Sargent refused the money; it went, instead to commission sculptor Derwent Wood to make a portrait bust (1913; Tate Britain).

212. James to William James, 13 May 1913, in Edel 1974–84, vol. 4, p. 675.

213. Letter to Ruth Draper, 15 June 1913, in Edel 1974–84, vol. 4, p. 677.

214. Young William James III's wife, Alice (née Runnells).

215. James to William James III, 18 June 1913, in Lubbock 1920, vol. 2, pp. 316–17.

216. Apparently the hand was among the final things done. James wrote after the final sitting: "yesterday was the last, the real last time—it terminated even at 12.30. Any touch more would be simply detrimental, and the hand, to my sense, is now all admirably there" (James to Mrs. Alfred Sutro, 25 June 1913; in Lubbock 1920, vol. 2, p. 320). On that same day he wrote of being "much handicapped as to the free brandish of arm and hand nowadays" (James to Rhoda Broughton, 25 June 1913; in ibid., vol. 2, pp. 317–18).

217. That the final sitting was on Tuesday the 24th is confirmed in James's pocket diary for the day: "sat to Sargent for the last time" (Edel and Powers 1987, p. 375). The pocket diaries record ten sittings: 18, 22, 25, 29 May and 1, 5, 8, 13, 15, and 24 June.

218. James to Rhoda Broughton, 25 June 1913, in Lubbock 1920, vol. 2, pp. 318–19.

219. James to Margaret, Lady Brooke, the Ranee of Sarawak, 8 December 1913, in Ormond and Kilmurray 2003, p. 230.

220. James to Emily Sargent, 17 December 1913, in Ormond and Kilmurray 2003, p. 230. Critical response to the portrait when it was at the Royal Academy in 1914, however, was, in the words of Ormond and Kilmurray, "distinctly muted" (ibid., p. 230). Unrelated to those views, on opening day, 4 May 1914, a suffragette slashed the work multiple times, so the picture was much in the news. Both James and Sargent took the attack with aplomb, and the canvas was restored. James wrote, humorously, of "sinking beneath the flood" of the 390 notes of condolence that had arrived, and that the suffragette "got at me thrice over before the tomahawk was stayed. I naturally feel very scalped and disfigured, but you will be glad to know that I seem to be pronounced curable" (James to Jessie Allen, 6 May 1914, in Edel 1974–84, vol. 4, p. 712). To William Dean Howells he wrote: "You will, I am sure, be glad to know that Sargent's extraordinarily fine portrait of me (as I didn't paint it myself I don't see why I

shouldn't unreservedly admire it), which was horribly gashed a while back by an idiotic suffragette, is under such successful treatment that I will probably be restored to effective life & bloom again. But those ladies really outrage humanity, & the public patience has to me a very imbecile side. Another of them has hacked with a chopper another picture today (a Herkomer portrait)" (13 May 1914; in Anesko 1997, p. 458). For an intricate and provocative consideration of the vandalism (albeit one that conflates documents concerning the 1912 drawing with the 1913 painting), see Otten 2006, pp. 60–85.

221. James to Edmund Gosse, 18 December 1913, in Hyde 1969, p. 245. I surmise that the reference to the portrait as a "perfect Omar Khayyam" means that it was a pure and absolute distillation of life.

222. [Henry James], "Notes," *The Nation* 520 (17 June 1875), p. 410. I am grateful to an anonymous reviewer for Penn State University Press for rightly pointing out that James writes something much like this about his own literary art: "Nothing, of course, will ever take the place of the good old fashion of 'liking' a work of art or not liking it: the more improved criticism will not abolish that primitive, that ultimate, test" (Henry James, "The Art of Fiction," *Longman's Magazine* 4 [September 1884], p. 514).

223. Charles Demuth, "Across a Greco Is Written," *Creative Art* 5 (September 1929), p. 634.

224. James to John La Farge, 21 September 1869, in Edel 1974–84, vol. 4, p. 134.

225. Henry James, "Our Artists in Europe," *Harper's New Monthly Magazine* 79, no. 169 (June 1889), p. 54.

226. Iris Murdoch, *The Bell* (1958; Harmondsworth: Penguin, 1962), pp. 195–96.

227. Henry James, "The Art of Fiction," *Longman's Magazine* 4 (September 1884), p. 510.

228. Ibid., pp. 510–11.

229. Henry James, "Charles S. Reinhart," *Harper's Weekly* (1890); reprinted in James 1893, p. 65.

230. Cortissoz 1911, p. 129.

231. Ibid., p. 131.

232. Henry James, "Houghton Journal III," 25 April 1894, in Edel and Powers 1987, p. 355.

233. Henry James, "The Art of Fiction," *Longman's Magazine* 4 (September 1884), p. 504.

234. Henry James, "Charles S. Reinhart," *Harper's Weekly* (1890); reprinted in James 1893, p. 65.

235. James 2011b, p. 79.

"PARDON MY TOO MANY WORDS": HENRY JAMES MANUSCRIPTS AND LETTERS AT THE MORGAN LIBRARY & MUSEUM

DECLAN KIELY

1. Henry James to Annie Fields, 2 January 1910, in Edel 1974–84, vol. 4, p. 541.

2. Quoted by MacFarland 2005, p. 198. Hawthorne recorded that "I burned great heaps of old letters and other papers, a little while ago, preparatory to going to England." Hawthorne burned the manuscripts of his works throughout his career, including, notoriously, that of *The Scarlet Letter.* Hawthorne once told an inquirer: "I threw that in the fire, put it up the chimney, long ago [and] never thought anybody would care for it." All that remains, a single sheet containing the title with the table of contents on its verso—is owned by the Morgan. It is part of the most important collection of Hawthorne manuscripts that survive. The collection also includes *The Blithedale Romance, Dr. Grimshawe's Secret, The Dolliver Romance, Septimus Felton, Tanglewood Tales,* and eighteen volumes of his notebooks.

3. Philip Horne has argued that James's "resistance to the prospect [of posthumous publication] was the rationale of the bonfires—of letters and other documents—whose smoke drifts across the trail of James studies to this day." See Horne 2010, p. 68.

4. Angus Easson in Schlicke 1999, p. 329.

5. Ibid., p. 329.

6. Quoted by Bowen 2011, p. 14.

7. Millgate 1992, p. 101.

8. From Leon Edel's introduction to Edel and Powers 1987, p. ix.

9. Published in *The Nation,* 14 March 1872. Wilson and Edel 1984, vol. 1, pp. 307–14.

10. James's candid assessment of the damage that the publication of Hawthorne's journals enacted upon the author's personal reputation is spelled out in the second paragraph of his review: "They represent him [Hawthorne], judged with any real critical vigor, as superficial, uninformed, inappreciative; but from beginning to end they cast no faintest shadow upon the purity of his peculiar gift."

11. James was himself one of those who gleaned amid the stubble; he

remained preoccupied with his antebellum New England precursor, publishing his biography *Hawthorne* (New York: Macmillan) in 1879, in which he positioned himself as Hawthorne's more advantaged literary successor. James wrote his biography of Hawthorne while residing in London and had no direct access to primary research material.

12. Henry James, "*Correspondance de H. de Balzac, 1819–1850,*" in Wilson and Edel 1984, vol. 2, pp. 68–69.

13. James was acutely concerned with how the revelation of an author's personal life, through the publication of his correspondence, might distract from or interfere with the evaluation of his literary work or consequently detract from critical appreciation. James's 1893 review of Flaubert's correspondence is a key document in tracing this issue; at the outset of his review, James reflects that "we may ask ourselves if the time has not come when it may well cease to be a leading feature of our homage to a distinguished man that we shall sacrifice him with sanguinary rites on the altar of our curiosity." Henry James, "*Correspondance de Gustave Flaubert,*" in Wilson and Edel 1984, vol. 2, pp. 296–97.

14. Henry James, "*Correspondance de H. de Balzac, 1819–1850,*" Wilson and Edel 1984, vol. 2, p. 69.

15. Henry James, review of *The Letters of Robert Louis Stevenson to His Family and Friends* published in the *North American Review,* January 1900, p. 63. James revised this sentence, but not its import, when he reprinted his review under the title "Robert Louis Stevenson" in *Notes on Novelists,* 1914. The revised sentence reads: "Nothing more belongs to our day than this question of the inviolable, of the rights of privacy and the justice of our claim to aid from editors and other retailers in getting behind certain eminent or defiant appearances." See Wilson and Edel 1984, vol. 1, p. 1257.

16. Adrian Poole proposed that "it is of some interest that the years in which James was writing these stories are those in which the modern laws and agreements governing international copyright got effectively settled. The business of writing was being transformed by the advances of technology and the extensions of markets into a massively organised and global industry. James attended closely to the consequences of an industry so indiscriminately dedicated to publicity and exhibition and celebrification, and its effects on the moral, emotional, and aesthetic lives of writers and readers. Needless to say, the attendant risks and rewards were for James more than crudely financial." See Poole in James 1983, pp. ix–x.

17. James signals his awareness of these competing claims in the case of the publication of Flaubert's letters, which "bring up with singular intensity the whole question of the rights and duties, the decencies and discretions of the insurmountable desire to *know.* To lay down a general code is perhaps as yet impossible, for there is no doubt that to know is good, or to want to know, at any rate, supremely natural." Henry James, "*Correspondance de Gustave Flaubert,*" in Wilson and Edel 1984, vol. 2, p. 297. This desire is an emotion that figures strongly in *The Aspern Papers.*

18. Henry James, *She and He: Recent Documents.* Wilson and Edel 1984, vol. 2, pp. 740 and 743.

19. In his notebook, meditating on "The Altar of the Dead" (1895), James reminded himself that "solidity of subject, importance, emotional capacity of subject, is the only thing on which, henceforth, it is of the slightest use for me to expend myself." Edel and Powers 1987, p. 99.

20. See James's entry for 17 November 1887 in Edel and Powers 1987, p. 40. James returns to this in 1894, describing what he calls "this age of advertisement and newspaperism" and "the phenomenon is the one that is brought home to one every day of one's life by the ravenous autograph-hunters, lion-hunters, exploiters of publicity." Ibid., p. 86. These musings are the seed of his short story *The Death of the Lion.*

21. Leon Edel suggested that James had Nathaniel Hawthorne in mind as the archetype for Jeffrey Aspern. Gary Scharnhorst argues persuasively in Scharnhorst 1990 that this story offers a "pointed commentary on the ethics of literary biography inspired in no small part by James's own research into the life of Nathaniel Hawthorne for his monograph in the English Men of Letters series in 1879 and by the controversy surrounding the publication of *Nathaniel Hawthorne and His Wife* by Hawthorne's son Julian five years later."

22. James 1999, p. 271.

23. It is also worth noting that a ruthlessly skeptical reader may be inclined to conjecture that the Aspern papers were really never extant and that the narrator's quest is entirely chimerical.

24. Gordon 1999, p. 5. James's interest in biography is evident in his review of Flaubert's letters, what we might loosely term *the biographical element* is evident in much of his critical writing and fiction.

25. *The Real Right Thing* also deals with the subject of biography; James's early story *A Bundle of Letters* presents a comic portrayal of just how misleading letters can be. In James's later fiction, there are incidents where the decision to keep or destroy a letter, to read or leave it unread, is essential to the unfolding dramatic action—two notable examples occur in *The Wings of the Dove* and the unfinished novel *The Ivory Tower.*

26. James wrote 112 short stories, several of which are often referred to as novellas because of their length. Fifty-seven of these stories were

included in the New York Edition; some may have been excluded because of space constraints or James's subsequent critical assessment.

27. It is not purely coincidental then, that James reused the term *literary remains* in *The Abasement of the Northmores.*

28. Follini 1996 considers the family controversy ignited by this publication. Follini reveals that James revised and edited the letters of his father, brother, and cousin Minny Temple.

29. Story's children commissioned James to write the biography and paid him well for his efforts. The commission enabled James to pay for the leasehold on Lamb House. See Chronology in James 1999, p. 934, which states, "In late September 1897 signs a twenty-one-year lease for Lamb House in Rye for £70 a year ($350). Takes on extra work to pay for setting up his house—the life of William Wetmore Story ($1,250 advance) and will furnish an 'America Letter' for new magazine *Literature* (precursor of *Times Literary Supplement*) for $200 a month."

30. Edel 1974–84, vol. 4, pp. 224–25.

31. James also explored the licit and illicit aspects of literary biography in his 1899 short story *The Real Right Thing.* Martin Scofield points out that this "story is about the biographer's awareness of his responsibility to his subject, and suggests James's reservations about that form of writing." See Scofield's introduction to James 2001, p. xiii.

32. Questions of privacy, and of what should and should not be made public in regard to an individual's life, were issues that concerned many authors and the families of the famous in the nineteenth century; it was a much debated question.

33. Edel 1974–84, vol. 4, p. 806.

34. Edel 1974–84, vol. 1, p. xxii.

35. Quoted by Greg W. Zacharias, "Timeliness and Henry James's Letters," in Zacharias 2008, p. 267. For a detailed discussion of the contested nature of relations between James's heirs and biographers, editors, and critics, see Anesko 2012.

36. Zacharias 2008, p. 267.

37. *Time* magazine's 30 November 1962 review of the second and third volumes of Edel's biography was titled "Who Owns Henry James?" The anonymous reviewer observed wryly: "Nobody has to ask 'Who owns Henry James?' A professor at New York University named Leon Edel has for years. Judging from the quality of the recently issued second and third volumes of his proposed four-volume biography, he may do so for decades more."

38. Zacharias 2008, p. 267. Zacharias argues that "the edition's influence resides in its power to shape our impression of James's letters overall and thus of Henry James himself." Horne posited that "The presentation of the evidence by a biographer [Edel] already massively influential in his construction of James's life and career matters because James's letters are of literary critical, not just biographical or cultural, interest." See Horne 2010, p. 75.

39. Edel 1974–84, vol. 1, pp. xxx and xxxvi.

40. See Greg W. Zacharias, "Timeliness and Henry James's Letters," in Zacharias 2008, p. 261.

41. Ibid., p. 270.

42. See Horne 2010, pp. 76 and 78.

43. Accession number ARC 3003.

44. The Princes Gate visitors' book (1901–12; accession number ARC 600) records that James's visit, with Dr. and Mrs. White, took place on 31 July 1907.

45. Jonathan Sturges was the cousin of Amelia ("Memie") Sturges, the first wife of Pierpont Morgan. Leon Edel has posited that Sturges, who brought James the original idea for *The Ambassadors,* is the archetype of the character John Bilham in that novel. See Edel 1972, p. 71. Sturges included Sargent and Whistler among his circle of friends and collaborated with Whistler on the magazines *The Baronet* and *The Butterfly*. It has also been suggested that Pierpont Morgan's art collection inspired James's vision of Adam Verver in *The Golden Bowl.* See Auchincloss 1990, pp. 56 and 58.

46. Strouse 1999, p. 264.

47. James describes Bender as having a "voracious integrity," but other characters in the novel refer to him as "a money-monster" and a "dreadful rich thing." See also Jean's Strouse's introduction to *The Outcry* (New York: New York Review Books, 2002). But Strouse points out that "the straightforward, energetic 'new man' with his big ambitions and deep pockets has far more of the author's amused affection than do the hypocritical aristocrats who try to use him." Ibid., p. ix.

48. It is likely that James was acquainted with Mrs. Sullivan through his friend Jonathan Sturges; Sturges was her nephew. Mrs. Morgan's brother, Frederick Sturges (1833–1917) was married to Mrs. Sullivan's sister, Mary Reed Fuller. I am grateful to Pamela Abernathy for the transcription of James's letter to Mrs. Sullivan and for tracing the relationships between Henry James, Mrs. Sullivan, and the Morgan family. Incidentally, Mrs. Sullivan is also the link between Henry James and Agatha Christie—she was Christie's godmother.

49. The envelope of James's letter, with postmark and stamps, is addressed to *Mrs. Sullivan / The Breakers / Palm Beach / Florida / c/o Frdk. Sturges / Esq.*
50. MA 4691. Except for the final seven pages at the Harry Ransom Humanities Research Center, University of Texas, these two chapters are all that exists of James's corrected typescript of *What Maisie Knew.*
51. In his personal correspondence, James usually apologized for the "fierce legibility" or "remingtonese" of typewritten letters.
52. MA 6152. Purchased on the Gordon N. Ray Fund, 2004.
53. *The Lesson of the Master* (Macmillan & Co.: New York and London, 1892).
54. James wrote a preface to Brooke's *Letters from America* (1916); see Wilson and Edel 1984, vol. 1, pp. 747–69.
55. MA 5464. This letter has been published. For the full text, see Edel 1974–84, vol. 4, pp. 775–76.
56. Horne 2010, p. 73.
57. At approximately 20,000 words, the synopsis is certainly "voluminous."
58. For the full transcription of this letter, see Horne 2000, pp. 375–76.
59. The box containing the typescript is inscribed *To Hyatt Mayor and Virginia with love / from / Bernard Bandler / June 22, 1932.*
60. There is a letter from Harry James to Kenneth Murdock in the Carter Burden Collection (MA 5297) concerning the publication of James's notebooks. Writing on 8 September 1943, James's nephew wrote: "Other notebooks undoubtedly existed once, but have never been found. I'm persuaded that they exist no more. I can tell you some time—if you don't know already–how my Uncle once destroyed a mass of unsorted material. . . . When I hear that somebody is going to do a job on my Uncle Henry, I'll confess to you that my first 'reaction'—here that overworked word is the only appropriate one—is to wince. For the greater part of what has been said about him, in so far as I've seen it, has been inept and silly if not quite absurdly false to the realities."
61. The text of Pinker's 19 October 1900 letter provides some visibility into the author fees that James received. The letter reads: "Mr. Lucas asked me last night to send you the terms for the Henry James serial. I gave Mr. McIlvaine a note of them when he was here last Friday, viz: for all serial rights One Thousand (£1000) [$5000]; for the American book rights Two Hundred Pounds (£200) [$1000] on account of the same royalties as you paid for the last book; and for the English book rights Two Hundred Pounds (£200) [$1000] on account of a royalty of 20 per cent. for the first 5000 and 25 per cent after, with 3½d. on the Colonial [rights]." An undated autograph note (MA 3140.5) states "Henry James / The Awkward Age / 15% serial rights U.S. & Canada £600 [$3000]. / Last year we had correspondence / about another book of his. / He suggested 15% with £150 [$750] / in advance & on a/c for U.S. / 20% & £250 [$1250] per J. B. Pinker / & Robt. McClure. / We proposed 15%, but thought £50 [$250] to £100 [$500] sufficient advance." $1.00 in 1900 is equivalent to approximately $26.90 today, so James's payment of $5000 for the serial rights of *The Ambassadors* would be, in terms of relative value, equivalent to $134,475 today.
62. MA 3140.2.
63. See Wilson and Edel 1984, vol. 2, p. 1306.
64. This collection was donated to the Morgan in 1968 by Dr. Baldwin's daughters, Cornelia Thayer Baldwin Lane (Mrs. Arthur Bliss Lane) and Margaret Elizabeth Baldwin Hawks (Mrs. Stanley B. Hawks).
65. There are two autograph letters and eleven telegrams from Pierpont Morgan to Dr. William Baldwin, written between 14 April 1905 and 22 March 1910 (MA 3564). Morgan enjoyed a professional and social relationship with Baldwin; the physician was invited to spend time on Morgan's yacht *The Corsair* when it was anchored in Venice. An insight into the closeness of Morgan's relationship with Baldwin is provided by his 27 September 1909 telegram, which reads: "I am at my library every morning from half past ten to half past eleven. Take first steamer that you can go by without regard to cost & I will gladly make up the difference." In 1905, in Rome, Morgan had written a check in the amount of $2,000 for Baldwin's medical services [the relative equivalent of $53,800 in 2016].
66. Edel 1974–84, vol. 3, p. 295.
67. Ibid., p. 349. In the same letter James noted that Baldwin was "detested, I don't know why, of [Francis] Boott."
68. Ibid., pp. 299–300, note 1.
69. Woolson fell from a window to her death in Venice on 24 January 1894. As Adrian Poole noted in his introduction to James 2013, p. x, the circumstances "strongly suggested suicide."
70. Talk of war between the United States and Great Britain had begun to circulate in the U. S. press after Lord Salisbury, the British prime minister and foreign secretary, declared that the Monroe Doctrine had no validity in international law and could not be invoked to settle a long-standing boundary dispute between Britain and Venezuela. Congress unanimously passed a measure to authorize the appointment of a boundary commission, and president Grover Cleveland urged that its findings be enforced "by every means."
71. Alice James died on 6 March 1892.

72. Despite its exclusion from the four-volume edition of James's letters, Edel does quote this passage from James's letter to Baldwin in Edel 1969, p. 139.

The only other mention of the Wilde scandal in James's correspondence is a letter to Edmund Gosse of 8 April 1895 in which he remarked: "it has been, it is, hideously, atrociously dramatic & really interesting—so far as one can say that of a thing of which the interest is qualified by such a sickening horribility. It is the squalid gratuitousness of it all—of the mere exposure—that blurs the spectacle. But the *fall*—from nearly 20 years of a really unique kind of 'brilliant' conspicuity (wit, 'art,' conversation—'one of our 2 or 3 dramatists &c,') to that sordid prison-cell & this gulf of obscenity over which the ghoulish public hangs and gloats—it is beyond any utterance of irony or any pang of compassion! He was never in the smallest degree interesting to me—but this hideous human history has made him so—in a manner." See Edel 1974–84, vol. 4, pp. 9–10. Oscar Wilde—and his brilliant career—may have been more publicly conspicuous than personally interesting to James, but there is a discernible note of disquiet in his letters to Baldwin and Gosse.

73. There are over seventy pages of handwritten letters.

74. *The Abasement of the Northmores*, in Bayley 2000, vol. 2, p. 606.

75. MA 8728.3.

76. James used this literary allusion again in a letter of 5 May 1914 to Henrietta Temple Pell-Clarke; see Horne 2000, p. 537. In Goldsmith's *The Vicar of Wakefield* (one of the most popular and widely read novels in the Victorian period, and for which James had written an introduction for a new edition in 1900), Mr. Primrose, the eponymous narrator, describes his domestic contentment in the following terms: "We had no revolutions to fear, nor fatigues to undergo; all our adventures were by the fire-side, and all our migrations from the blue bed to the brown."

77. Coburn 1913. Hazlitt 1821–22, vol. 1, ch. v, p. 98. Hazlitt was referring to William Wordsworth.

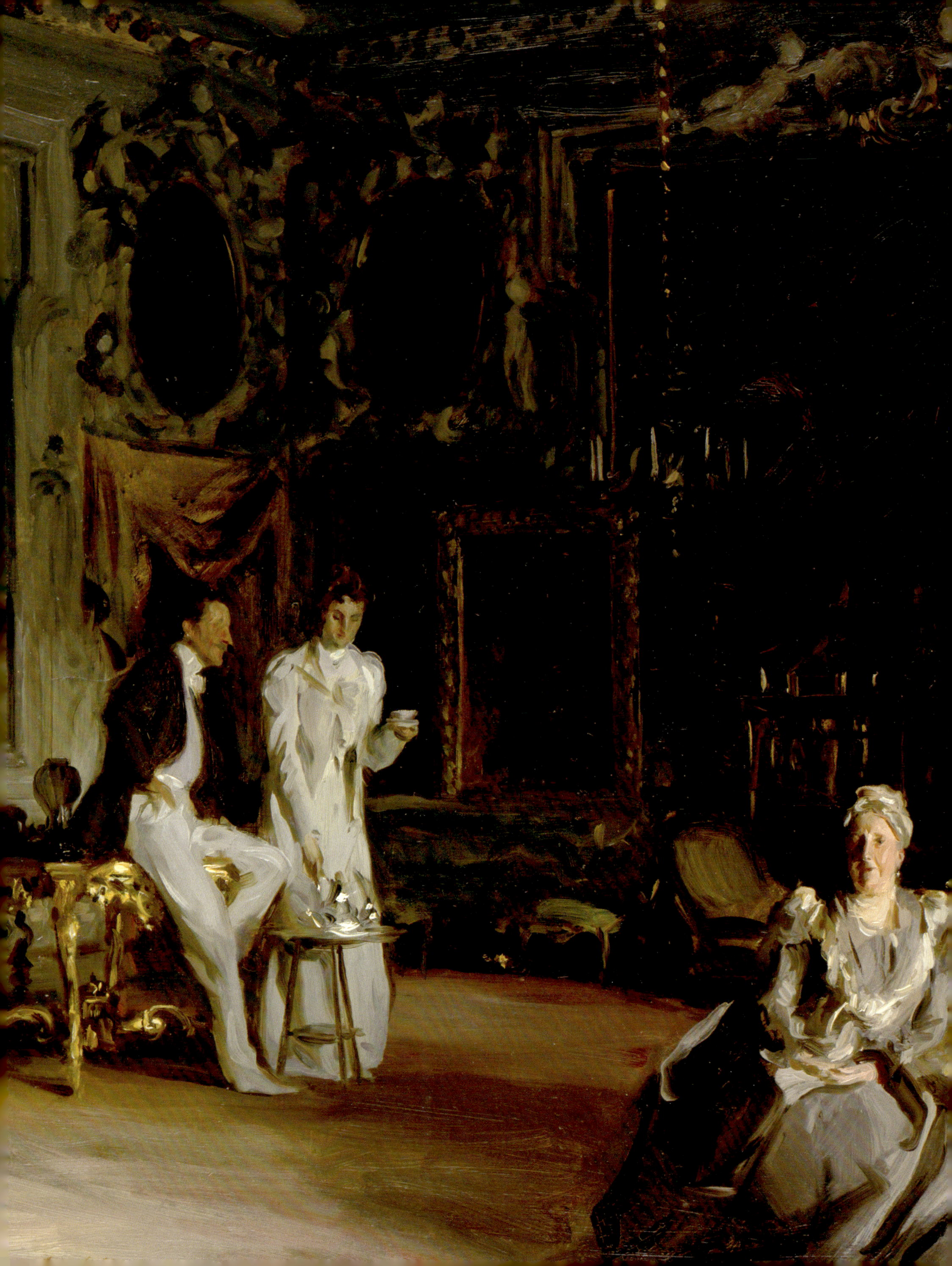

Checklist of Henry James Manuscripts and Letters in the Morgan Library & Museum

DECLAN KIELY

MANUSCRIPTS

Impressions of a Cousin. Autograph manuscript, signed, 1883. MA 203.

What Maisie Knew. Typescript of two chapters with autograph corrections, 1897. MA 4691.

The Ambassadors. Typescript, signed, 1 September 1900. MA 3140.1.

Notes of a Son and Brother. Revised typescript, signed, 1914. MA 7319.

"The Novel in *The Ring and the Book*." Typescript with autograph revisions, undated. MA 6092.

COLLECTION OF LETTERS TO DR. WILLIAM W. BALDWIN

1887

Autograph letter, signed, to Dr. William W. Baldwin, [1887?]. MA 8732.1.

Autograph letter, signed, to Dr. William W. Baldwin, [5 or 6 February 1887]. MA 8732.2.

Autograph letter, signed, to Dr. William W. Baldwin, 8 March 1887. MA 8732.3.

Autograph letter, signed, to Dr. William W. Baldwin, 13 March 1887. MA 8732.4.

Autograph letter, signed, to Dr. William W. Baldwin, 23 March 1887. MA 8732.5.

1888

Autograph letter, signed, to Dr. William W. Baldwin, 31 July 1888. MA 8732.6.

1889

Autograph letter, signed, to Dr. William W. Baldwin, 17 May [1889]. MA 8732.7.

Autograph envelope to Dr. William W. Baldwin, 19 May 1889. MA 8732.8.

1890

Autograph letter, signed, to Dr. William W. Baldwin, 10 June 1890. MA 8732.9.

Autograph letter, signed, to Dr. William W. Baldwin, 20 June 1890. MA 8732.10.

Autograph letter, signed, to Dr. William W. Baldwin, 19 July 1890. MA 9832.11.

Autograph letter, signed, to Dr. William W. Baldwin, 25 July 1890. MA 8732.12.

Autograph letter, signed, to Dr. William W. Baldwin, 5 September 1890. MA 8732.13.

Autograph letter, signed, to Dr. William W. Baldwin, 29 September 1890. MA 8732.14.

Autograph letter, signed, to Dr. William W. Baldwin, 19 December 1890. MA 8732.15.

1891

Autograph letter, signed, to Dr. William W. Baldwin, 6 February 1891. MA 8732.16.

Autograph letter, signed, to Dr. William W. Baldwin, 15 July 1891. MA 8732.17.

Autograph letter, signed, to Dr. William W. Baldwin, 19 July 1891. MA 8732.18.

Autograph letter, signed, to Dr. William W. Baldwin, 24 July 1891. MA 8732.19.

Autograph letter, signed, to Dr. William W. Baldwin, 25 July 1891. MA 8732.20.

Autograph letter, signed, to Dr. William W. Baldwin, 6 September 1891. MA 8732.21.

Autograph letter, signed, to Dr. William W. Baldwin, 19 October 1891. MA 8732.22.

Autograph letter, signed, to Dr. William W. Baldwin, 29 December 1891. MA 8732.23.

1892

Autograph letter, signed, to Dr. William W. Baldwin, 8 June 1892. MA 8732.24.

Autograph letter, signed, to Dr. William W. Baldwin, 9 June 1892. MA 8732.25.

Autograph letter, signed, to Dr. William W. Baldwin, 11 June 1892. MA 8732.26.

Autograph letter, signed, to Dr. William W. Baldwin, 18 June 1892. MA 8732.27.

Autograph letter, signed, to Dr. William W. Baldwin, 25 June 1892. MA 8732.28.

Autograph letter, signed, to Dr. William W. Baldwin, 26 June 1892. MA 8732.29.

Autograph letter, signed, to Dr. William W. Baldwin, 29 June 1892. MA 8732.30.

Autograph letter, signed, to Dr. William W. Baldwin, 3 August 1892. MA 8732.31.

Autograph letter, signed, to Dr. William W. Baldwin, 16 August 1892. MA 8732.32.

Autograph letter, signed, to Dr. William W. Baldwin, 20 August 1892. MA 8732.33.

Autograph letter, signed by William James, to Dr. William W. Baldwin, 18 August 1892. MA 8732.34 (enclosed in the letter from Henry James to Baldwin of 20 August 1892, MA 8732.33).

Autograph letter, signed, to Dr. William W. Baldwin, 15 November 1892. MA 8732.35.

1893

Autograph letter, signed, to Dr. William W. Baldwin, 25 June 1893. MA 8732.36.

Autograph letter, signed, to Dr. William W. Baldwin, 10 November 1893. MA 8732.37.

Autograph letter, signed, to Dr. William W. Baldwin, 31 December 1893. MA 8732.38.

1894

Autograph letter, signed, to Dr. William W. Baldwin, 26 January 1894. MA 8732.39.

Autograph letter, signed, to Dr. William W. Baldwin, 2 February 1894. MA 8732.40.

Autograph letter, signed, to Mrs. William W. Baldwin, 3 March 1894. MA 8732.41.

Autograph letter, signed, to Dr. William W. Baldwin, 3 April 1894. MA 8732.42.

Autograph letter, signed, to Dr. William W. Baldwin, 17 April 1894. MA 8732.43.

Autograph letter, signed, to Dr. William W. Baldwin, 27 May 1894. MA 8732.44.

Autograph letter, signed, to Dr. William W. Baldwin, 29 May 1894. MA 8732.45.

Autograph letter, signed, to Dr. William W. Baldwin, 30 May 1894. MA 8732.46.

Autograph letter, signed, to Dr. William W. Baldwin, 4 June 1894. MA 8732.47.

Autograph letter, signed, to Dr. William W. Baldwin, 7 June 1894. MA 8732.48.

Telegram to Dr. William W. Baldwin, 9 June 1894. MA 8732.49.

Autograph letter, signed, to Dr. William W. Baldwin, 29 June 1894. MA 8732.50.

Autograph letter, signed, to Dr. William W. Baldwin, 19 August 1894. MA 8732.51.

Autograph letter, signed, to Dr. William W. Baldwin, 23 August 1894. MA 8732.52.

Autograph letter, signed, to Dr. William W. Baldwin, [17 December 1894]. MA 8732.53.

Autograph letter, signed, to Dr. William W. Baldwin, 18 December 1894. MA 8732.54.

1895

Autograph letter, signed, to Dr. William W. Baldwin, 2 June 1895. MA 8732.55.

Autograph letter, signed, to Dr. William W. Baldwin, 8 October 1895. MA 8732.56.
Autograph letter, signed, to Dr. William W. Baldwin, 16 November 1895. MA 8732.57.

1896

Autograph letter, signed, to Dr. William W. Baldwin, 2 January 1896. MA 8732.58.
Autograph letter, signed, to Mrs. William W. Baldwin, 2 January 1896. MA 8732.59.
Autograph letter, signed, to Dr. William W. Baldwin, 15 March 1896. MA 8732.60.
Autograph letter, signed, to Dr. William W. Baldwin, 14 July 1896. MA 8732.61.
Autograph letter, signed, to Dr. William W. Baldwin, 26 July 1896. MA 8732.62.

1897

Autograph letter, signed, to Dr. William W. Baldwin, 17 January 1897. MA 8732.63.
Typed letter, signed, to Dr. William W. Baldwin, 22 March 1897. MA 8732.64.
Autograph letter, signed, to Dr. William W. Baldwin, 2 July 1897. MA 8732.65.
Typed letter, signed, to Dr. William W. Baldwin, 28 November 1897. MA 8732.66.

1898

Autograph letter, signed, to Dr. William W. Baldwin, 4 February 1898. MA 8732.67.
Autograph letter, signed, to Dr. William W. Baldwin, 29 May 1898. MA 8732.68.
Telegram to Dr. William W. Baldwin, 22 June 1898. MA 8732.69.
Autograph letter, signed, to Dr. William W. Baldwin, 23 August 1898. MA 8732.70.

1899

Autograph letter, signed, to Dr. William W. Baldwin, 22 July 1899. MA 8732.71.
Typed letter, signed, to Dr. William W. Baldwin, 30 August 1899. MA 8732.72.

1900

Autograph letter, signed, to Dr. William W. Baldwin, 4 December 1900. MA 8732.73.

1907

Autograph letter, signed, to Dr. William W. Baldwin, [1907]. MA 8732.74.
Autograph letter, signed, to Mrs. William W. Baldwin, [1907]. MA 8732.75.

INDIVIDUAL LETTERS (IN CHRONOLOGICAL ORDER)

1872

Autograph letter, signed, to John S. Clark, 21 March 1872. MA 2032.

1876

Autograph letter, signed, to Arthur Sedgwick, 29 February 1876. MA 4799.
Autograph letter, signed, to Arthur Sedgwick, 25 May 1876. MA 4799.
Autograph letter, signed, to Arthur Sedgwick, 6 July 1876. MA 4799.
Autograph letter, signed, to Arthur Sedgwick, 29 September 1876. MA 4799.

1877

Autograph letter, signed, to Richard Watson Gilder, 7 July 1877. MA 4500.

1878

Autograph letter, signed, to W. E. Henley, 9 March [1878]. MA 1617.1.

Autograph letter, signed, to W. E. Henley, 24 August [1878]. MA 1617.7.

Autograph letter, signed, to W. E. Henley, 28 August [1878]. MA 1617.9.

Autograph letter, signed, to W. E. Henley, 6 October [1878]. MA 1617.9.

Autograph letter, signed, to W. E. Henley, [11, 18, or 25 October 1878]. MA 1617.2.

1879

Autograph letter, signed, to W. E. Henley, 5 February [1879]. MA 1617.3.

Autograph letter, signed, to W. E. Henley, 9 April [1879]. MA 1617.4.

Autograph letter, signed, to W. E. Henley, 26 May [1879]. MA 1617.5.

Autograph letter, signed, to W. E. Henley, 21 June [1879]. MA 1617.6.

1880

Autograph letter, signed, to Jane Octavia Brookfield, 9 March [1880]. MA 470.53.

1886

Autograph letter, signed, to Miss Langdon (later Mrs. Royal Phelps Carroll), 15 June 1886. MA 3256.

1888

Autograph letter, signed, to Harry Quilter, 29 May [1888]. MA 5004.

Autograph letter, signed, to Harry Quilter, 31 May [1888]. MA 5004.

Autograph letter, signed, to Harry Quilter, "Thursday night," [possibly 1888]. MA 5004.

Autograph letter, signed, to Harry Quilter, 28 June [1888]. MA 5004.

Autograph letter, signed, to Harry Quilter, 4 July [1888]. MA 5004.

Autograph letter, signed, to Harry Quilter, 6 July [1888]. MA 5004.

Autograph letter, signed, to Harry Quilter, 7 July [1888]. MA 5004.

Autograph letter, signed, to Harry Quilter, 17 July [1888]. MA 5004.

Autograph letter, signed, to Harry Quilter, 20 July [1888]. MA 5004.

Autograph letter, signed, to Harry Quilter, 24 July [1888]. MA 5004.

1889

Autograph letter, signed, to Harry Quilter, 16 March [1889]. MA 5004.

1890

Autograph letter, signed, to Harry Quilter, 25 February [1890]. MA 5004.

Autograph letter, signed, to Harry Quilter, 19 December [1890]. MA 5004.

1891

Autograph letter, signed, to Madame Helena Modjeska, 17 November 1891. MA 5459.

1892

Autograph letter to George Higginson, 6 April 1892. MA 8728.1.

Autograph letter, signed, to Harry Quilter, 11 May [1892]. MA 5004.

Autograph letter, signed, to Harry Quilter, 17 May [1892]. MA 5004.

1894

Autograph letter to George Higginson, 5 November 1894. MA 8728.2.

1895

Autograph letter, signed, to Mrs. George Washburn Smalley, 15 November 1895. MA 4977.

Autograph letter, signed, to Sir J. E. Millais, "Xmas" 1895. MA 1485 K443.

1896

Autograph letter, signed, to Clement K. Shorter, 24 February 1896. MA 6091.1. All eight letters from James to Shorter are interleaved in Henry James, *Letters to an Editor* (London: Privately printed by Clement Shorter, 1916).

Autograph letter, signed, to Clement K. Shorter, 26 February 1896. MA 6091.2.

Autograph letter, signed, to Clement K. Shorter, 14 March 1896. MA 6091.3.

Autograph letter, signed, to Clement K. Shorter, 6 May 1896. MA 6091.4.

Autograph letter, signed, to Clement K. Shorter, 13 May 1896. MA 6091.5.

Autograph letter, signed, to Clement K. Shorter, 29 August 1896. MA 6091.6.

Autograph letter, signed, to William James, 11 September 1896. MA 7448.

1898

Autograph letter, signed, to Émile Zola, 24 February 1898. MA 6152.

Autograph letter, signed, to Clement K. Shorter, 5 April 1898. MA 6091.7.

Autograph letter, signed, to Hester Ritchie, 2 November 1898. MA 4500.

1899

Autograph letter, signed, to Mrs. George Washburn Smalley, 22 February 1899. MA 4977.

1900

Autograph letter, signed, to Clement Shorter, 8 November 1900. MA 6091.8.

1903

Copy of a typed letter, signed, to Harper & Brothers, 13 October 1903. MA 3140.6.

1905

Autograph letter, signed, to Mrs. James (Catherine A. Fuller) Sullivan, 11 March 1905. MA 8731.

Autograph letter, signed, to Walter Berry, 11 June 1905. Bound in PML 137461, a copy of *Letters of Henry James* to Walter Berry (Paris: Black Sun Press, 1928).

1906

Autograph letter to George Higginson, 7 June 1906. MA 8728.3.

Autograph letter to George Higginson, 4 July 1906. MA 8728.4.

Autograph letter to Emily Higginson, 3 August 1906. MA 8728.5.

Autograph letter to George Higginson, 6 August 1906. MA 8728.6.

Autograph letter to George Higginson, 9 August 1906. MA 8728.7.

Autograph letter to George Higginson, 13 August 1906. MA 8728.8.

1907

Autograph letter to George and Emily Higginson, 11 January 1907. MA 8728.9.

Autograph letter to Emily Higginson, 14 August 1907. MA 8728.10.

1908

Autograph letter to Emily Higginson, 7 January 1908. MA 8728.11.

Autograph letter, signed, to Gay, 16 June 1908. MA 4500.

1909

Autograph letter, signed, to Sir Arthur Wing Pinero, 29 September 1909. MA 4500.

1910

Autograph letter to George and Emily Higginson, 2 January 1910. MA 8728.12.

Autograph letter to George Higginson, 26 October 1910. MA 8728.13.

1911

Autograph letter, signed, to Robert Underwood Johnson, 26 January 1911. MA 8915.

Autograph letter to George and Emily Higginson, 25 December 1911. MA 8728.14.

1914

Autograph letter, signed, to Mrs. Christopher, 16 June 1914. MA 4500.

Autograph letter, signed, to Alice Runnells James, 20 August 1914. MA 4640.

1915

Typed letter, signed, to Miss Betham Edwards, 5 January 1915. MA 4500.

Autograph letter, signed, to Marie Belloc Lowndes, 6 February 1915. MA 5460.

Autograph letter, signed, to Marie Belloc Lowndes, 8 February 1915. MA 5461.

Autograph letter, signed, to A. B. Walkley, 15 April 1915. MA 4500.

Autograph letter, signed, to Marie Belloc Lowndes, 27 April 1915. MA 5462.

Autograph letter, signed, to Marie Belloc Lowndes, 20 May 1915. MA 5463.

Autograph letter, signed, to Marie Belloc Lowndes, 17 August 1915. MA 5464.

UNDATED LETTERS AND MISCELLANEA

Autograph letter, signed, to Mrs. George Washburn Smalley, undated. MA 4977.

Autograph letter, signed, to W. E. Henley, undated. MA 1617.10.

Receipt, signed, London, 18 February 1890. MA 1950.

Exhibition Checklist

COLM TÓIBÍN AND DECLAN KIELY

PORTRAITS OF HENRY JAMES

Cabinet photograph of Henry James, inscribed to Emerson Smalley, [1890s]. The Morgan Library & Museum, New York; MA 4977.4.

Cecilia Beaux (1855–1942), *Henry James*, 1911. National Portrait Gallery, Smithsonian Institution, Washington, DC; NPG. 87.248.

Alice Boughton (1865–1943), *Henry James*, 1905. National Portrait Gallery, Smithsonian Institution, Washington, DC; NPG. 87.36.

Alice Boughton (1865–1943), *Henry James*, 1906. National Portrait Gallery, Smithsonian Institution, Washington, DC, gift of Allan M. Price; NPG. 72.118.

Alvin Langdon Coburn (1882–1966), *Henry James*, photogravure, 12 June 1906. Private collection.

John La Farge (1835–1910), *Henry James*, 1862. The Century Association, New York; 1949.2.

Emil Otto (E. O.) Hoppé, *Henry James*, vintage bromide print, 1911. National Portrait Gallery, London; NPG X132910.

William James (1882–1961), *Henry James*, 1910. Isabella Stewart Gardner Museum, Boston; P3n18.

Ellen Gertrude Emmet Rand (1875–1941), *Henry James*, 1900. National Portrait Gallery, Smithsonian Institution, Washington, DC, gift of Marjorie Edel in memory of Leon Edel; NPG. 98.74.

Ellen Gertrude Emmet Rand (1875–1941), *Henry James*, 1900. National Portrait Gallery, Smithsonian Institution, Washington, DC, gift of Marjorie Edel in memory of Leon Edel; NPG. 98.75.

John Singer Sargent (1856–1925), *Henry James*, 1913. National Portrait Gallery, London; NPG 1767.

Abbott Handerson Thayer (1849–1921), *Henry James*, ca. 1881. Courtesy of the American Academy of Arts and Letters, New York.

PAINTINGS

Elizabeth Boott Duveneck (1846–1888), *Poppies*, 1882. Brooklyn Museum of Art; 2005.54.5.

Frank Duveneck (1848–1919), *Francis Boott*, 1881. Cincinnati Art Museum, The Edwin and Virginia Irwin Memorial; 1969.633.

Frank Duveneck (1848–1919), *Elizabeth Boott Duveneck*, 1888. Cincinnati Art Museum, gift of the artist; 1915.78.

John La Farge (1835–1910), *William James*, 1859. National Portrait Gallery, Smithsonian Institution, Washington, DC, gift of William James, IV; NPG. 91.6.

William Morris Hunt (1824–1879), *Girl at the Fountain*, 1852–54. Lent by the Metropolitan Museum of Art, New York; 08.88.

Lilla Cabot Perry (1848–1933), *The Green Hat*, 1913. Terra Foundation for American Art, Chicago, Daniel J. Terra Collection; 1987.25.

John Singer Sargent (1856–1925), *Venetian Women in the Palazzo Rezzonico*, ca. 1880. Private collection, courtesy of David Nisinson.

John Singer Sargent (1856–1925), *A Venetian Interior*, ca. 1880. Sterling and Francine Clark Institute, Williamstown, Massachusetts; 1955.580.

John Singer Sargent (1856–1925), *Robert Louis Stevenson and His Wife*, 1885. Crystal Bridges Museum of American Art, Bentonville, Arkansas; 2005.3.

John Singer Sargent (1856–1925), *Mrs. Edward Darley Boit (Mary Louisa Cushing)*, 1887. Museum of Fine Arts, Boston; 63.2688.

John Singer Sargent (1856–1925), *An Interior in Venice (The Curtis Family)*, 1899. Royal Academy of Arts, London; 03/1387.

James McNeill Whistler (1834–1903), *Nocturne, Blue and Silver: Battersea Reach*, 1872–78. Isabella Stewart Gardner Museum, Boston; P1e1.

James McNeill Whistler (1834–1903), *Arrangement in Black and Brown: The Fur Jacket*, 1877. Worcester Art Museum, museum purchase; 1910.5.

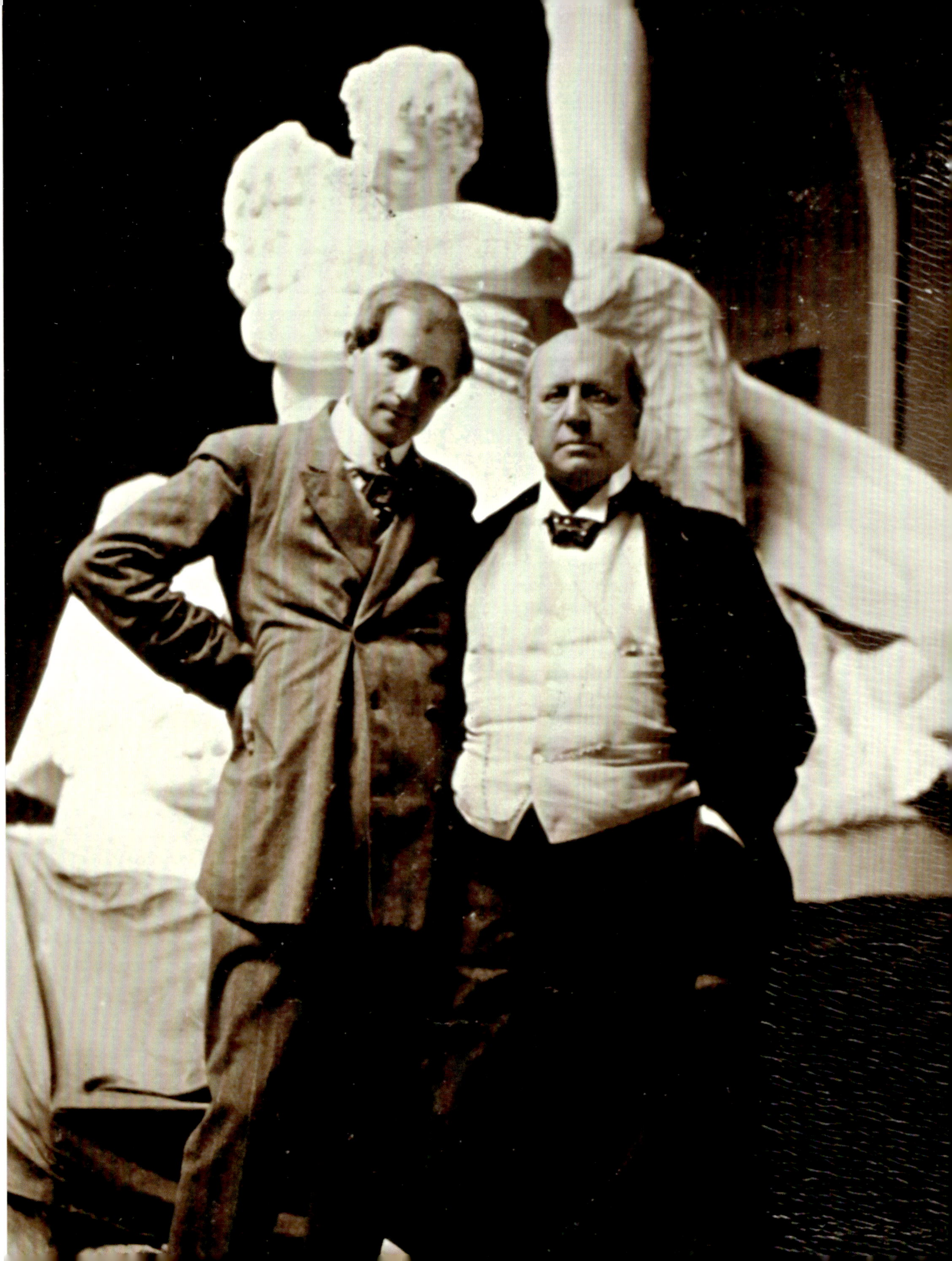

Works Cited in Abbreviated Form

ANDERSON AND KOVAL 1994
Ronald Anderson and Anne Koval, *James McNeill Whistler: Beyond the Myth,* London: Carroll and Graff, 1994.

ANESKO 1997
Michael Anesko, *Letters, Fictions, Lives: Henry James and William Dean Howells,* New York: Oxford University Press, 1997.

ANESKO 2012
Michael Anesko, *Monopolizing the Master: Henry James and the Politics of Modern Literary Scholarship,* Stanford: Stanford University Press, 2012.

AUCHINCLOSS 1990
Louis Auchincloss, *J. P. Morgan: The Financier as Collector,* New York: H.N. Abrams, 1990.

BACHER 1909
Otto Bacher, *With Whistler in Venice,* New York: Hardpress, 1909.

BAYLEY 2000
Henry James: Collected Stories, Volume 2 (1892–1910), selected and introduced by John Bayley, New York: Alfred A. Knopf, 2000.

BOGARDUS 1978
Ralph F. Bogardus, "Henry James and the Art of Illustration," *The Centennial Review* 22, no. 1 (Winter 1978), pp. 77–94.

BOGARDUS 1984
Ralph F. Bogardus, *Pictures and Texts: Henry James, A. L. Coburn, and New Ways of Seeing in Literary Culture,* Ann Arbor: University of Michigan Press, 1984.

BOWDEN 1956
Edwin T. Bowden, *The Themes of Henry James: A System of Observation Through the Visual Arts,* New Haven: Yale University Press, 1956.

BOWEN 2011
John Bowen, "The Life of Dickens 2: After Ellen Ternan," in *Charles Dickens in Context,* Sally Ledger and Holly Furneaux, eds., New York: Cambridge University Press, 2011, pp. 11–17.

BOYD 2010
Ailsa Boyd, "'Something vibrates back': Whistler and Henry James," in *Connecting Whistler: Essays in Honour of Margaret F. MacDonald,* Erma Hermens, Joanna Meacock, and Grischka Petri, eds., Glasgow: Glasgow University, 2010 (online publication: http://www.gla.ac.uk/media/media_182035_en.pdf), pp. 63–70.

CHARTERIS 1927
Evan Charteris, *John Sargent,* New York: Charles Scribner's Sons, 1927.

COBURN 1913
Alvin Langdon Coburn, *Men of Mark,* London: Duckworth & Company, 1913.

COLLISTER 2007
Peter Collister, *Writing the Self: Henry James and America*, London: Pickering & Chatto, 2007.

CONRADS 2000
Margaret C. Conrads, "'In the Midst of an Era of Revolution': The New York Art Press and the Annual Exhibitions of the National Academy of Design in the 1870s," in *Rave Reviews: American Art and Its Critics, 1826–1925*, David B. Dearinger, ed., New York: National Academy of Design, 2000, pp. 93–106.

CONRADS 2001
Margaret C. Conrads, *Winslow Homer and the Critics: Forging a National Art in the 1870s*, Princeton: Princeton University Press, 2001.

CORTISSOZ 1911
Royal Cortissoz, *John La Farge: A Memoir and a Study*, Boston and New York: Houghton Mifflin, 1911.

DINNERSTEIN 1992
Lois Dinnerstein, "From Private Grief to Public Monument: The Funeral Effigy of Elizabeth Boott Duveneck," in *The Italian Presence in American Art 1860–1920*, Irma B. Jaffe, ed., New York: Fordham University Press, 1992, pp. 200–213.

EDEL 1953
Leon Edel, *Henry James: The Untried Years: 1843–1870*, Philadelphia and New York: J. B. Lippincott, 1953.

EDEL 1953 (1978)
Leon Edel, *Henry James: The Untried Years: 1843–1870*, New York: Avon Books, 1978.

EDEL 1962
Leon Edel, *Henry James: The Conquest of London: 1870–1881*, Philadelphia and New York: J. B. Lippincott, 1962.

EDEL 1962 (1978)
Leon Edel, *Henry James: The Conquest of London: 1870–1881*, New York: Avon Books, 1978.

EDEL 1962A
Leon Edel, *Henry James: The Middle Years: 1882–1895*, London: Rupert Hart-Davis, 1962.

EDEL 1962A (1978)
Leon Edel, *Henry James: The Middle Years: 1882–1895*, New York: Avon Books, 1978.

EDEL 1969
Leon Edel, *Henry James: The Treacherous Years: 1895–1901*, Philadelphia and New York: J. B. Lippincott, 1969.

EDEL 1972
Leon Edel, *Henry James: The Master, 1901–1916*, Philadelphia and New York: J. B. Lippincott, 1972.

EDEL 1972 (1978)
Leon Edel, *Henry James: The Master, 1901–1916*, New York: Avon Books, 1978.

EDEL 1974
Leon Edel, "Henry James as an Art Critic," *The American Art Journal* 6, no. 2 (November 1974), pp. 5–14.

EDEL 1974–84
Henry James Letters, Leon Edel, ed., 4 vols.: vol. 1 (1974), *1843–1875*; vol. 2 (1975), *1875–1883*; vol. 3 (1980), *1883–1895*; vol. 4 (1984), *1895–1916*, Cambridge, Massachusetts: The Belknap Press of Harvard University Press, 1984.

EDEL AND LIND 1957
Henry James, *Parisian Sketches: Letters to the* New York Tribune, *1875–1876*, Leon Edel and Ilse Dusoir Lind, eds., New York: New York University Press, 1957.

EDEL AND POWERS 1987
The Complete Notebooks of Henry James: The Authoritative and Definitive Edition, introduction and notes by Leon Edel and Lyall H. Powers, eds., New York: Oxford University Press, 1987.

FAIRBROTHER 1981
Trevor J. Fairbrother, "John Singer Sargent and America," PhD thesis, Boston University, 1981.

FISHER 2000
Paul Fisher, *Artful Itineraries: European Art and American Careers in High Culture, 1865–1920,* New York: Garland Publishing, 2000.

FLORENCE 2012
Palazzo Strozzi, Florence, *Americans in Florence: Sargent and the American Impressionists,* Francesca Bardazzi and Carlo Sisi, eds., 2012.

FOLLINI 1996
Tamara Follini, "Pandora's Box: The Family Correspondence in *Notes of a Son and Brother,*" *The Cambridge Quarterly* 25 (Winter 1996), pp. 26–40.

GERNSHEIM 1966
Alvin Langdon Coburn, Photographer: An Autobiography, Helmut and Alison Gernsheim, eds., New York: Praeger, 1966.

GLESMANN 2002
Amanda J. Glesmann, "Sentimental Journey: Envisioning the American Past in George Henry Boughton's *Pilgrims Going to Church,*" MA thesis, University of Delaware, 2002.

GORDON 1999
Lyndall Gordon, *A Private Life of Henry James: Two Women and His Art,* New York: W. W. Norton & Company, 1999.

GUNTER 1999
Dear Munificent Friends: Henry James's Letters to Four Women, Susan E. Gunter, ed., Ann Arbor: University of Michigan Press, 1999.

GUNTER 2009
Susan E. Gunter, *Alice in Jamesland: The Story of Alice Howe Gibbens James,* Lincoln: University of Nebraska Press, 2009.

GUNTER AND JOBE 2004
Dearly Beloved Friends: Henry James's Letters to Younger Men, Susan E. Gunter and Steven H. Jobe, eds., Ann Arbor: University of Michigan Press, 2004.

HARALSON AND JOHNSON 2009
Critical Companion to Henry James: A Literary Reference to His Life and Work, Eric Haralson and Kendall Johnson, eds., New York: Facts on File, 2009.

HAZLITT 1821–22
William Hazlitt, *Table-Talk; or, Original Essays,* 2 vols., London: John Warren, 1821–22.

HONOUR AND FLEMING 1991
Hugh Honour and John Fleming, *The Venetian Hours of Henry James, Whistler and Sargent,* London: Walker, 1991.

HORNE 1999
Henry James: A Life in Letters, Philip Horne, ed., London: Allen Lane, 1999.

HORNE 2000
Henry James: A Life in Letters, Philip Horne, ed., Harmondsworth, UK: Penguin, 2000.

HORNE 2010
Philip Horne, "Letters and Notebooks," in *Henry James in Context,* David McWhirter, ed., New York: Cambridge University Press, 2010, pp. 68–79.

HORNE 2016
Henry James, *Autobiographies,* Philip Horne, ed., New York: Library of America, 2016.

HOWARD 1993
Henry James, *Collected Travel Writings: The Continent,* Richard Howard, ed., New York: Library of America, 1993.

HOWARD 1993A
Henry James, *Collected Travel Writings: Great Britain and America,* Richard Howard, ed., New York: Library of America, 1993.

HOWELLS 2004
William Dean Howells, *Indian Summer,* New York: New York Review Books Classics, 2004.

HYDE 1969
H. Montgomery Hyde, *Henry James at Home,* New York: Farrar, Straus & Giroux, 1969.

JAMES 1892
Henry James, *The Lesson of the Master,* New York and London: Macmillan and Co., 1892.

JAMES 1893
Henry James, *Picture and Text,* New York: Harper's, 1893.

JAMES 1934
Henry James, *The Art of the Novel,* New York: Charles Scribner's Sons, 1934.

JAMES 1983
Henry James, *The Aspern Papers and Other Stories,* Adrian Poole, ed., Oxford: Oxford University Press, 1983.

JAMES 1986
Henry James, *Roderick Hudson,* London: Penguin Classics, 1986.

JAMES 1986A
Henry James, *The Ambassadors,* London: Penguin Books, 1986.

JAMES 1989
Henry James, *Novels 1886–1890,* New York: Library of America, 1989.

JAMES 1999
Henry James, *Complete Stories 1884–1891,* Edward Said, ed., New York: Library of America, 1996.

JAMES 2001
Henry James, *Ghost Stories of Henry James,* Martin Scofield, intr., Ware, UK: Wordsworth Editions, 2001 (reissued 2008).

JAMES 2008
Henry James, *The Wings of the Dove,* London: Penguin Classics, 2008.

JAMES 2011
Henry James, *The Portrait of a Lady,* London: Penguin Classics, 2011.

JAMES 2011A
Henry James, *A Small Boy and Others,* Peter Collister, ed., 1913; Charlottesville: University of Virginia, 2011.

JAMES 2011B
Henry James, *Notes of a Son and Brother* and *The Middle Years,* Peter Collister, ed., 1914 and 1917; Charlottesville: University of Virginia, 2011.

JAMES 2013
Henry James, *The Aspern Papers and Other Stories*, Adrian Poole, ed., Oxford: Oxford University Press, 2013, updated edition.

KAPLAN 1992
Fred Kaplan, *Henry James: The Imagination of Genius, A Biography*, New York: William Morrow & Company, 1992.

DE LEEUW 1995
Ronalde de Leeuw, "George Henry Boughton and the 'Beautiful Picture' in Van Gogh's 1876 Sermon," *Van Gogh Museum Journal* (1995), pp. 48–61.

LONDON AND ELSEWHERE 1998
Tate Gallery, London, National Gallery of Art, Washington, DC, and Boston Museum of Fine Arts, *John Singer Sargent*, Elaine Kilmurray and Richard Ormond, eds., 1998.

LONDON AND NEW YORK 2015
National Portrait Gallery, London, and the Metropolitan Museum of Art, New York, *Sargent: Portraits of Artists and Friends*, catalogue by Richard Ormond, 2015.

LUBBOCK 1920
The Letters of Henry James, Percy Lubbock, ed., 2 vols., New York: Charles Scribner's Sons, 1920.

MACDONALD ET AL. 2003–
The Correspondence of James McNeill Whistler, 1855–1903, Margaret F. MacDonald, Patricia de Montfort, and Nigel Thorp, eds.; including *The Correspondence of Anna McNeill Whistler, 1855–1880*, Georgia Toutziari, ed., Glasgow: University of Glasgow (online edition: http://www.whistler.arts.gla.ac.uk/correspondence), 2003–.

MACFARLAND 2005
Philip MacFarland, *Hawthorne in Concord*, New York: Grove Press, 2005.

MATTHIESSEN AND MURDOCK 1947
The Notebooks of Henry James, F. O. Matthiessen and Kenneth B. Murdock, eds., New York: Oxford University Press, 1947.

MERRILL 1992
Linda Merrill, *A Pot of Paint: Aesthetics on Trial in Whistler v. Ruskin*, Washington, DC: Smithsonian Institution Press, 1992.

MILLGATE 1992
Michael Millgate, *Testamentary Acts: Browning, Tennyson, James, Hardy*, Oxford: Clarendon Press, 1992.

MILLS 2014
Cynthia Mills, *Beyond Grief: Sculpture and Wonder in the Gilded Age Cemetery*, Washington, DC: Smithsonian, 2014.

MIYABE 2007
Kyoko Miyabe, "Reading Henry James Through John Singer Sargent," PhD thesis, University of Cambridge, 2007.

NEWPORT 1995
William Vareika Fine Arts, Newport, Rhode Island, *John La Farge in Paradise: The Painter and His Muse*, catalogue by James L. Yarnall, 1995.

NEW YORK 1996
Owen Gallery, New York, *Duveneck: Frank Duveneck & Elizabeth Boott Duveneck*, catalogue by Carol Margot Osborne, 1996.

NEW YORK 2002
The Metropolitan Museum of Art, New York, *Manet/ Velázquez: The French Taste for Spanish Painting,* catalogue by Gary Tinterow et al., 2002.

ORMOND AND KILMURRAY 2003
Richard Ormond and Elaine Kilmurray, *John Singer Sargent: The Later Portraits (Complete Paintings Volume 3),* New Haven: Yale University Press, 2003.

OSBORNE 1992
Carol M. Osborne, "Lizzie Boott at Bellosguardo," in *The Italian Presence in American Art, 1860–1920,* Irma B. Jaffe, ed., New York: Fordham University Press, 1992, pp. 188–99.

OTT 2016
James Ott, *The Greatest Brush: Love, Tragedy and Redemption of Artist Frank Duveneck,* Wellesley, Massachusetts: Branden Books, 2016.

OTTEN 2006
Thomas J. Otten, *A Superficial Reading of Henry James: Preoccupations with the Material World,* Columbus: Ohio State University Press, 2006.

POWERS 1990
Lyall Harris Powers, *Henry James and Edith Wharton: Letters, 1900–1915,* New York: Scribner's, 1990.

RAWLINGS 1996
Henry James: Essays on Art and Drama, Peter Rawlings, ed., Aldershot, UK: Scolar Press, 1996.

RIOUX 2016
Anne Boyd Rioux, *Constance Fenimore Woolson,* New York: W. W. Norton & Company, 2016.

SCHARNHORST 1990
Gary Scharnhorst, "James, 'The Aspern Papers,' and the Ethics of Literary Biography," *Modern Fiction Studies* 36, no. 2 (Summer 1990), pp. 211–17.

SCHLICKE 1999
Oxford Reader's Companion to Charles Dickens, Paul Schlicke, ed., New York: Oxford University Press, 1999.

SEATTLE 2000–2001
Seattle Art Museum, *John Singer Sargent: The Sensualist,* catalogue by Trevor J. Fairbrother, New Haven: Yale University Press, 2000–2001.

SIMPSON 1993
Marc Alfred Simpson, "Reconstructing the Golden Age: American Artists in Broadway, Worcestershire, 1885 to 1889," PhD thesis, Yale University, 1993.

SIMPSON 2000
Marc Simpson, "Revelations for the Eye: Winslow Homer's Milkmaids," *Belvedere: Zeitschrift für bildende Kunst* 6, no. 1 (2000), pp. 48–63, 96–104.

SKRUPSKELIS AND BERKELEY 1992–2004
The Correspondence of William James, Ignas K. Skrupskelis and Elizabeth M. Berkeley, eds., 12 vols.: vol. 1 (1992), *William and Henry 1861–1884*; vol. 2 (1993), *William and Henry 1885–1896*; vol. 3 (1994), *William and Henry 1897–1910,* Charlottesville: University Press of Virginia, 1992–2004.

SPASSKY ET AL. 1985
Natalie Spassky et al., *American Paintings in the Metropolitan Museum of Art, Volume 2: A Catalogue of Works by Artists Born Between 1816 and 1845,* New York: The Metropolitan Museum of Art, 1985.

STROUSE 1982
Jean Strouse, *Alice James: A Biography,* 1980; Toronto: Bantam Books, 1982.

STROUSE 1999
Jean Strouse, *Morgan: American Financier,* New York: Random House, 1999.

SWEENEY 1956
The Painter's Eye: Notes and Essays on the Pictorial Arts by Henry James, John L. Sweeney, ed., London: Grafton Books, 1956.

SWEENEY 1956A
The Painter's Eye: Notes and Essays on the Pictorial Arts by Henry James, John L. Sweeney, ed., Cambridge, Massachusetts: Harvard University Press, 1956.

TINTNER 1986
Adeline R. Tintner, *The Museum World of Henry James,* Ann Arbor: University of Michigan Press, 1986.

TUCKER 2010
Amy B. Tucker, *The Illustration of the Master: Henry James and the Magazine Revolution,* Stanford, California: Stanford University Press, 2010.

VANDERLAAN 2008
Kimberly Vanderlaan, "The Painter Henry James Might Have Been," *American Literary Realism* 41, no. 1 (Fall 2008).

WALKER AND ZACHARIAS 2009
The Complete Letters of Henry James, 1872–1876, 2 vols., Pierre A. Walker and Greg W. Zacharias, eds., Lincoln: University of Nebraska Press, 2009.

WALKER AND ZACHARIAS 2014–15
The Complete Letters of Henry James, 1878–1880, vols. 1 (2014) and 2 (2015), Pierre A. Walker and Greg W. Zacharias, eds., Lincoln: University of Nebraska Press, 2014–15.

WASHINGTON AND ELSEWHERE 1987–88
National Museum of American Art, Washington, DC, Carnegie Museum of Art, Pittsburgh, and Museum of Fine Arts, Boston, *John La Farge,* with essays by Henry Adams, Kathleen A. Foster, Henry A. La Farge, H. Barbara Weinberg, Linnea H. Wren, and James L. Yarnall, 1987–88.

WILLIAMSTOWN 1997
Sterling and Francine Clark Art Institute, Williamstown, Massachusetts, *Uncanny Spectacle: The Public Career of the Young John Singer Sargent,* catalogue by Marc Simpson with contributions by Richard Ormond and H. Barbara Weinberg, 1997.

WILSON AND EDEL 1984
Henry James, *Literary Criticism,* Mark Wilson and Leon Edel, eds., 2 vols.: vol. 1, *Essays on Literature, American Writers, English Writers;* vol. 2, *French Writers, Other European Writers, the Prefaces to the New York Edition,* New York: Library of America, 1984.

WINNER 1970
Viola Hopkins Winner, *Henry James and the Visual Arts,* Charlottesville: University Press of Virginia, 1970.

YARNALL 2012
James L. Yarnall, *John La Farge, A Biographical and Critical Study,* Burlington, Vermont: Ashgate, 2012.

ZACHARIAS 2008
A Companion to Henry James, Greg W. Zacharias, ed., London: Blackwell Publishing Ltd., 2008.

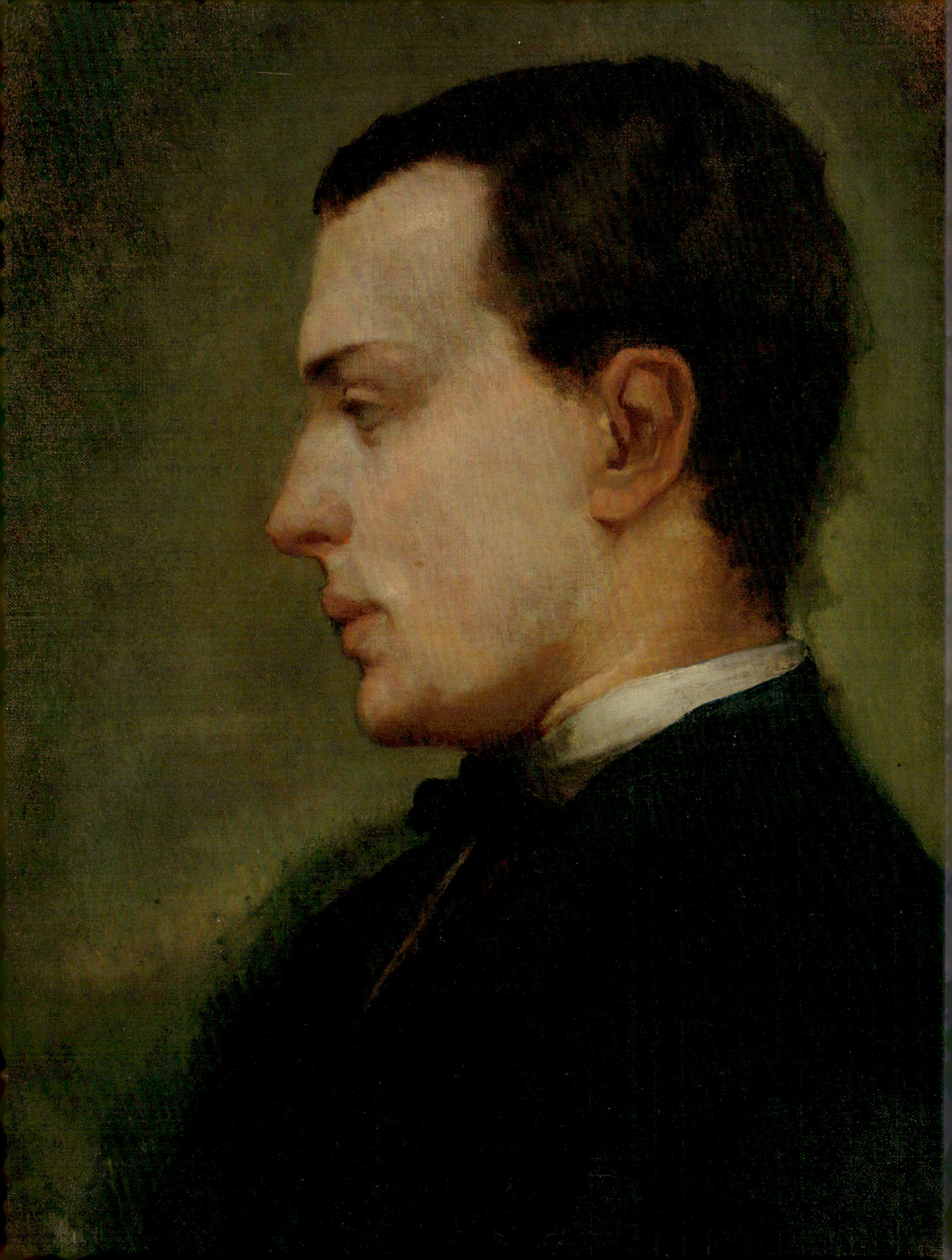

Index

Page numbers in *italics* refer to illustrations.

Acknowledgments

The authors would like to thank the following individuals for their invaluable assistance during the making of the exhibition and catalogue: Pamela Abernathy, John Alexander, Colin B. Bailey, Karen Banks, John Bidwell, Linden Chubin, James Donchez, Patricia Emerson, Peggy Fogelman, Maria Fredericks, Graham Haber, V. Heidi Hass, Eliza Heitzman, Keith Johnson, Hannah Judd, Joan Kiely, Phineas and Benedict Kiely, Anita Masi, Patrick Milliman, Winona Packer, Christina Lee Padden, Marilyn Palmeri, Michelle Perlin, Chad Petrovay, Paula Pineda, Stephen Saitas, Tom Shannon, Reba Fishman Snyder, Eva Soos, Ian Umlauf, Carolyn Vega, and Scott Whipkey.

Credits

Every effort has been made to trace copyright owners and photographers. The Morgan apologizes for any unintentional omissions and would be pleased in such cases to add an acknowledgment in future editions.

TEXT:

Unpublished Henry James texts by kind permission of the James Family. Bay James, literary executor. *The Bell* by Iris Murdoch © 1958. Reprinted by kind permission of the Estate of Iris Murdoch, p. 95.

PHOTOGRAPHIC COPYRIGHT:

Collection of the American Academy of Arts and Letters, New York City, p. 102; Amon Carter Museum of American Art, Fort Worth, Texas; 1975.28, p. 68; Rome, Hendrik C. Andersen Museum, by permission of Ministero dei Beni e delle Attività Culturali e del Turismo, p. 162; Frank and Elizabeth Boott Duveneck papers, 1851–1972, bulk 1851–1919, Archives of American Art, Smithsonian Institution, pp. viii and 14; courtesy of the Berkshire Museum, Pittsfield, Massachusetts, USA, p. 71; Brooklyn Museum, Healy Purchase Fund B, 78.176, p. 12; courtesy of the Century Association, New York, pp. 8 and 170; Cincinnati Art Museum, Ohio, USA, gift of the artist / Bridgeman Images, pp. 16 and 18, gift of Frank Duveneck / Bridgeman Images, p. 29; image © Sterling and Francine Clark Art Institute, Williamstown, Massachusetts, USA, p. 80; The Cleveland Museum of Art, 1961.39, p. 51, Fig. 1; Crystal Bridges Museum of American Art, Bentonville, Arkansas, 2005.3, p. 39; Freer Gallery of Art and Arthur M. Sackler Gallery Archives, Smithsonian Institution, Washington, DC, gift of the estate of Charles Lang Freer, FSA A.01 12.02.1.02, p. 23; Imaging Department © President and Fellows of Harvard College, p. 9, Fig. 5, p. 45; Isabella Stewart Gardner Museum, Boston, pp. 40 and 47; image copyright © The Metropolitan Museum of Art, image source: Art Resource, NY, pp. 31, 48, 51, Fig. 2, pp. 59, 61, 69, 73, 75, 78, 83, 88, and 134; The Morgan Library & Museum, ARC 3003, pp. 109–10; MA 203, p. 111; MA 3140.1, pp. 121–22; MA 3140.3, p. 124; MA 4691, p. 113, Fig. 7; MA 4640, p. 115; MA 4977.4, p. 116; MA 5462, p. 120, Figs.16–17; MA 6092, p. 117; MA 7319, p. 113, Fig. 8, p. 114; MA 8728, pp. 98 and 128; MA 8728.5, p. 130; MA 8732.6, p. 125; MA 8732.58, p. 126, Fig. 22; MA 8732.55, p. 126, Fig. 23, p. 127; PML 134805, p. 92; PML 196394, by kind permission of The Universal Order, p. 132; PML 198149-50, p. 118; photograph © 2017 Museum of Fine Arts Boston, pp. 46, 54, and 84; courtesy National Gallery of Art, Washington, Corcoran Collection (Museum Purchase, Anna E. Clark Fund), 2014.79.25, p. 9, Fig. 4; courtesy National Gallery of Art, Washington, Gaillard F. Ravenel and Frances P. Smyth-Ravenel Fund 2000.144.1, p. 56; © National Portrait Gallery, London, front cover, pp. 2 and 38; National Portrait Gallery, Smithsonian Institution, gift of Marjorie Edel in memory of Leon Edel, pp. 36–37; National Portrait Gallery, Smithsonian Institution, gift of Allan M. Price, back cover, pp. ii and 106; courtesy of the National Museum of Women in the Arts, Washington, DC, gift of Frank Duveneck, p. 11; © National Trust / Charles Thomas, p. 3; Princeton University Art Museum / Art Resource, NY, p. 86; private collection, Courtesy David Nisinson, p. 77; © Royal Academy of Arts, London, pp. 43 and 152; Royal Collection Trust / © Her Majesty Queen Elizabeth II 2016, p. 100; Tate, London / Art Resource, NY, p. 94; Terra Foundation for American Art, Daniel J. Terra Collection, 1987.25, p. 41.

PHOTOGRAPHY:

Michael Agee, p. 80; John Bigelow Taylor, pp. 8 and 170; Alice Boughton, back cover, pp. ii and 106; Geoffrey Clements, p. 102; Alvin Langdon Coburn, p. 132; Prudence Cuming Associates Limited, pp. 43 and 152; M. Dornac, p. 23; Graham S. Haber, pp. 92, 98, 109–11, 113–18, 120–22, 124–28, and 130; Dwight Primiano, p. 39; Lee Stalsworth, p. 11; photography © Terra Foundation for American Art, Chicago, p. 41.

The Penn State Series in the History of the Book

James L. W. West III, General Editor

PREVIOUSLY PUBLISHED TITLES IN THE PENN STATE SERIES IN THE HISTORY OF THE BOOK

Peter Burke, *The Fortunes of the "Courtier": The European Reception of Castiglione's "Cortegiano"* (1996)

Roger Burlingame, *Of Making Many Books: A Hundred Years of Reading, Writing, and Publishing* (1996)

James M. Hutchisson, *The Rise of Sinclair Lewis, 1920–1930* (1996)

Julie Bates Dock, ed., *Charlotte Perkins Gilman's "The Yellow Wall-paper" and the History of Its Publication and Reception: A Critical Edition and Documentary Casebook* (1998)

John Williams, ed., *Imaging the Early Medieval Bible* (1998)

Ezra Greenspan, *George Palmer Putnam: Representative American Publisher* (2000)

James G. Nelson, *Publisher to the Decadents: Leonard Smithers in the Careers of Beardsley, Wilde, Dowson* (2000)

Pamela E. Selwyn, *Everyday Life in the German Book Trade: Friedrich Nicolai as Bookseller and Publisher in the Age of Enlightenment* (2000)

David R. Johnson, *Conrad Richter: A Writer's Life* (2001)

David Finkelstein, *The House of Blackwood: Author-Publisher Relations in the Victorian Era* (2002)

Rodger L. Tarr, ed., *As Ever Yours: The Letters of Max Perkins and Elizabeth Lemmon* (2003)

Randy Robertson, *Censorship and Conflict in Seventeenth-Century England: The Subtle Art of Division* (2009)

Catherine M. Parisian, ed., *The First White House Library: A History and Annotated Catalogue* (2010)

Jane McLeod, *Licensing Loyalty: Printers, Patrons, and the State in Early Modern France* (2011)

Charles Walton, ed., *Into Print: Limits and Legacies of the Enlightenment; Essays in Honor of Robert Darnton* (2011)

James L. W. West III, *Making the Archives Talk: New and Selected Essays in Bibliography, Editing, and Book History* (2012)

John Hruschka, *How Books Came to America: The Rise of the American Book Trade* (2012)

A. Franklin Parks, *William Parks: The Colonial Printer in the Transatlantic World of the Eighteenth Century* (2012)

Roger E. Stoddard, comp., and David R. Whitesell, ed., *A Bibliographic Description of Books and Pamphlets of American Verse Printed from 1610 Through 1820* (2012)

Nancy Cervetti, *S. Weir Mitchell: Philadelphia's Literary Physician* (2012)

Karen Nipps, *Lydia Bailey: A Checklist of Her Imprints* (2013)

Paul Eggert, *Biography of a Book: Henry Lawson's "While the Billy Boils"* (2013)

Allan Westphall, *Books and Religious Devotion: The Redemptive Reading of an Irishman in Nineteenth-Century New England* (2014)

Scott Donaldson, *The Impossible Craft: Literary Biography* (2015)

John Bidwell, *Graphic Passion: Matisse and the Book Arts* (2015)

Peter L. Shillingsburg, *Textuality and Knowledge: Essays* (2017)

Steven Carl Smith, *An Empire of Print: The New York Publishing Trade in the Early American Republic* (2017)

PUBLISHED BY THE PENNSYLVANIA STATE
UNIVERSITY PRESS
AND THE MORGAN LIBRARY & MUSEUM

The Morgan Library & Museum
Karen Banks, *Publications Manager*
Patricia Emerson, *Senior Editor*
Eliza Heitzman, *Editorial Assistant*

PROJECT STAFF

Marilyn Palmeri, *Imaging and Rights Manager*
Eva Soos, *Imaging and Rights Assistant Manager*
Graham S. Haber, *Photographer*

The Pennsylvania State University Press
Jennifer Norton, *Design and Production Manager*
Laura Reed-Morrisson, *Managing Editor*
Patty Mitchell, *Production Coordinator*
Alex Vose, *Editorial Assistant*

Designed by Jo Ellen Ackerman / Bessas & Ackerman
Typeset in Monotype Baskerville and DIN Next Pro
Printed on Garda Silk and bound by Friesens

The Morgan wishes to thank
Catherine Dorsey and Min Tian.